I08105б2

IMAGES
of America

SHARON AND SHARON SPRINGS

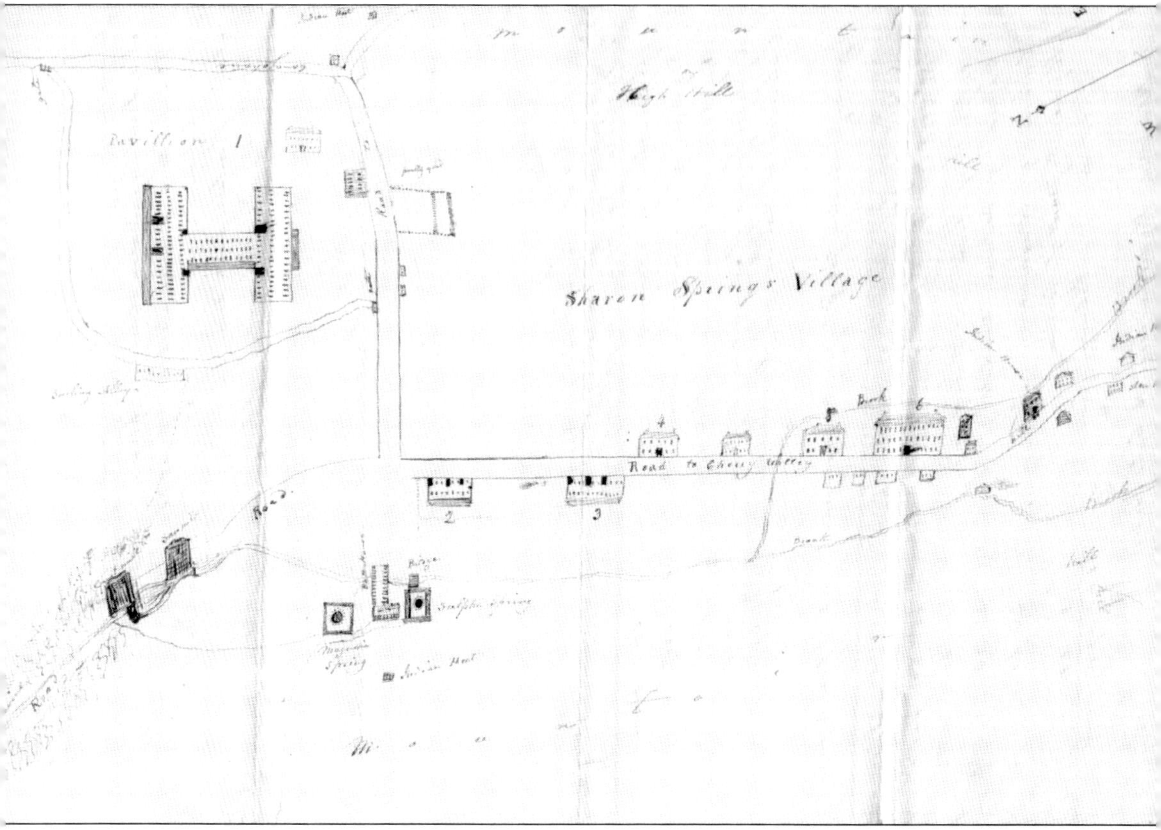

This 1847 hand-drawn map shows the lower Village of Sharon Springs in the early stages of the spa era. The H-shaped Pavilion Hotel appears at upper left, the Eldredge House is labeled no. 3, and no. 6 is the newly built American Hotel. Most interesting are the three indications of "Indian Huts," one south of the Pavilion, one north of the Sulphur Spring, and the third at the southwest extension of the "Road to Cherry Valley." A building just to the south of the American Hotel, labeled "Indian House," is the home of the Brazille family, who were of Abenaki heritage and lived in the village for many years in the 19th century. (Courtesy of James Whitelaw.)

On the Cover: This 1888 photograph shows three generations of the Gardner family on the Stone House front porch. This family owned and operated the Pavilion Hotel for over 100 years, from 1838 to 1940. The family patriarch, John Henry Gardner (seated in chair left of center), and his wife, Almeda (in chair to her husband's left), pose with their sons, daughters, and their spouses, as well as their grandchildren. Seated in front of John is Lorenzo Delmonico of the New York restaurant family, husband of Julia Gardner. (Courtesy of Sharon Historical Society.)

IMAGES
of America

SHARON AND SHARON SPRINGS

Sharon Historical Society
with Nancy DiPace Pfau

ARCADIA
PUBLISHING

ISBN 978-1-4671-2275-7

Published by Arcadia Publishing
Charleston, South Carolina

Printed in the United States of America

Library of Congress Control Number: 2014943083

For all general information, please contact Arcadia Publishing:
Telephone 843-853-2070
Fax 843-853-0044
E-mail sales@arcadiapublishing.com
For customer service and orders:
Toll-Free 1-888-313-2665

Visit us on the Internet at www.arcadiapublishing.com

For my children, Bradley and Aleksandra, and grandsons, Sebastian and Tobias.

Contents

ACKNOWLEDGMENTS

Like other writers, I have stood on the shoulders of many to compose this short look at the history of Sharon and Sharon Springs, New York. I am most indebted to the work of Sandra Manko, Jean Bakkom, and others of the Sharon Historical Society, whose books, *Reflections on Sharon: 1797–1997, A Pictorial History; A Touch of Nostalgia: Sharon Springs Spa;* and *Sibs of Sharon: The Happy Hamlets*, have provided invaluable help. These books are still available from the society. Hansi Durlach and Stuart Blumin's *The Short Season of Sharon Springs* offered insights into the Jewish era, and I have used some of the photographs Hansi gave to the Sharon Historical Museum. Emily Lang's thesis, "The Othering of Sharon Springs," offered additional insight into the Jewish culture. Also helpful was *A Sharon Springs Timeline* by Carl Waldman and Chris Campbell. Archivists at the New York State Historical Association Library in Cooperstown and the Old Stone Fort in Schoharie provided helpful information. Several friends have lent photographs and shared stories: Dorcas Comrie, Nan Fisherman Goodman, Peter Mauhs, Maureen Lodes, Douglas Plummer, Joshua Kilmer-Purcell, Betty Gavin Singer, Bruce Button, Chris Stout-Hazard, Leila Durkin, Sandra Lane Manko, James Whitelaw, and Megan Mast Holken. Officers of the Sharon Historical Society, president Mary Ann Larkin, vice president Sandra Manko, and treasurer Bernadetta Vrooman read the entire text and made dozens of helpful suggestions. Thomas Reynolds, Anthony M. DiPace, and Lori Webb at Sharon Springs Central School kindly allowed me access to photographs and files. My most valiant collaborator has been my husband, Richard Pfau, whose encouragement, technical support, and editorial genius have assured the book's completion. I wish to send a special thank-you also to Sharon McAllister, my Arcadia acquisitions editor, who promptly answered any and all questions. If I have forgotten anyone, I hope they can forgive my lapse of memory. It does take a village and a town to write a book on Sharon and Sharon Springs!

Unless otherwise noted, all images appear courtesy of the Sharon Historical Society, which will receive the author's royalties.

INTRODUCTION

Situated in the northwest corner of Schoharie County, the Village of Sharon Springs and the Town of Sharon have created a fascinating history over the centuries. With a combination of award-winning mineral springs, spectacular views of the Mohawk Valley, enduring farms, and committed citizens, the town and the village enjoy a special place in New York State history.

Thousands of years before the first Europeans arrived, native peoples used the various springs to prevent or soothe many ailments. Even before European settlements, different cultures intermingled in the area. Archeological evidence suggests that the tribes commonly known as the Iroquois Nation came to this region from the Southwest about 3,000 years ago and mixed with the people already here. The Iroquois considered the area around the springs a sacred place, where shamans from many tribes would gather to purify themselves. Native peoples continued to visit and live in Sharon for many years following European possession of the land.

The earliest European settlers were Palatine German and Dutch farmers, who arrived around 1750 to work the land and worship as they pleased. Ever since, churches have been an important part of the culture; indeed, Sharon Springs has the only synagogue in Schoharie County. Many pastors, priests, and rabbis played significant roles in the life of the village and town.

A European-style spa opened in 1825. During the latter half of the 19th century, it was a destination for the rich and famous. Every summer, U.S. presidents—among them Martin Van Buren, Ulysses S. Grant, Theodore Roosevelt, and Franklin Roosevelt—graced the grandest hotels, and ladies arrived with their trunks full of gowns from such fashionable dressmakers as Worths' in Paris. The baths anchored the economy for over 100 years, but fell out of fashion in the late 20th century, were sold to new investors, and finally closed in 2005.

Agriculture has remained crucially important to Sharon, from surpluses that fed the Revolution and early Republic, through the profitable time of hop production, the difficult years of foreclosures, to today's mix of dairy farming, maple-syrup production, cheese making, apple orchards, and organic farming.

Volunteers continue to keep the town and village alive. Community organizations like the fire department, emergency rescue service, library, historical society, sports teams, and others are powered by committed citizens. That same sense of civic duty led many local men and women to serve in the armed forces, with several earning decorations for bravery during the nation's wars.

Even before the establishment of the first one-room school in 1799, education occupied an important role in the lives of the residents. For many years, young people attended tiny local schools, until the school district was centralized in the 1930s. Although the centralized school remains small, with graduating classes between 16 and 35, because of the committed faculty and staff, the alumni remain loyal, and many go on to successful careers

Each era has brought new diversity and challenges to Sharon and its spa. From its earliest history, the region has seen difficult times and profitable ones. In the late 19th century, wealthy visitors to the spa included Vanderbilts, Roosevelts, ambassadors, Oscar Wilde, and other famous people. In the 20th century, visitors and residents included Holocaust survivors. Today's renaissance has been spurred by artists, entrepreneurs, and artisans.

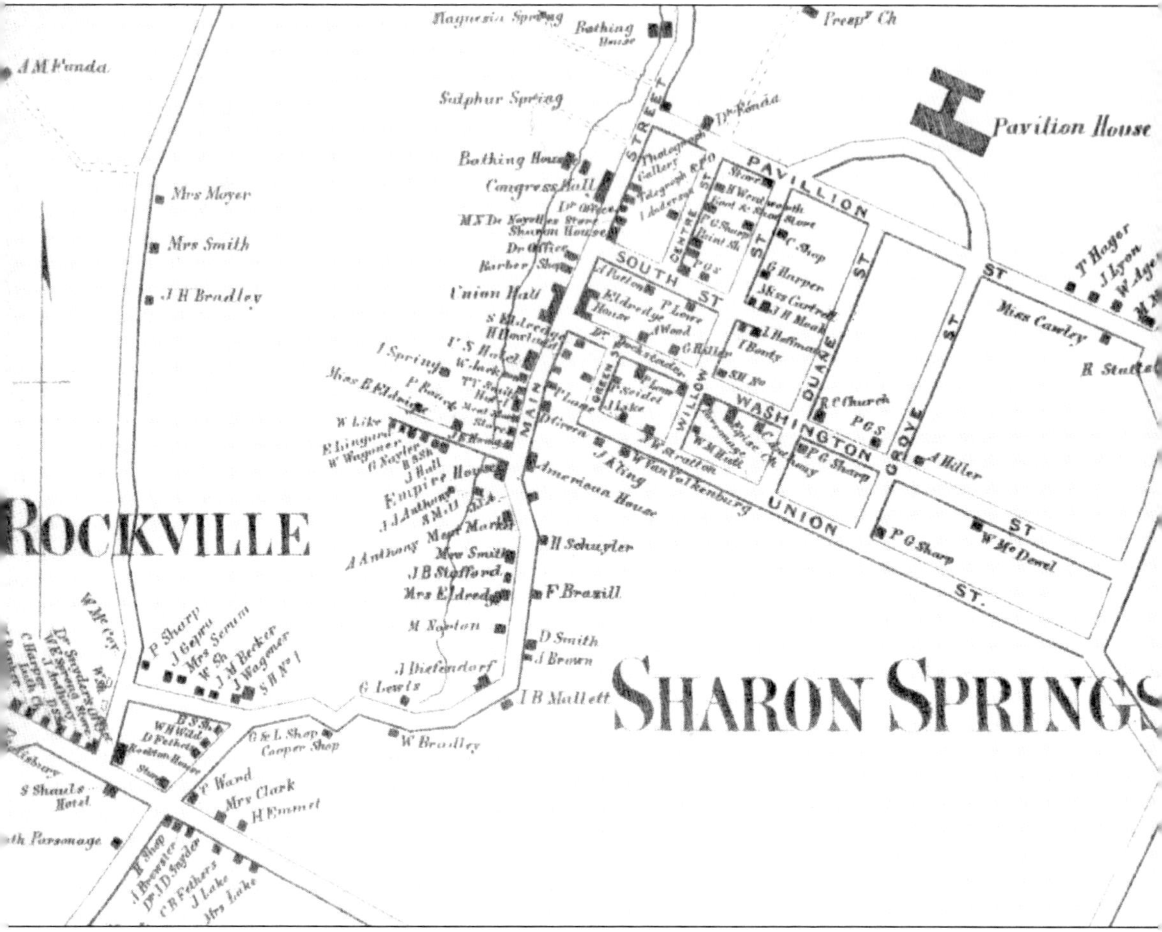

This 1866 map shows the Village of Sharon Springs divided into Rockville, the "upper village" along the Great Western Turnpike, and Sharon Springs, or "downstreet," the spa area. Of the 11 hotels pinpointed on this map, only one remained open in 2014: the recently restored American Hotel. A comparison with the map on page 2 shows how many new hotels were built in only 19 years.

One

Early Settlements

The first Europeans to settle in Sharon did not come for the healing waters but to farm the good lands, to worship as they pleased, and to free themselves from the tyranny of heavy taxation and war. The German people from the Palatinate were themselves displaced persons, arriving in Schoharie Valley in 1712 with permission from the Mohawk chief Karighondonte to settle along the Schoharie and Cobleskill Creeks.

These original European settlers enjoyed friendly relations with their Mohawk neighbors, often sending their sons to live among the native tribes for a year or more. Unfortunately, the Palatines did not obtain a permit from the English governor, so the colonial government rejected their land titles, leading many to flee. Some went to Pennsylvania, and others moved to vacant land in Sharon, which they named New Dorlach.

Next came Dutch settlers, who, as Russell Shorto asserts, brought tolerance for pluralism to what would become New York State; they eventually built the Dutch Reformed Church. New waves of German settlers also arrived, including, in 1732, Rev. Peter Nicholas Sommer, the first Lutheran pastor, who preached in several of the hamlets comprising the town. Perhaps the best-known resident, William Beekman arrived around 1785.

The Revolutionary War changed the character of the town dramatically. Many local families remained loyal to the British crown, some fleeing the frontier for Canada or the more settled and fortified area of Albany. During the latter years of the war, raiding parties from both sides foraged the towns' farms to feed soldiers and animals. In 1781, two opposing groups met at Cedar Swamp, east of what was then called New Dorlach, and the colonists defeated the loyalists and Indians. After the war, most of these loyalists' property was awarded to Yankee families.

Although the majority of Native American tribes were removed from this area after the treaty ending the American War of Independence, the wave of newcomers settling in the town created a mixture of languages, culture, and religious preferences, a pattern that would continue over the ensuing centuries and bring with it challenges and opportunities.

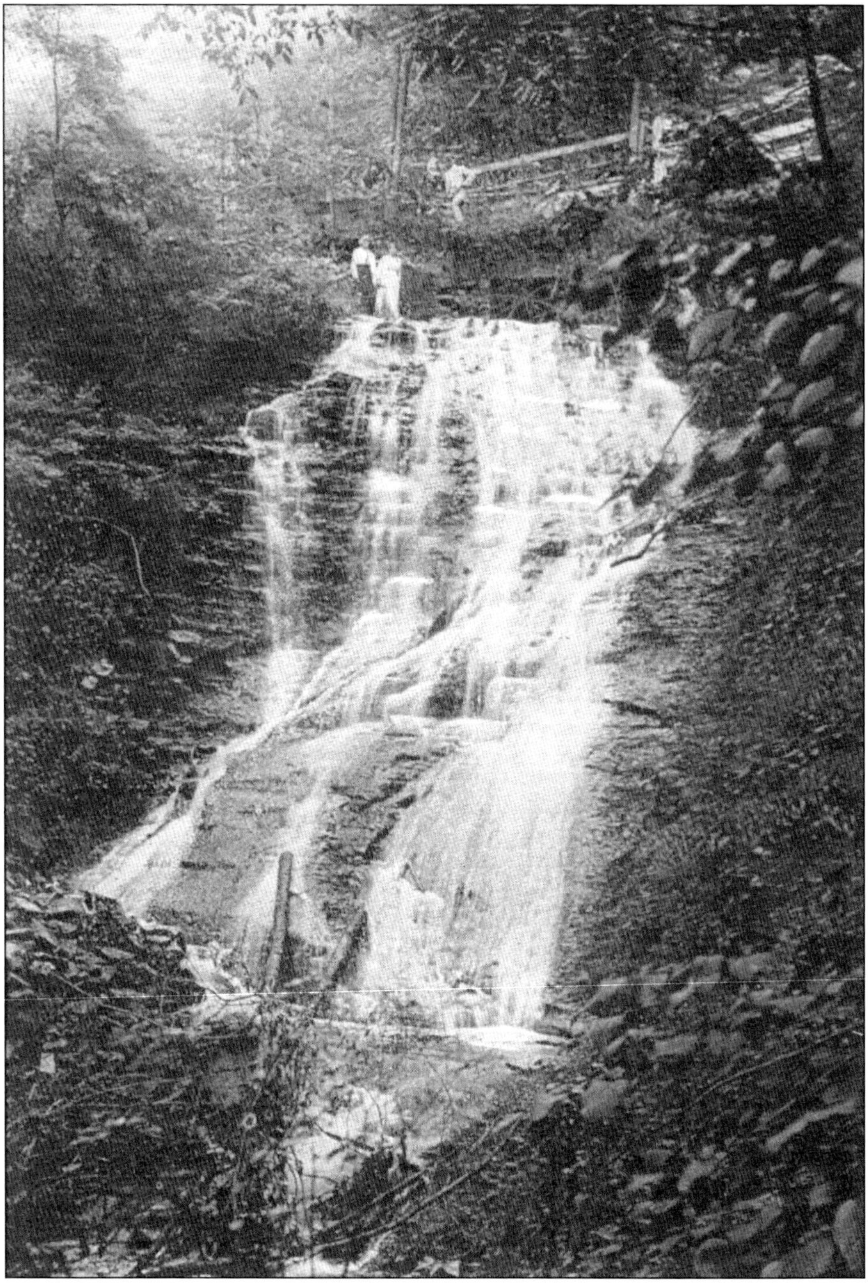

This early photograph from the 1800s shows the falls just north of the village, where the sulphur water gushes over the rock face. "The flow of sulphur water is enormous," reports the August 30, 1875, *New York Times*. "The village creek turns milky white below the springs." Native tribes were attracted to the waters for their curative powers and shared their knowledge with the first Europeans to settle in Sharon. The waters were used both internally and externally for a variety of ailments: skin lesions, arthritis, "biliary derangements," malaria, asthma, vertigo, and headaches, among others. The beauty of the surrounding hills, woodlands, falling waters, and the clear air wafting in from the nearby Adirondacks provided the impetus for the resort that flourished in Sharon for more than a century.

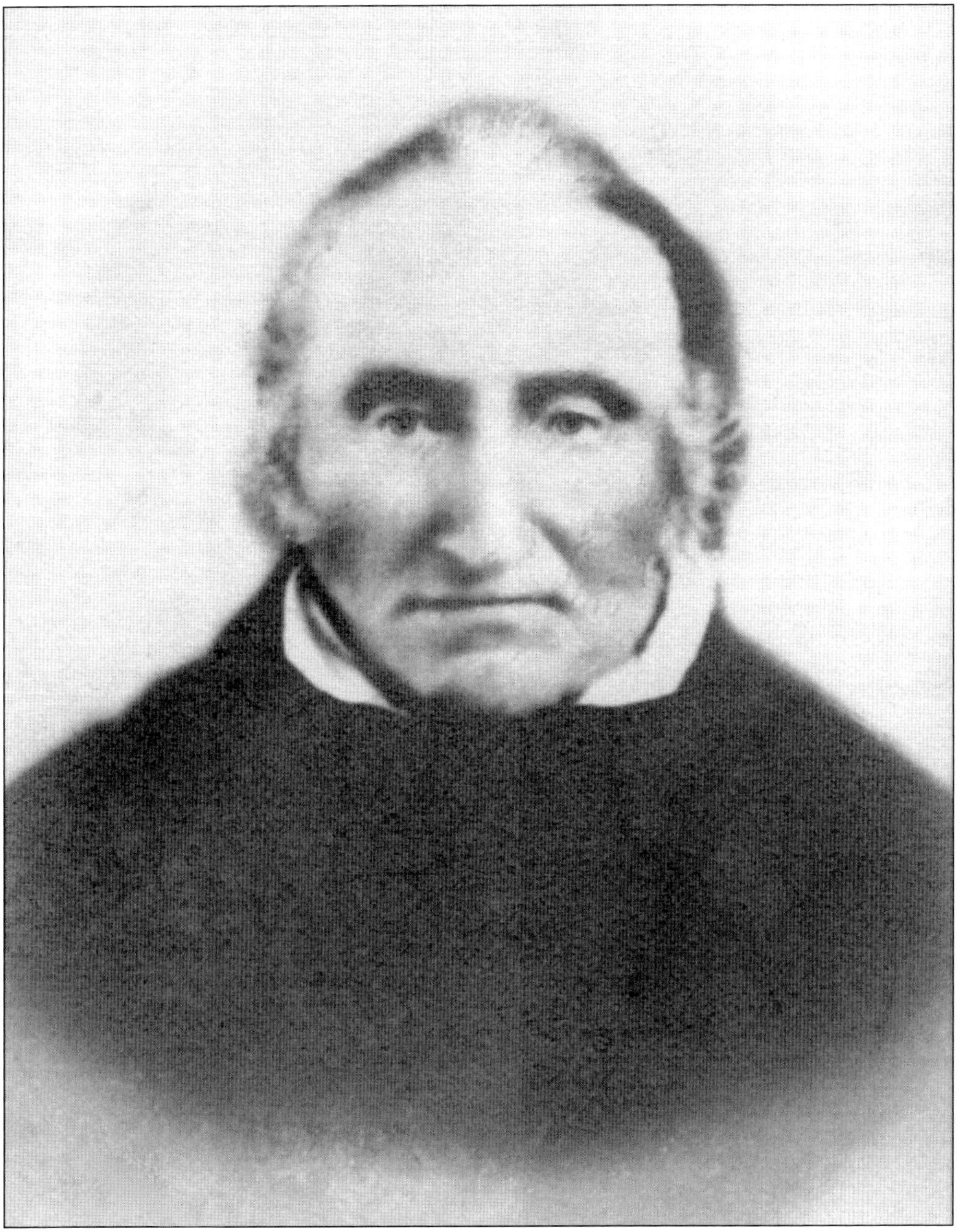

Jacob Dievendorff, captured by loyalists and Indians in July 1781, was force-marched to Sharon. When he attempted to escape, he was scalped and left for dead. He recovered and went on to live a long, productive life with a metal plate in his head, becoming a local legend. His captors were part of a raiding party that burned farms and seized crops as part of the vicious irregular war along the frontier in New York. The group that had seized Dievendorff, about 300 strong, encamped east of Sharon Springs, then called New Dorlach, at a cedar swamp. It was there that a smaller group of local militia under Colonel Willett ambushed and defeated them. Historical markers along Route 20, east of the village, indicate the sites of the Sharon Battle and the Camp of Cedar Swamp.

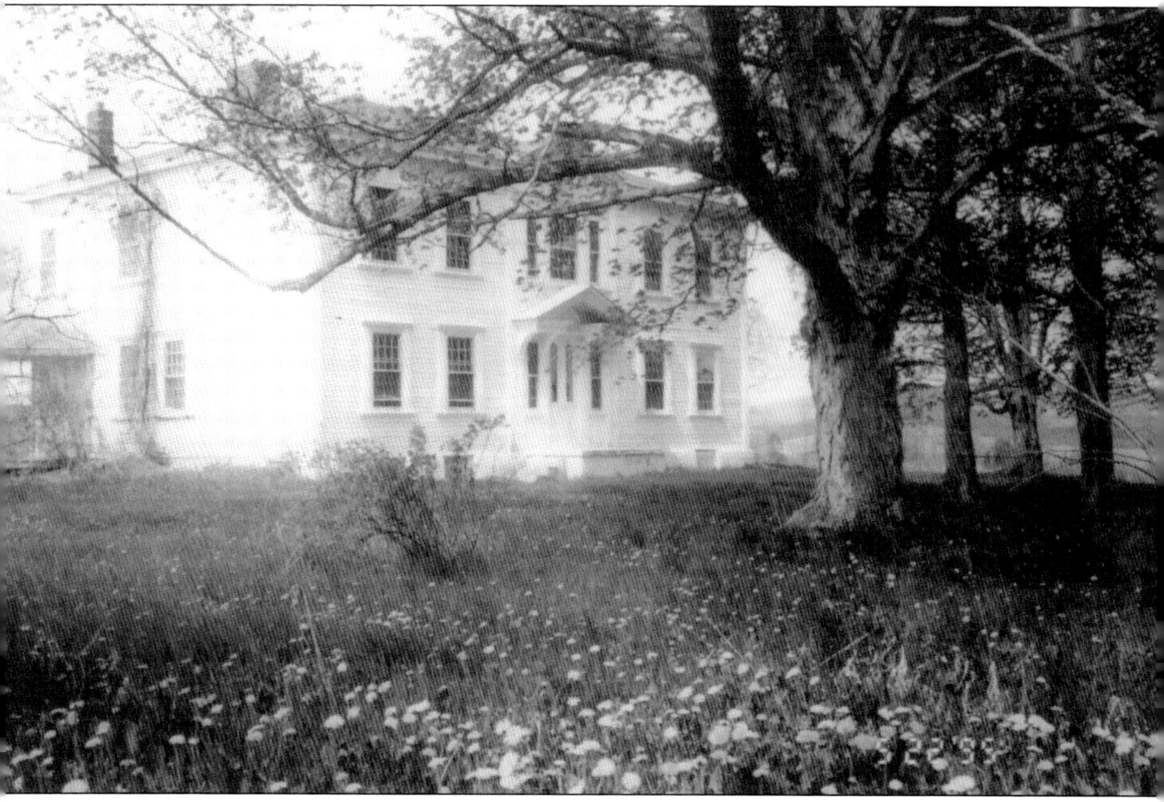

Built in 1802–1804, this spacious, Palladian-style home of William Beekman stands today as a monument to his legacy. Carpenters were brought in from Connecticut to construct the mansion at a cost of $10,000, an unusually vast sum at that time. At age 14, Beekman became private secretary to Col. Marinus Willet, who commanded the border militia. While serving the colonel, Beekman met the family of prominent landowner Nicholas Low and married his daughter, Joanna, in 1785. William and Joanna Beekman settled in the town of Sharon in 1787. His appointment as the first judge of Schoharie County by Gov. Dewitt Clinton created controversy, as many older lawyers expected the honor. But Beekman served with dignity until his retirement at age 66. He and Joanna had 10 children; seven died young, giving rise to the many ghost stories haunting the house today.

William Beekman was born on the Atlantic Ocean in 1767 while his parents were emigrating from Holland; sadly, his mother died when he was only a few months old. A successful farmer, businessman (he owned the first mercantile store in town), and the first judge in Schoharie County, Beekman was fluent in Dutch, German, and English. (Courtesy of the Mitchell Collection at Sharon Springs Central School.)

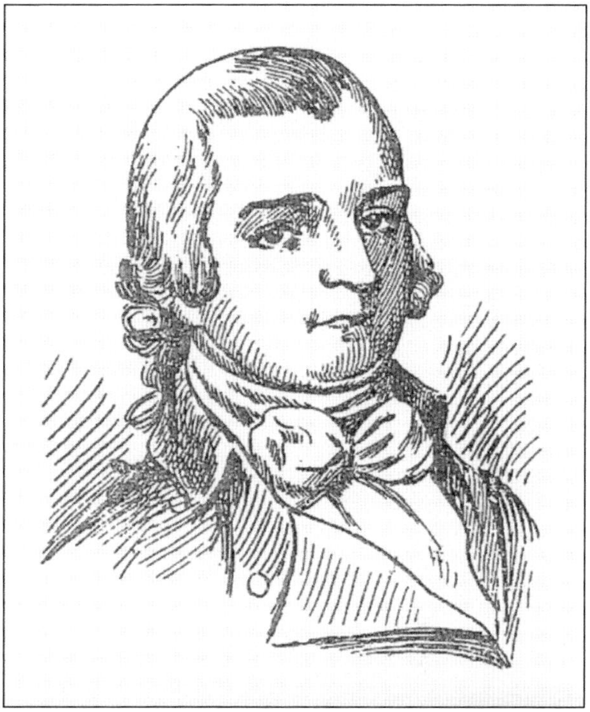

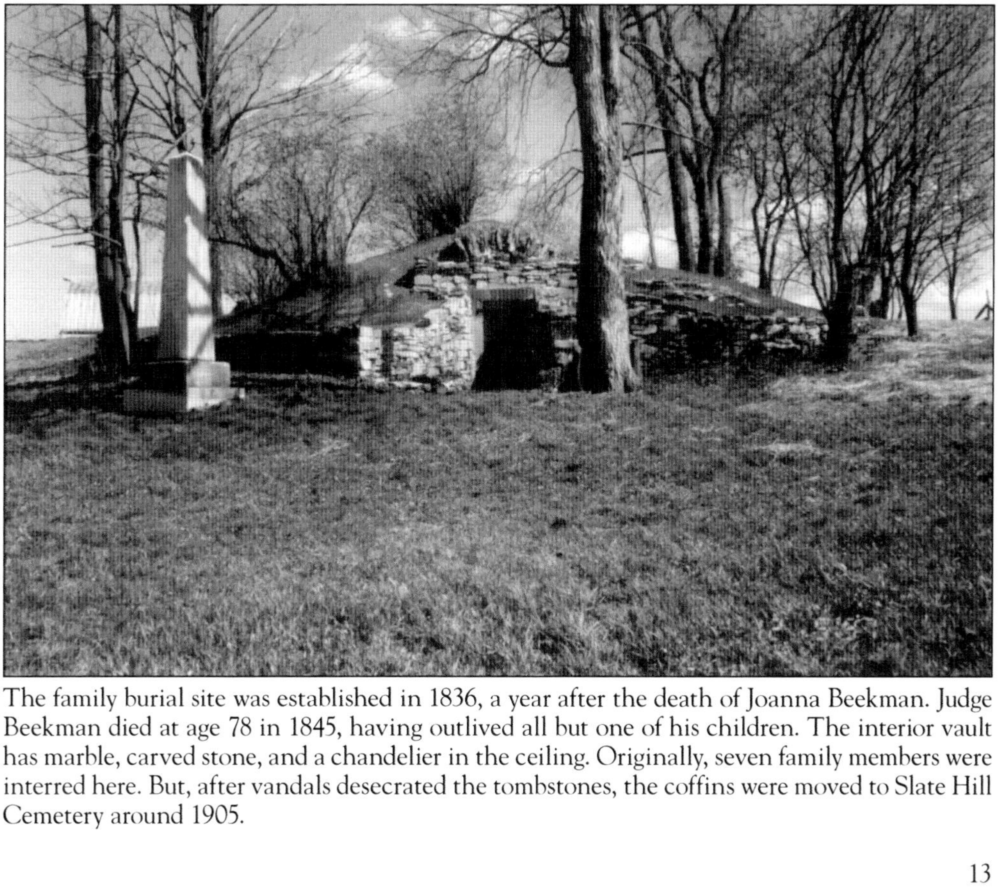

The family burial site was established in 1836, a year after the death of Joanna Beekman. Judge Beekman died at age 78 in 1845, having outlived all but one of his children. The interior vault has marble, carved stone, and a chandelier in the ceiling. Originally, seven family members were interred here. But, after vandals desecrated the tombstones, the coffins were moved to Slate Hill Cemetery around 1905.

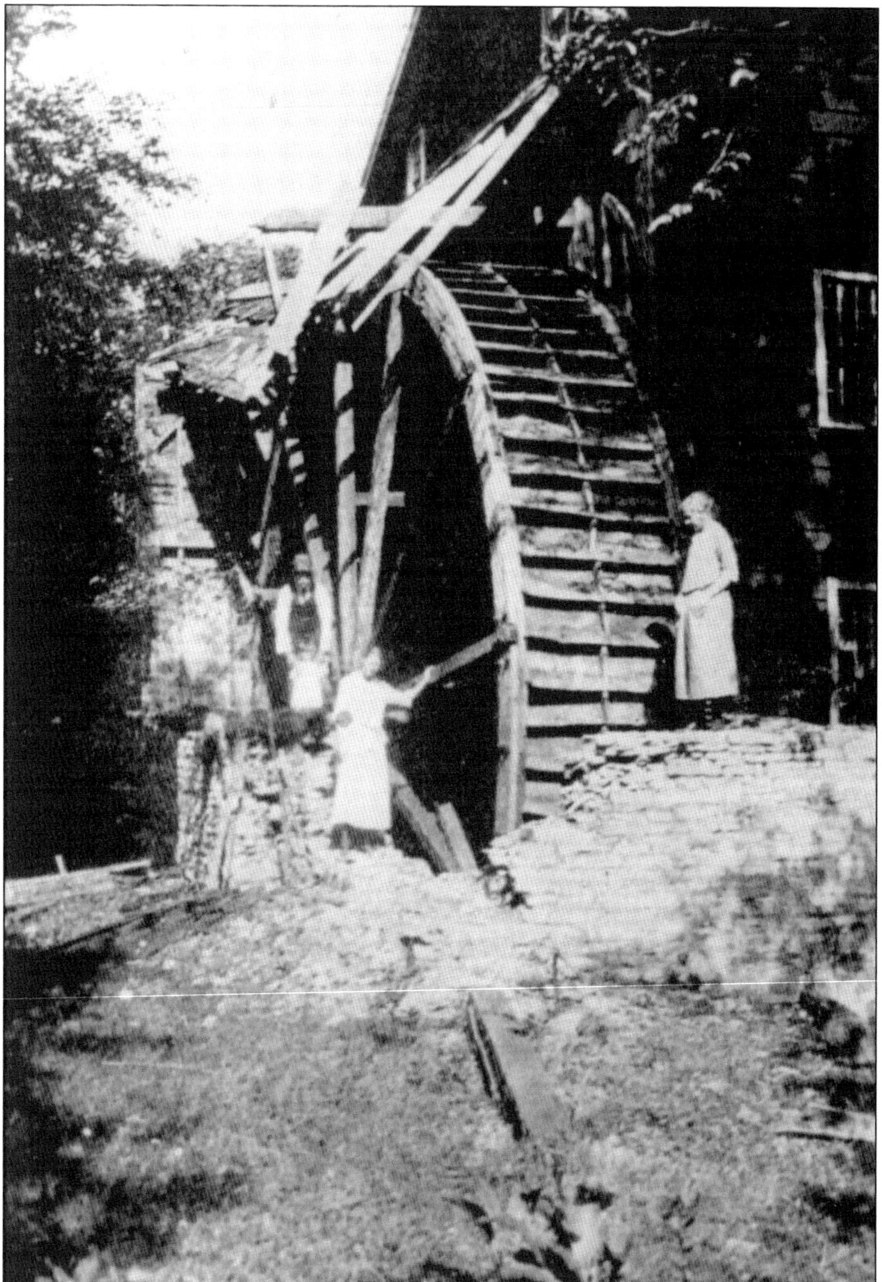

The first mill on this site was built by Peter Engell in 1810. In 1869, his son, Moses Engell, built the one pictured here, which stood just southeast of Engleville Pond. The large overshot waterwheel was 32 feet in diameter and could generate 60 horsepower. The mill had three stone "runs," one for feed, one for buckwheat flour, and one for wheat flour. Adam Engell, one of six sons of Moses, was the miller. The Engell family (spelled Engle, Engel, or Engell) were early arrivals, dating back to Peter Engell from the Palatinate of Germany, who settled in the area in 1749. Many descendants can be found in Sharon today. Although the mill is gone, a stone wall from the original foundation survives.

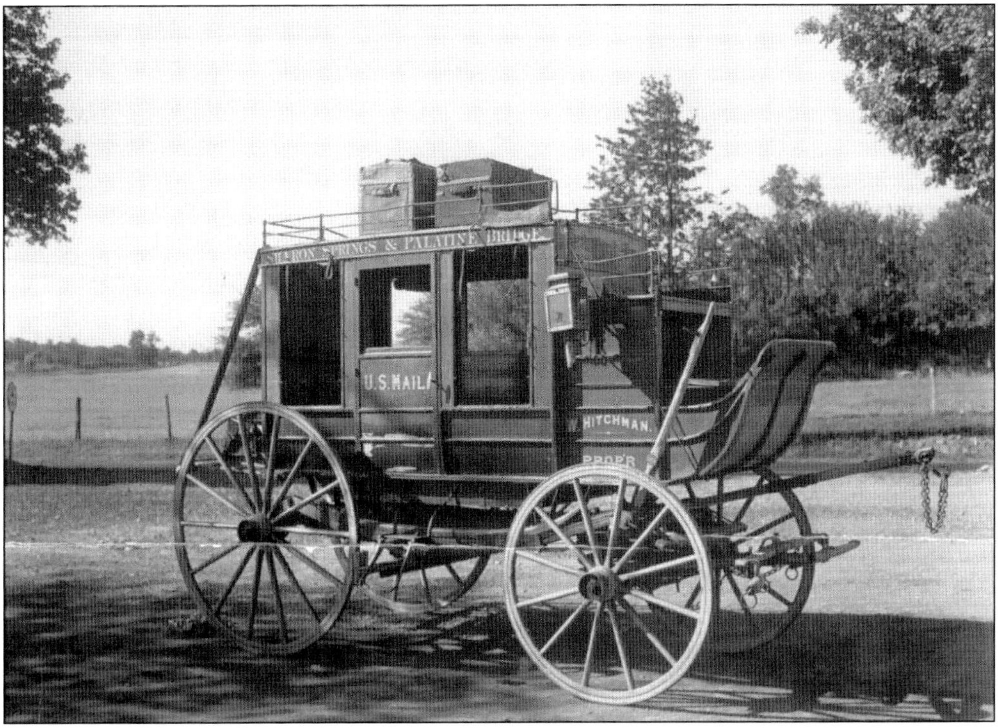

Transportation to and from Sharon has been a challenge because of the rolling, often steep terrain. One early mode of access was to journey by water to Palatine Bridge, located on the Erie Canal, 11 miles north of the village. Travelers then proceeded via this stagecoach to Sharon Springs. The route from the canal was an arduous climb up a challenging grade.

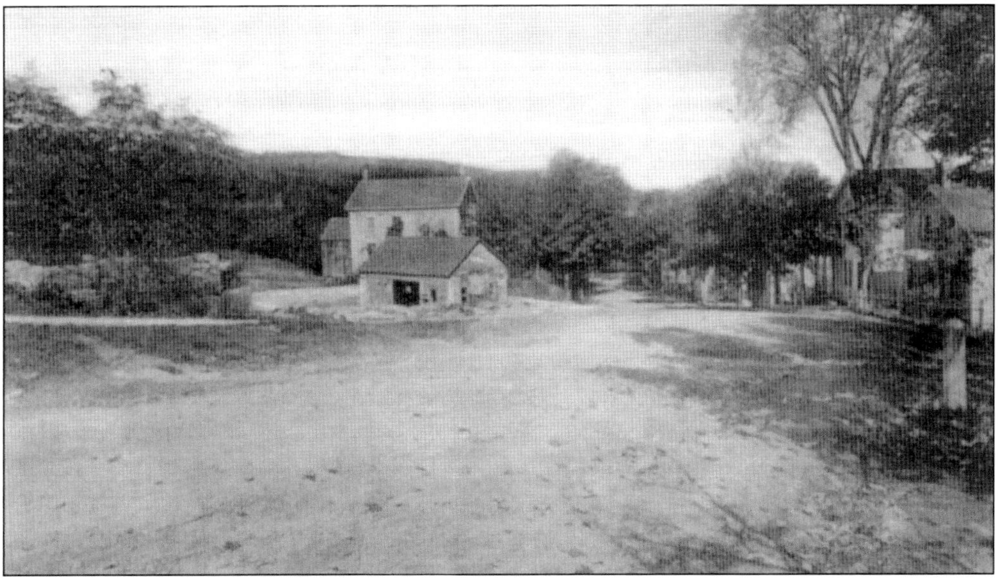
Shown here is Rockville, located at the top of the hill above the springs. When the Town of Sharon was chartered in 1797, Rockville was one of the hamlets, but in 1871, it was absorbed into the Village of Sharon Springs. No longer referred to as Rockville, the upper village continues to feel a separation from the springs area in the lower part of the village.

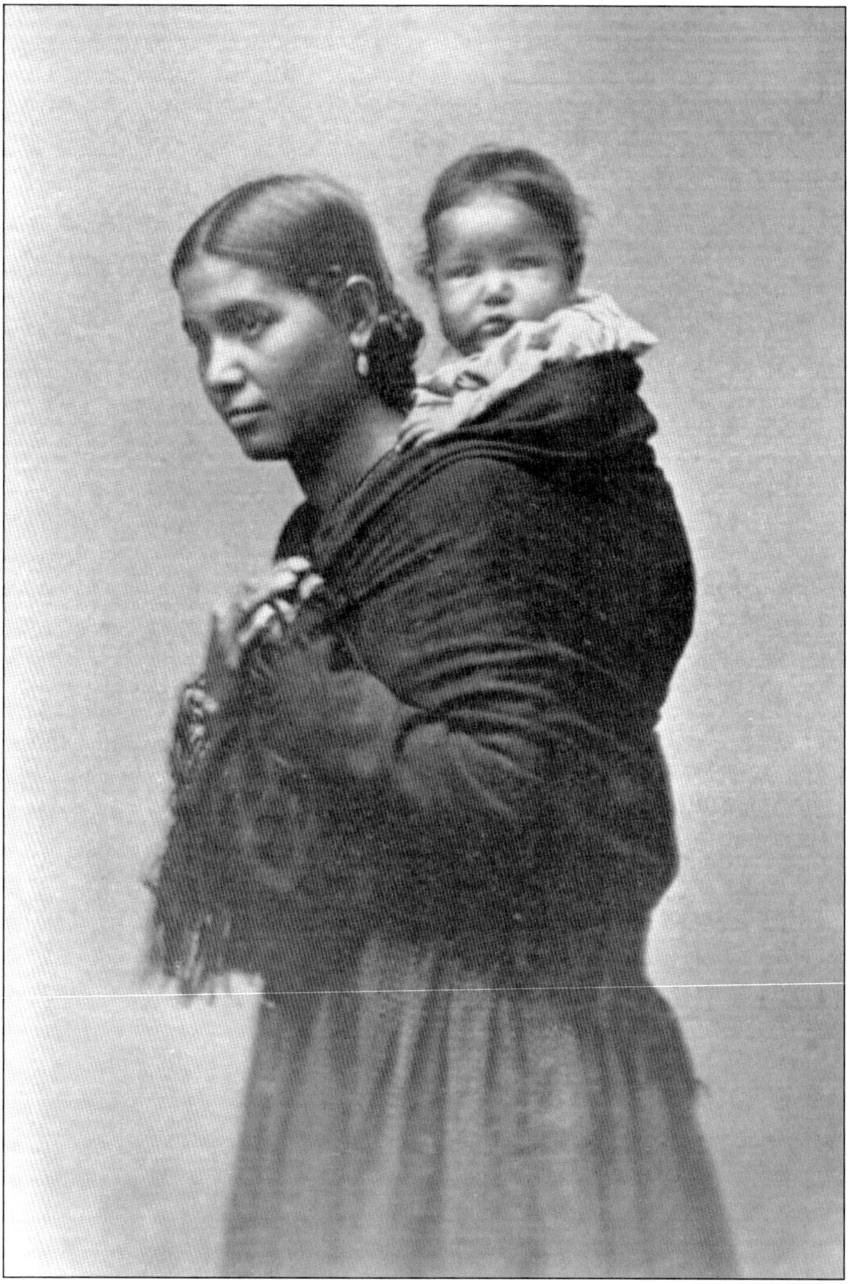

Although most Native Americans were removed from the area after 1787, several continued to come to Sharon Springs over the centuries. Lucinda Brazille and her family of the Abenaki tribe owned a home here in the 19th century. This 1872 photograph shows her with a son born in Sharon. The Brazille family eventually immigrated to California, but they had lived in Sharon for much of the 19th century. A lithograph of the area around the springs of Sharon in the June 1856 issue of *Harper's Monthly* shows "a small encampment of St. Francis Indians, who have occupied the spot for several seasons, make and sell baskets, fans, and other splintwork, and give pleasure to visitors by their novelty and the picturesqueness of their little village." See the map on page 2 for locations of Native Americans' homes in 1847.

Two

THE SPA ERA

It was a quiet beginning. David Eldredge moved a house next to the springs to serve as a boardinghouse in 1825. Despite the health-enhancing properties of the springs and the popularity of spas, lack of transportation slowed development. Eventually, guests arrived via the Erie Canal to Canajoharie, then a stagecoach ride up the steep ridge to the spa. By 1870, one could arrive by train directly to Sharon Springs.

In addition to the award-winning mineral waters, the location 1,100 feet above sea level with sweeping vistas of the Mohawk Valley and Adirondack Mountains inspired many visitors. One wrote in her diary of "a stretch of country marked off into squares like a chequer board. . . . Uncle said he had seen a great many splendid prospects but this was the finest."

Construction began on the Pavilion Hotel in 1836. This soon became the elegant resort of the wealthy. By the end of the 1840s, prominent Bostonians, wealthy New York socialites, and visitors from France, Spain, Cuba, and Mexico could be found enjoying the summer season at Mr. Gardner's Pavilion Hotel. Their doings can be found in the society pages of the *New York Times* from that era. The newspaper sent a reporter to cover the scene in Sharon Springs. One can imagine the local farmers and their families driving into the village to observe the flower parades, the promenades, and the society damsels wearing the latest fashions from Paris. Several songs and poems exist chronicling the courtships prevalent among the elite families sojourning in Sharon Springs. A Gardner daughter married Lorenzo Delmonico of the famous restaurant family, who spent his summers at the palatial hotel and often catered wedding receptions on-site.

While much of Sharon Springs enjoyed this resort boom, some residents were not so fortunate. The resort trade can be fickle, and a few bad seasons can spell ruin, as happened with H.L. Bang and his Congress Hall. Fires could spell disaster to large wooden hotel structures, and many succumbed. The spa era cast its spell, and the village would never be the same.

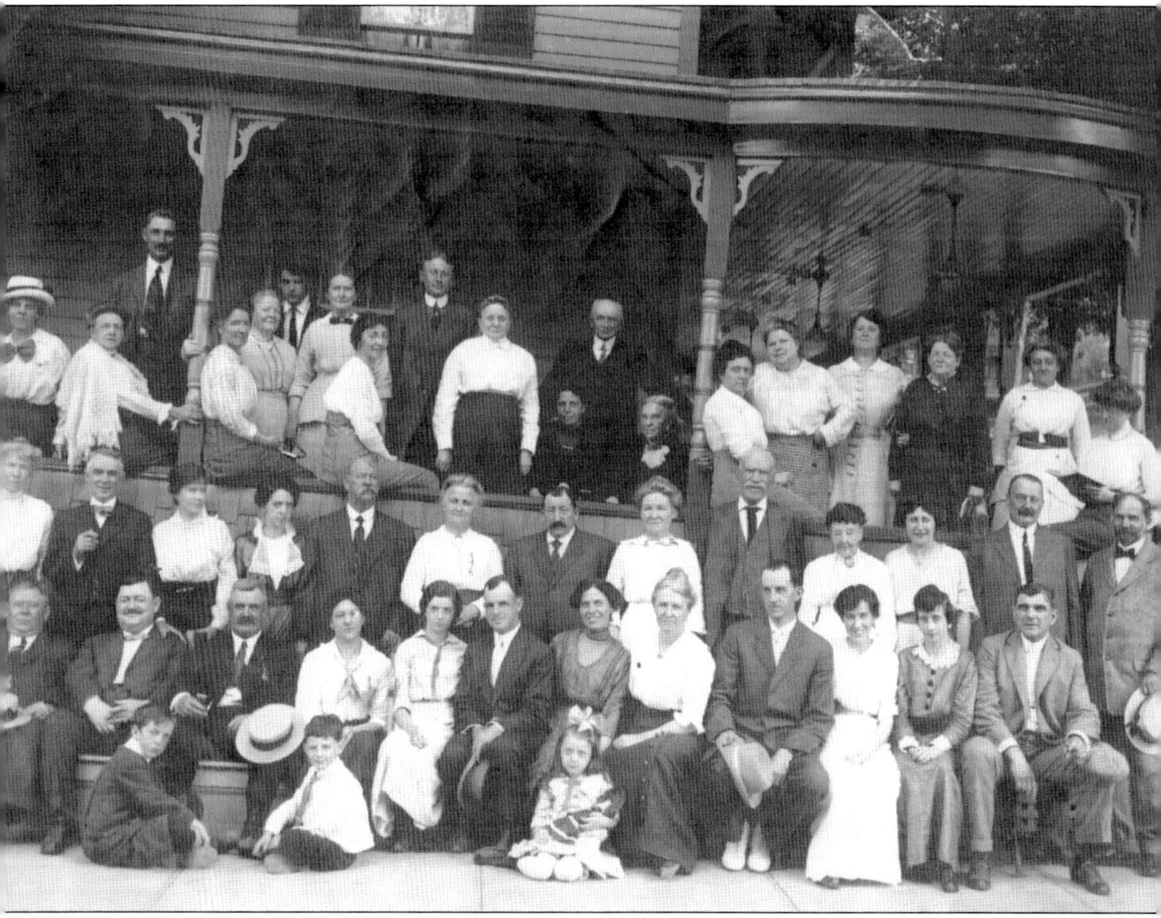

Guests relax in 1890 on the porch of the Eldredge House, one of the more fashionable boardinghouses in the 19th century. The Eldredge family started the spa resort when entrepreneur David Eldredge established the first boardinghouse near the mineral springs in 1825. Eldredge's vision soon proved profitable, and within a few years, many hotels, each larger and more magnificent than the last, sprouted along the village streets. By 1866, there were 12 hotels welcoming guests for the summer season. Families would come for several weeks to escape the heat and stale air of the cities at a time when coal, the prevalent source of power, created a miasma of smog over urban areas. Another reason for the popularity of Sharon was the quality of the springs, described by analysts as "very powerful" for healing and general health.

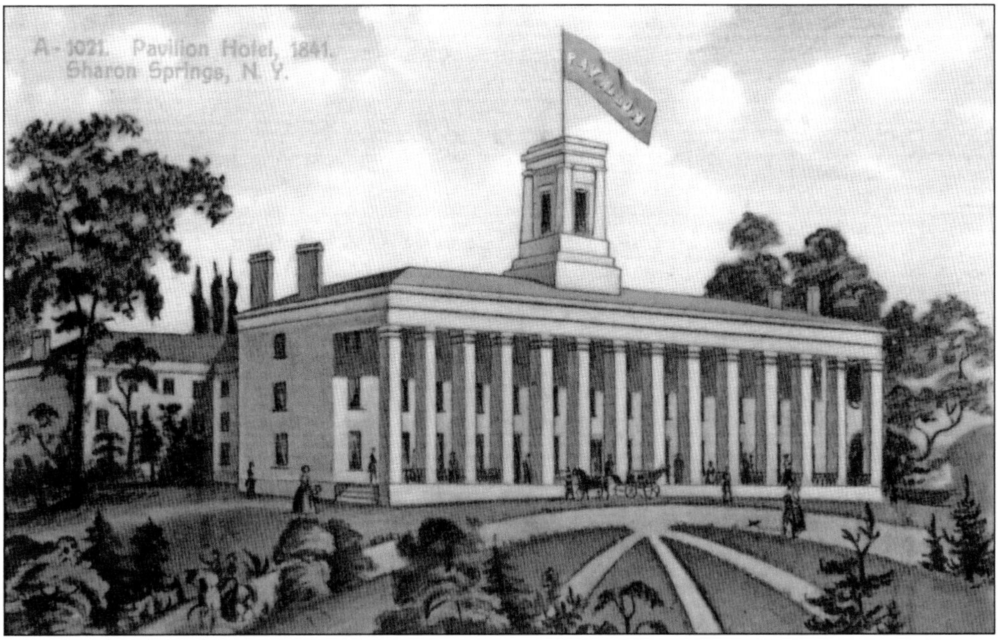

Built in 1836, the Pavilion Hotel, with its 220-foot-long porch overlooking the Mohawk Valley, attracted many prominent families of the 19th century. A *New York Times* reporter in 1849 wrote: "My home is the Pavilion . . . which is at present the home of more beauty, and fashion, and gaiety, that can be found. . . . The most prominent members of the 'Upper Ten' of New York . . . are [here] for the season."

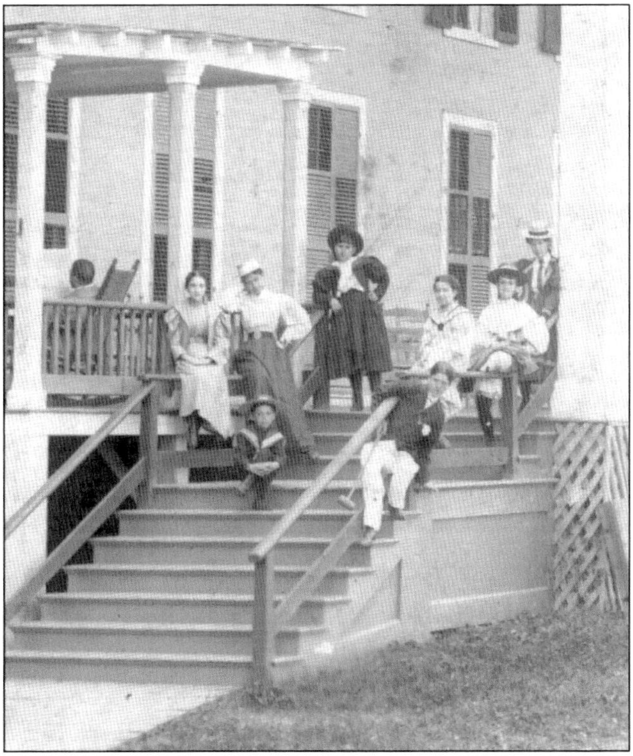

This c. 1880 photograph shows children at the Pavilion dressed for a lively game of croquet on the lawn. Their leisure is very different from the summer lives of full-time resident farm children, who would be working in the fields or employed in the hotels, restaurants, or bathing facilities.

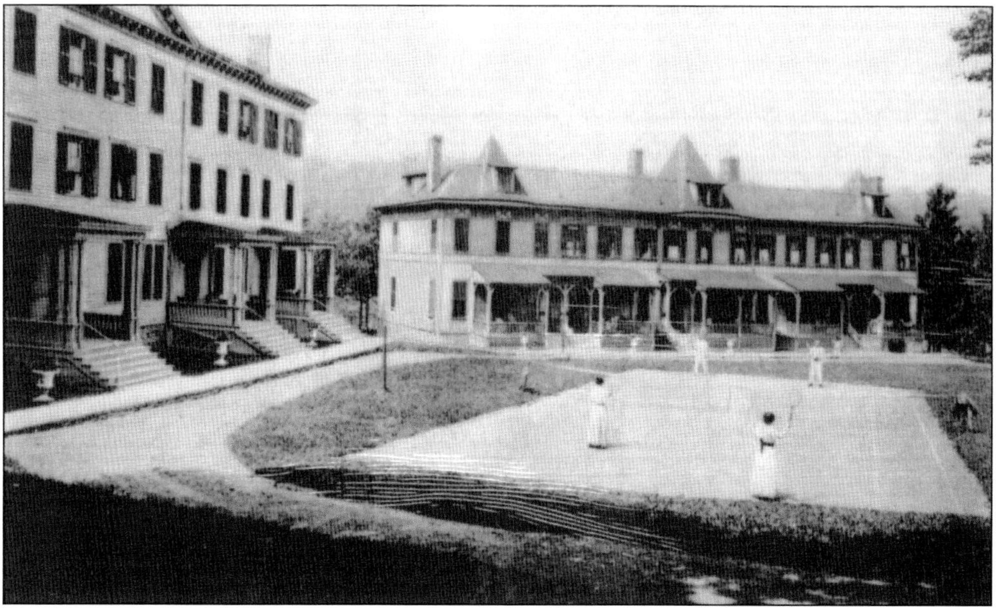

The Pavilion cottages offered tennis courts, croquet courts, and other amenities, including fireplaces, two-story piazzas, and conveniently located "water closets." Families wishing more privacy than a hotel could afford preferred renting a cottage for the season. Although in a state of decay today, the West building (center) remains.

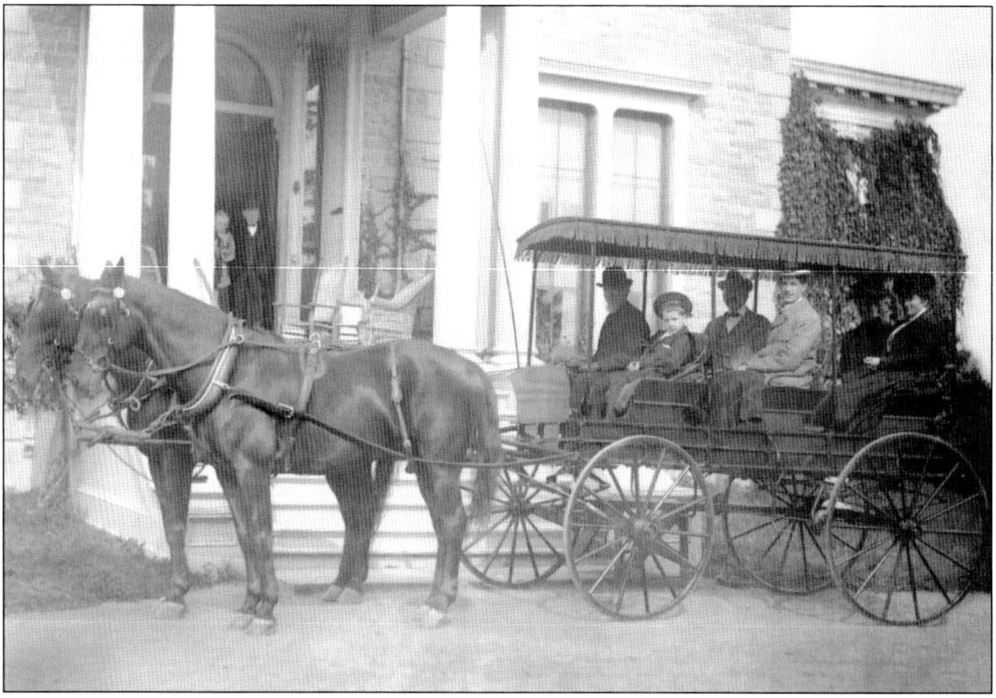

Members of the Gardner family arrive at the Stone House for a summer retreat around 1885. This was the family summer residence from 1838 until 1940. The Gardners owned the Imperial Baths and the Pavilion Hotel, and they were prominent in local affairs. John Gardner held mortgages on several other hotel properties in Sharon and was instrumental in establishing Trinity Church.

A young relative of John Gardner poses in front of the Stone House around 1890. Several generations of Gardners enjoyed the ambience of summers in Sharon Springs with the healthy mountain air, clear-running streams, and the opportunity to play on the Pavilion grounds with children from elite families.

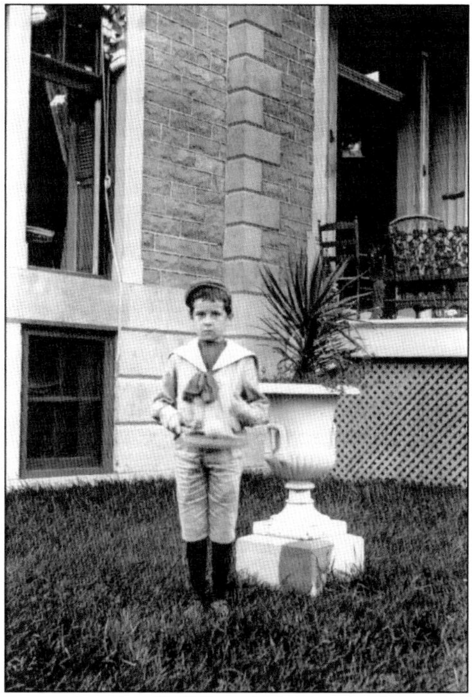

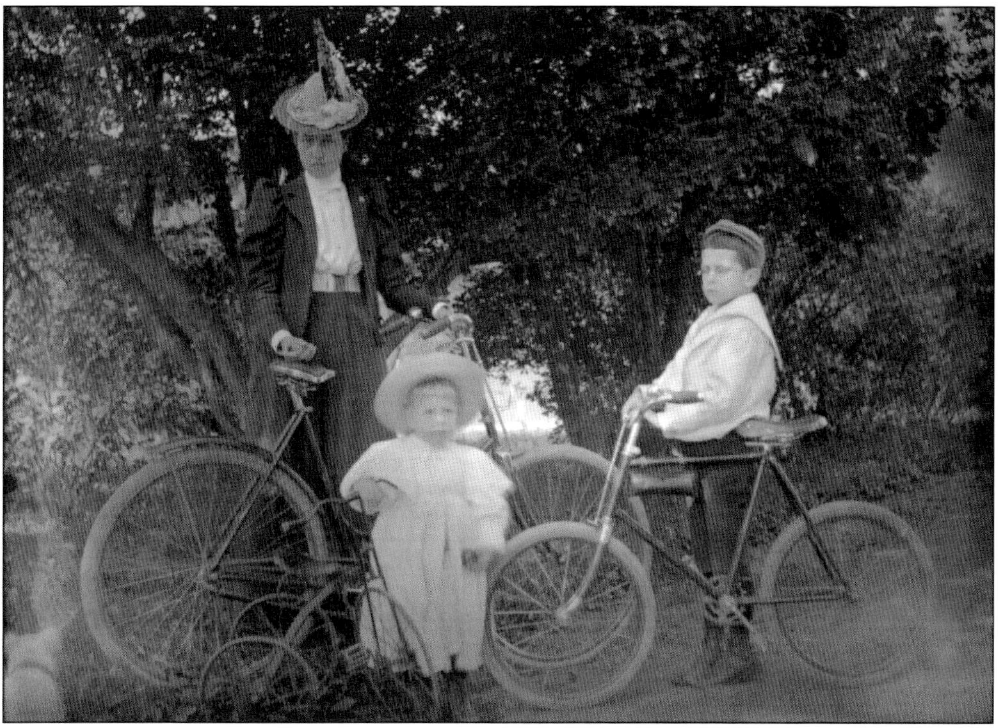

Members of the Gardner family pose before a bicycle outing in the 1890s. The mother wears the obligatory hat and long-skirted suit, which was the style before the change to more comfortable women's clothing. Her older son sports knickers, while the younger boy is still in a dress, as was customary at the time. He stands beside his three-wheeled velocipede.

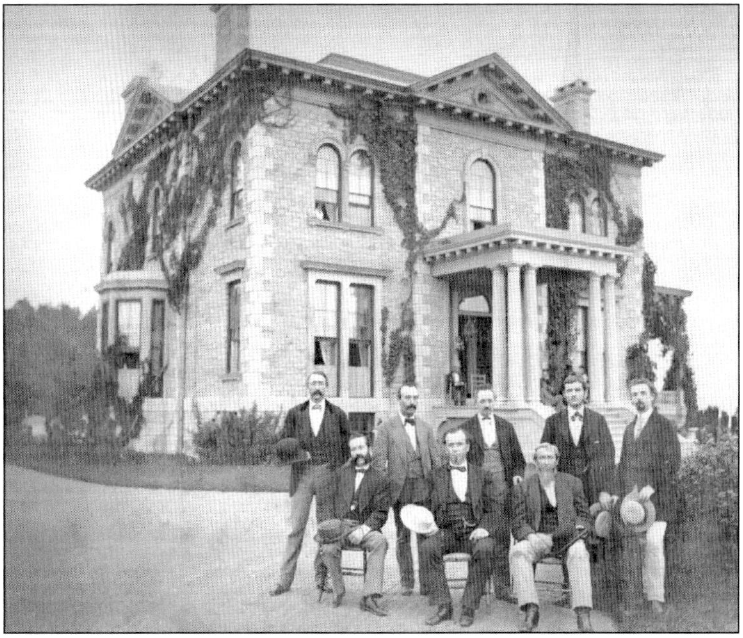

This 1880s photograph shows employees of the Gardner estate posed in front of the Stone House Mansion. The home was built in 1863 with stone from the Sharon Springs limestone quarry. The low-pitched roof, bracketed eaves, and round-head windows identify the style as Italianate. Located on a hilltop overlooking the Mohawk Valley, the house symbolizes the family's stature in the community.

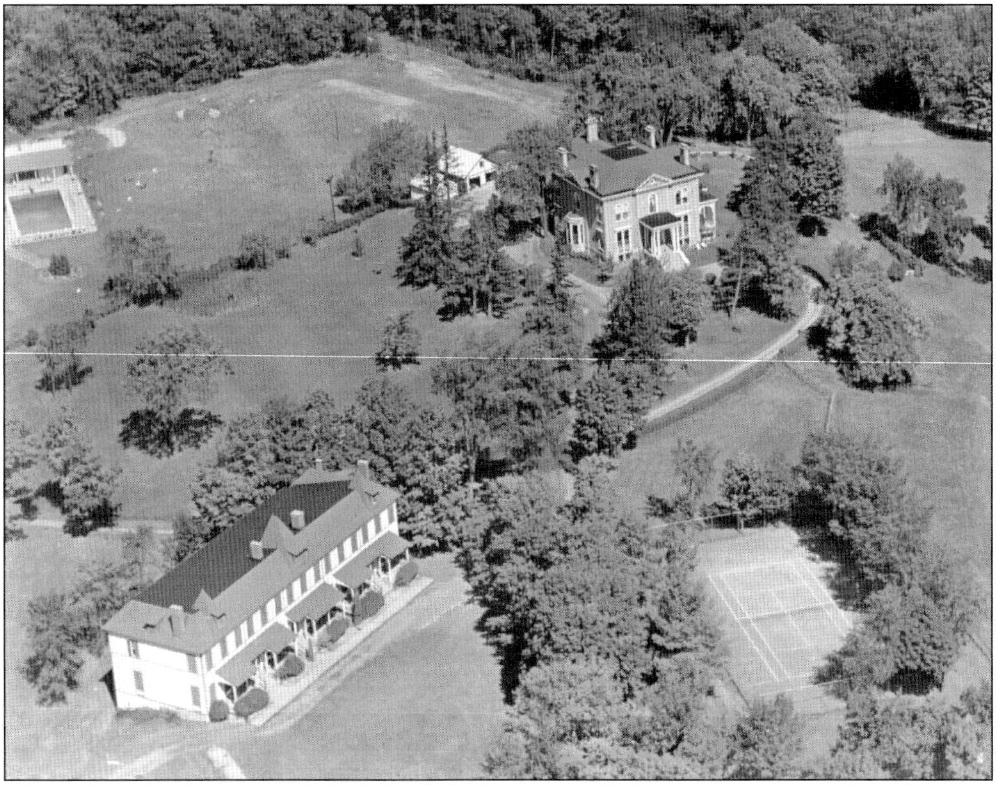

This 1940s aerial photograph of the Gardner Stone House Mansion shows the Pavilion cottages in the foreground, as well as the tennis court. The Adler Hotel pool is at upper left. To the right of the mansion is part of the golf course that was created by the Gardner family to encourage more tourism.

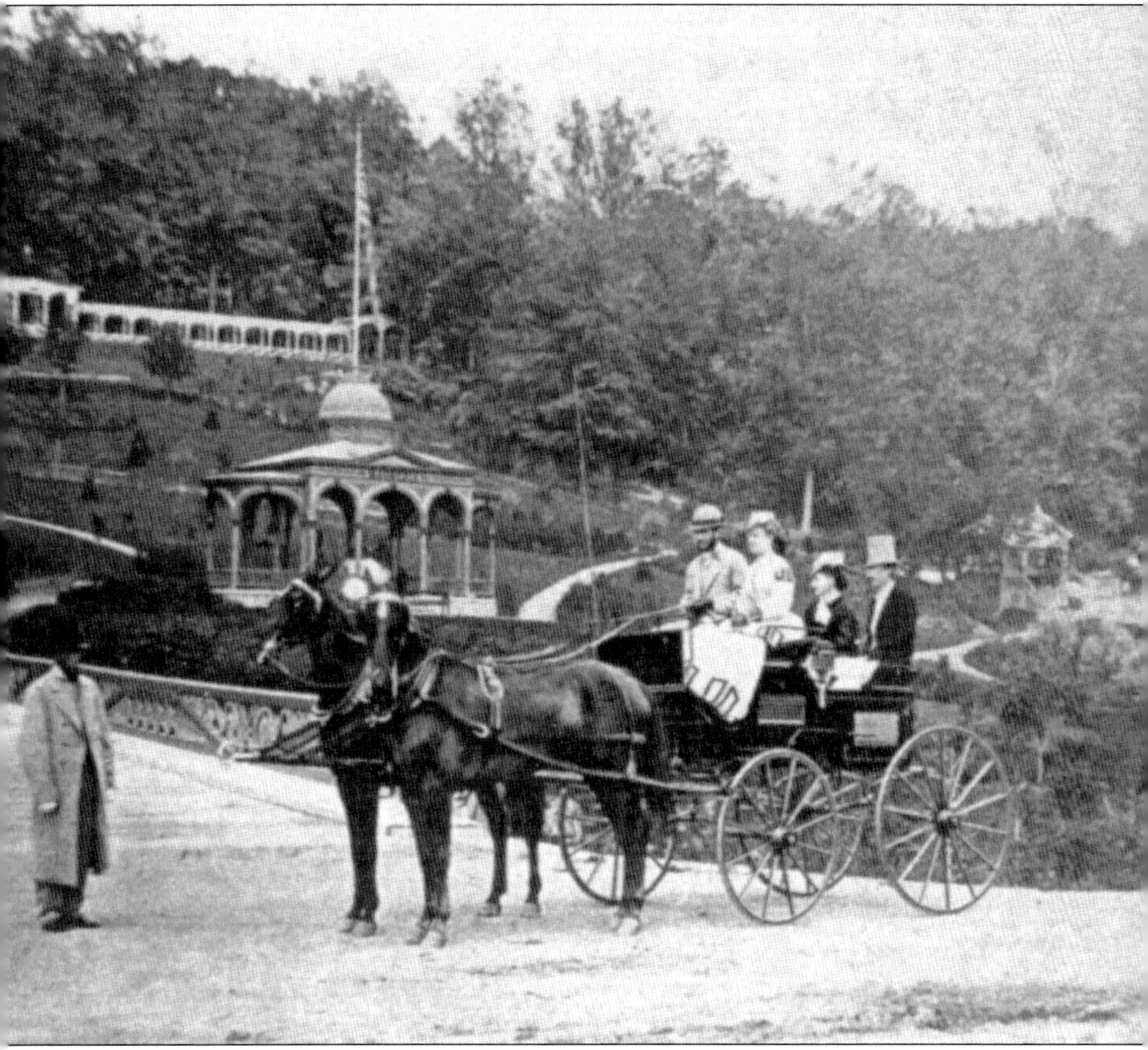

This stereoscopic image from 1870 shows the grounds of Congress Park Hotel, with its gracious arbors, walkways, and Magnesia Temple. The occupants dressed for a daytime outing and sitting in a carriage are representative of spa visitors of this era. The success of Gardner's Pavilion Hotel inspired many others, one of whom was H.L. Bang, who, in 1860, built Congress Hall in a park near the springs. He surrounded the hotel with magnificent landscaping and the exquisite Magnesia Temple. By the 1870s, Bang was beset by financial troubles; one day in 1875, all the furniture was removed from the hotel, which burned to the ground the very next day (the first of many "insurance fires" in the village). Bang sold his home, untouched by the fire, to the Schaeffer brewing family.

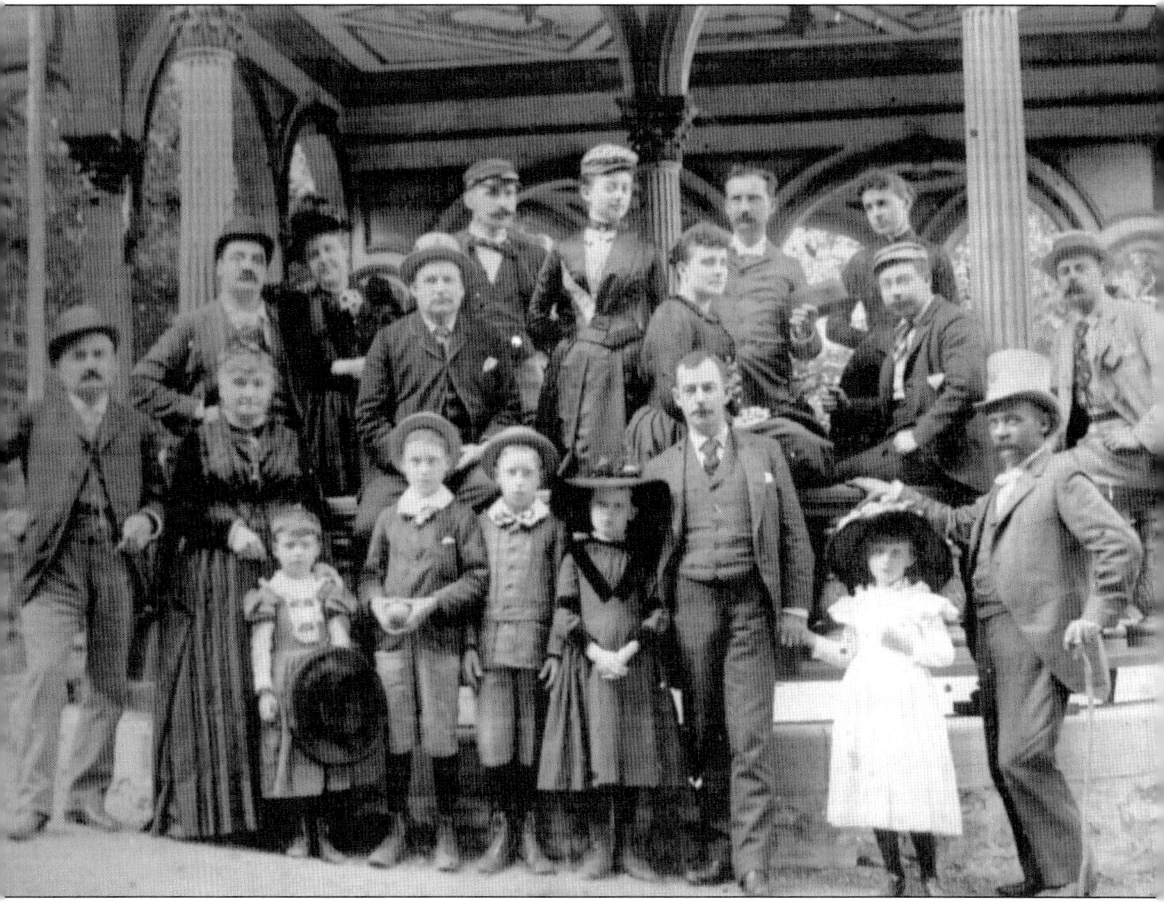

The Barnard family poses at the Magnesia Temple in 1888. This magnificent wrought-iron structure was built in 1863 as part of H.L. Bang's Congress Hall Park. The temple is an example of the Renaissance Revival, one of many Victorian Revival styles. The triangular pediment, dentils in the cornice, and Corinthian columns indicate Classical influence. The cast-iron temple was created in New York City. It is believed that the structure was ferried to Palatine Bridge via riverboat and loaded on a sled in the winter and pulled up the steep incline to Sharon. For a century, although privately owned, this was a favorite spot for photographs, picnics, and gatherings. The water was valued as a curative for intestinal disorders (think "milk of magnesia") and turns the surrounding hillside white at times.

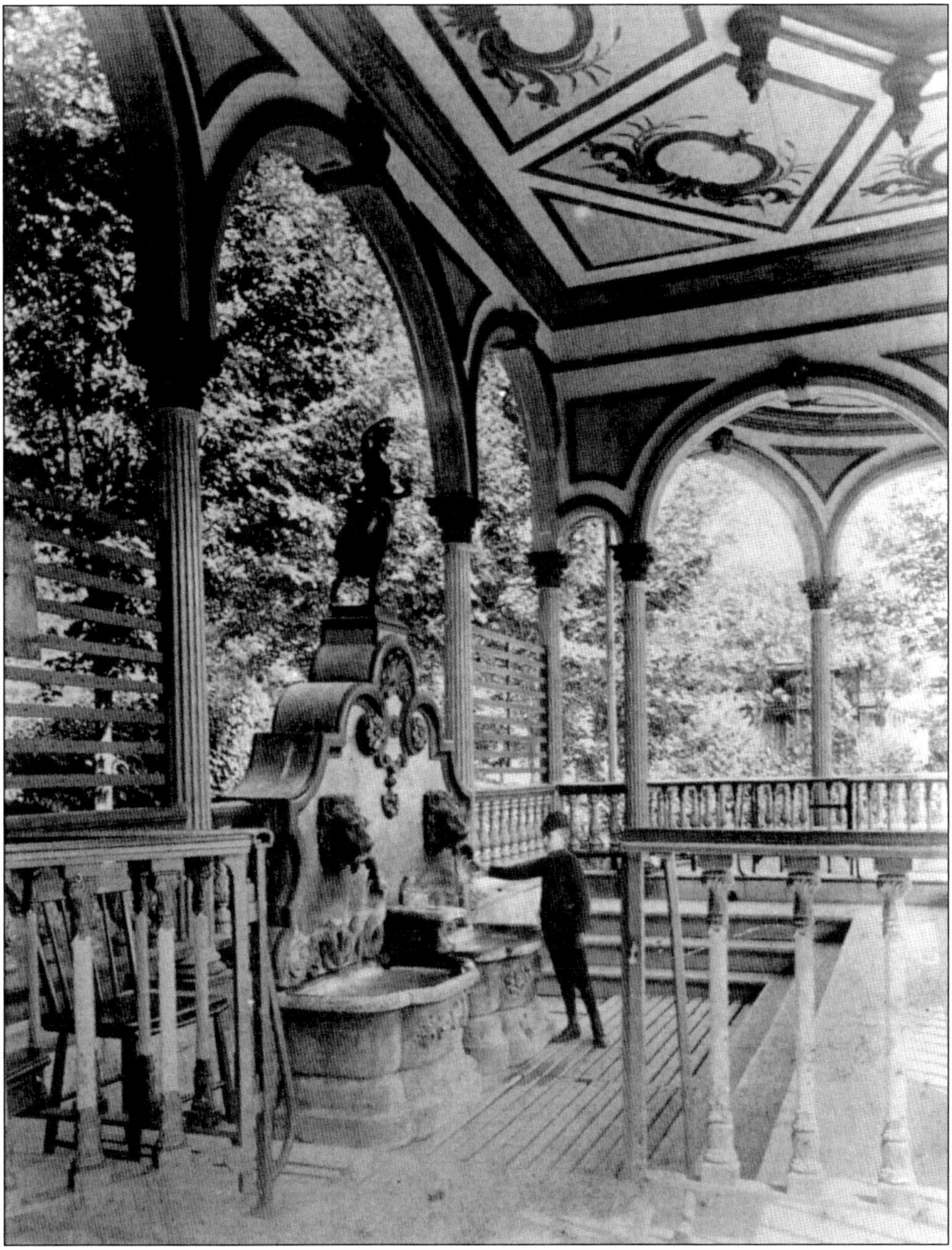

The interior of the Magnesia Temple is shown here in 1880, with its Oriental motifs: acanthus leaf dentils under the cornice, grapevine motifs throughout the structure, and graceful arches. The mineral water once spouted from the mouths of twin stone lion heads, which have since disappeared. Here, a young boy fills a cup with the water. He was probably hired for the season to serve guests.

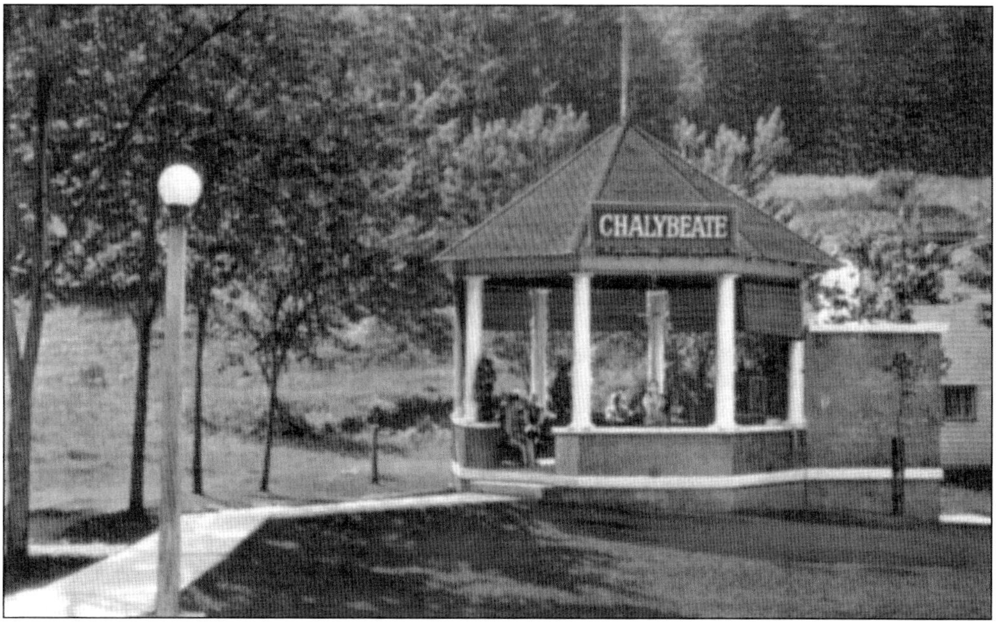

Located a few blocks south of the Magnesia and Sulphur Temples, the Chalybeate Temple, seen here on a 1920s postcard, marks the chalybeate, or iron, spring, considered beneficial for women's health because of the heavy concentration of iron, so much that it would turn teeth brown! Today, the village owns and is restoring the Chalybeate Temple, the only spring not in private hands.

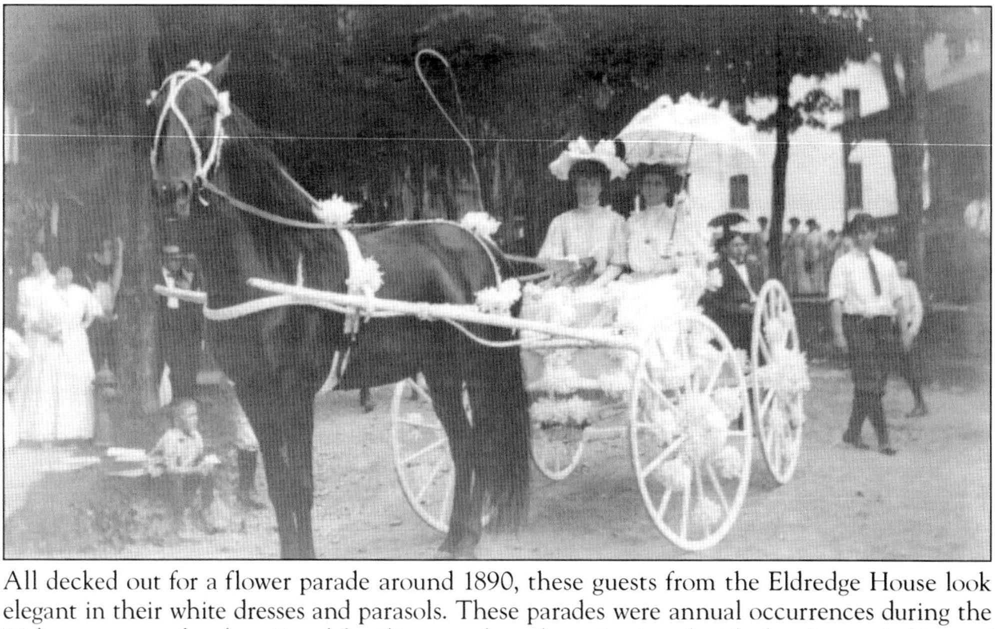

All decked out for a flower parade around 1890, these guests from the Eldredge House look elegant in their white dresses and parasols. These parades were annual occurrences during the 19th-century spa heydays. Local families must have been intrigued with the elegant fashions of the day and the chance to hobnob with elite families.

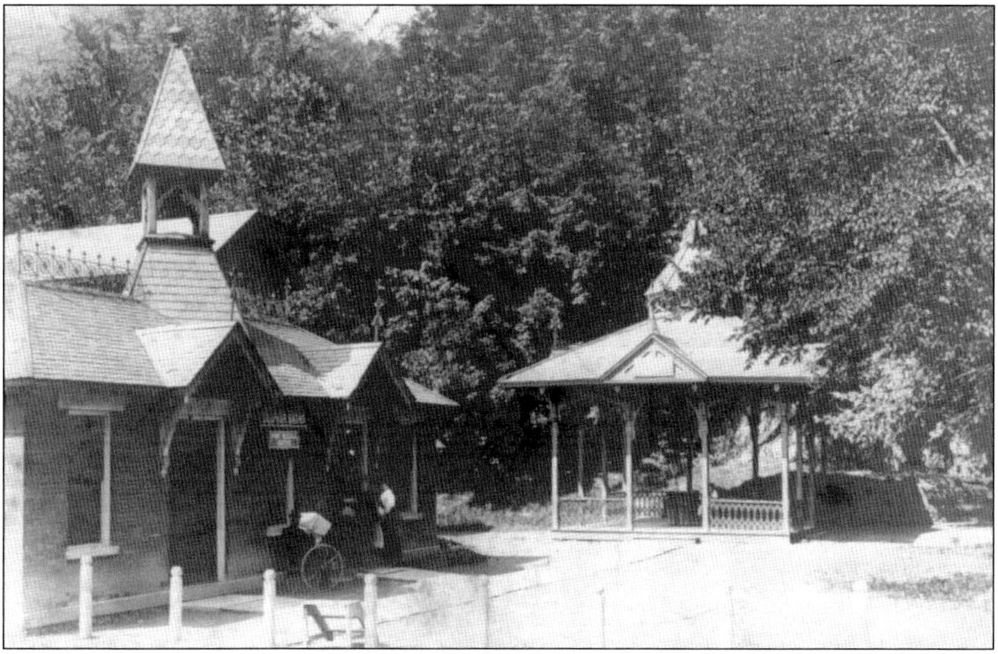

The lower Sulphur Bath House and Sulphur Temple are seen here in the 1880s. The wooden temple was replaced in the 20th century, and the bathhouse was enlarged. The sign offering "Pine Needle Baths" refers to the preferred additive to a sulphur bath to mitigate the "rotten egg" smell of sulphur. The lower bathhouse offered a less expensive option, with no resting room available.

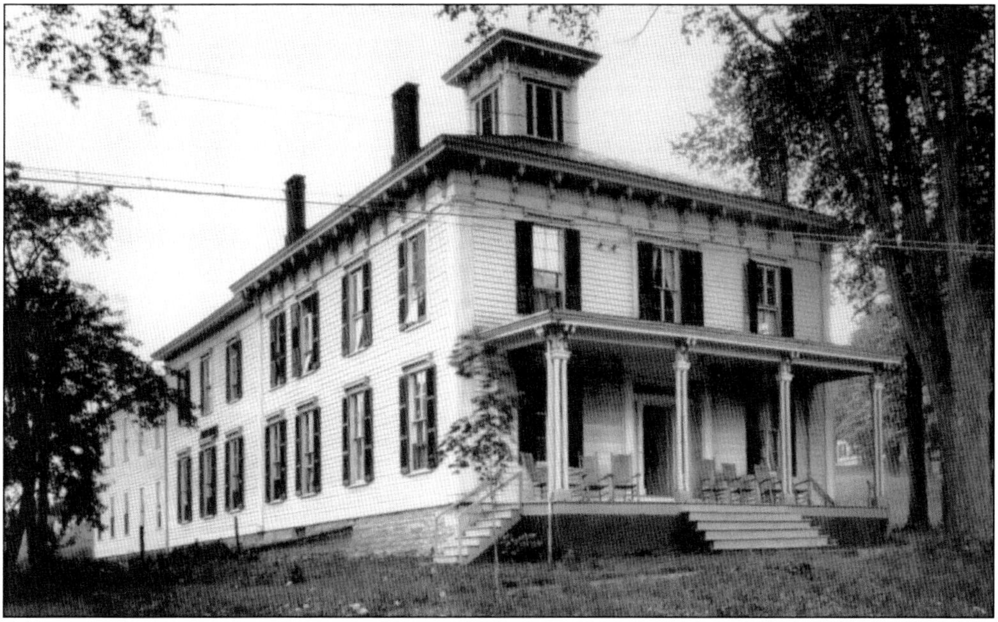

Dr. John Fonda built the Italianate Fonda Cottage in 1850, and Sebastian Fonda wrote the first thorough analysis of the mineral waters here (the actor Henry Fonda was a direct descendant). By 1890, Emily Fonda operated the home as a boardinghouse until the 1920s. In the mid-20th century, the house served as a dormitory for White Sulphur employees. Today, it has been restored by Phoebe MacGillivary as a private residence.

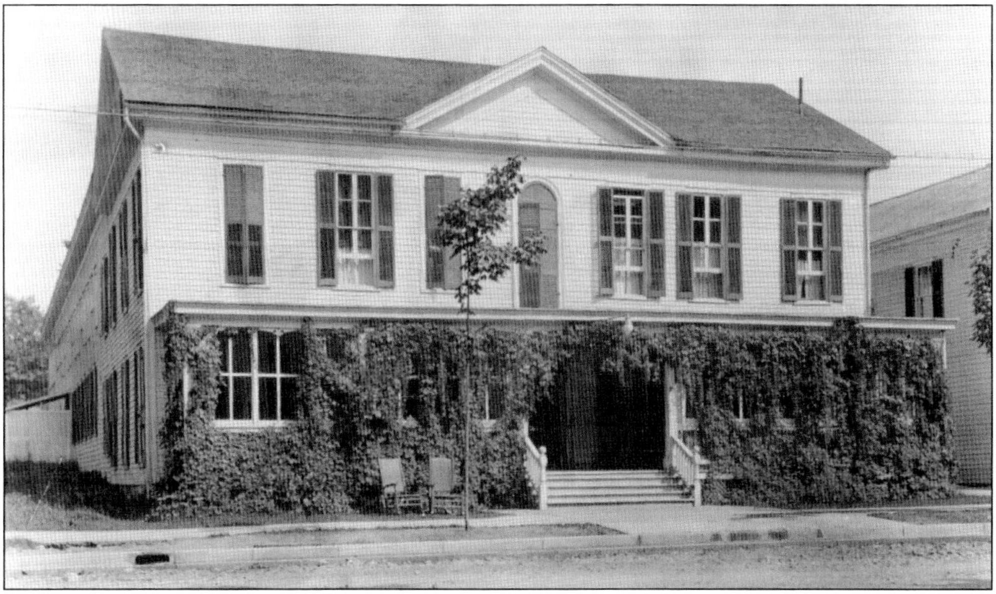

This photograph of the Park View Hotel was taken around 1908. Frederick Mauhs owned the hotel from 1900 to 1911, when he was tragically killed in a sledding accident. Mauhs was an enterprising entrepreneur who added a spa annex to the hotel. Located across the street from the Sulphur Temple Park, the hotel was a popular spot with tourists from its beginning in 1870. (Courtesy of Peter Mauhs.)

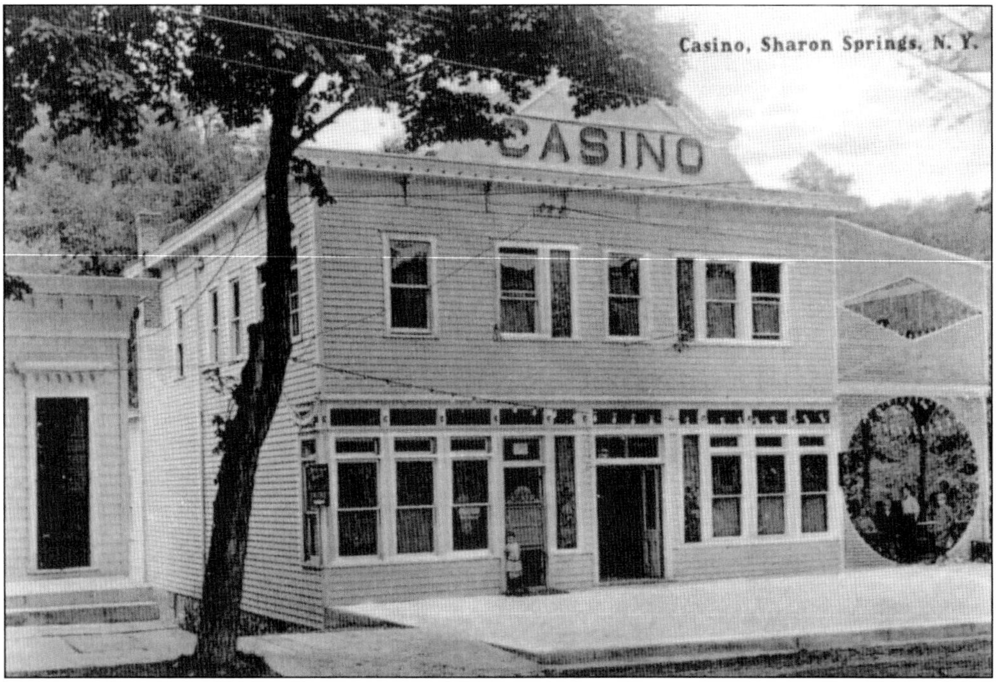

Located on Main Street, the Casino Hotel was a project conceived and designed by Frederick Mauhs around 1905. Offering rooms and entertainment, this was an attempt to compete with Saratoga Spa's gambling and other entertainments. The Gardner family sponsored Mauhs's enterprises and held the mortgages until his untimely death in 1911. (Courtesy of Peter Mauhs.)

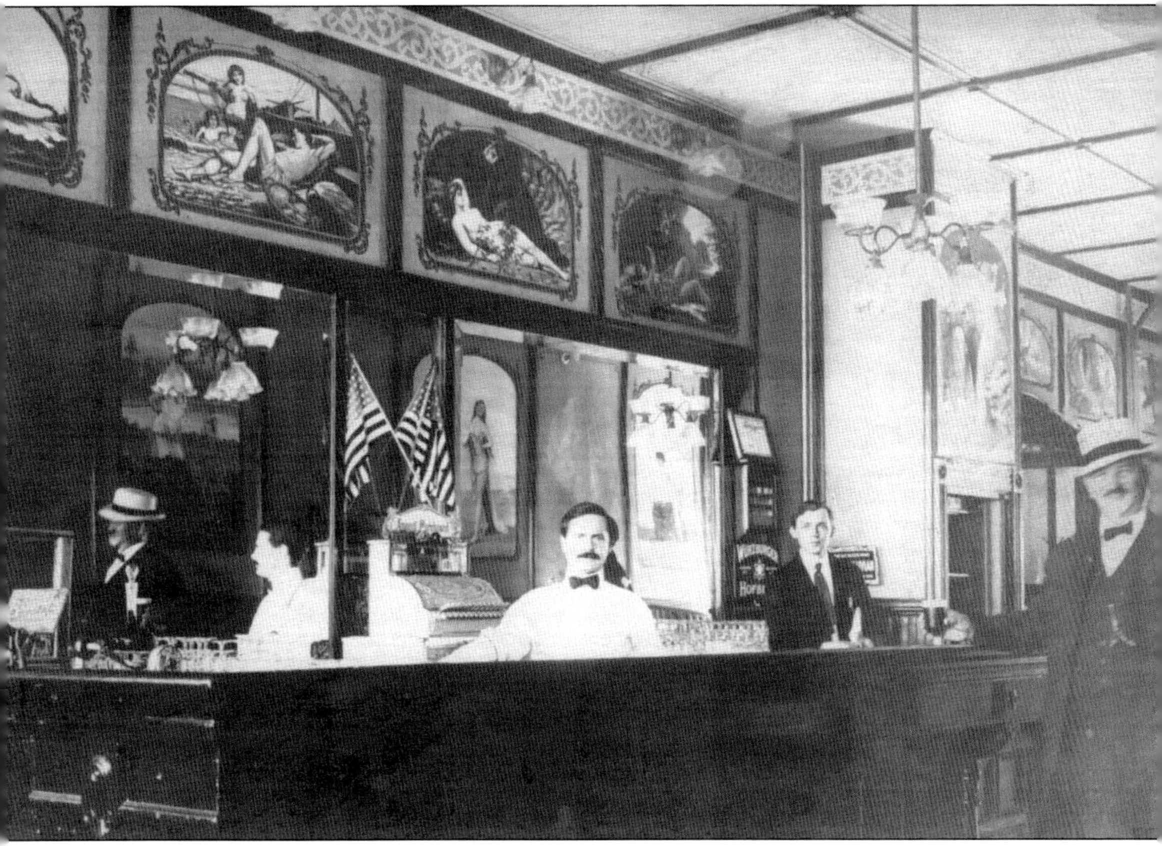

This bar at the Casino Hotel, with risqué paintings on the wall, was for male customers only. Women had a separate area. The hotel survived a devastating fire in 1926, only to perish in flames in 1949. Fire by arson has continued to be a scourge, the latest victim being the Park View Hotel in 1996. (Courtesy of Peter Mauhs.)

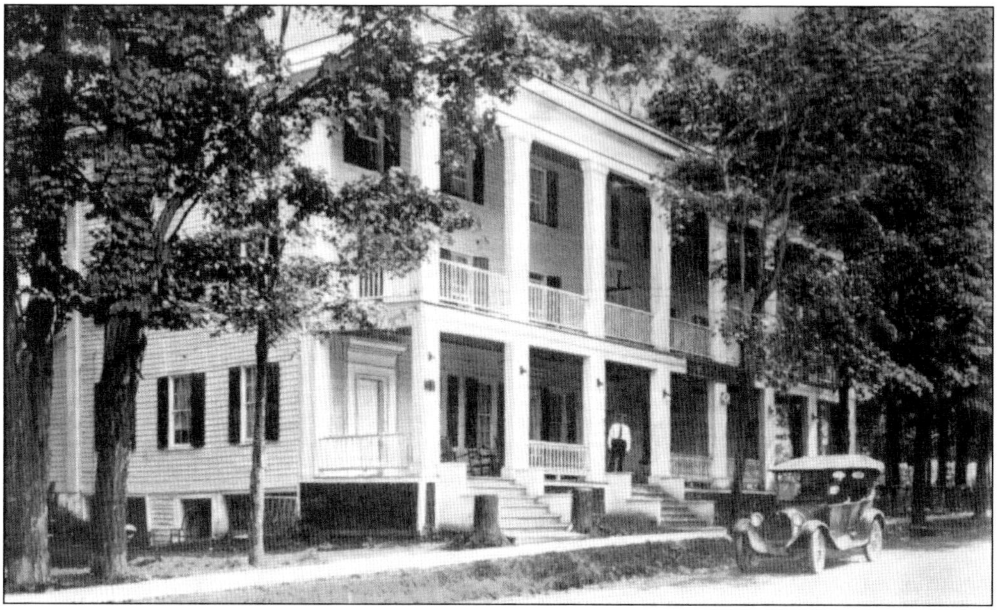

Built between 1847 and 1851, the American Hotel became the village's second Greek Revival hotel, joining the grand Pavilion. The LaRue family ran the hotel for more than 40 years in the 19th century. The 20th century marked a gradual decline in the hotel's fortunes, until it was abandoned by its owners, a Hasidic group from New York City, in the 1970s. New owners Garth Roberts and Doug Plummer renovated and reopened it 30 years later.

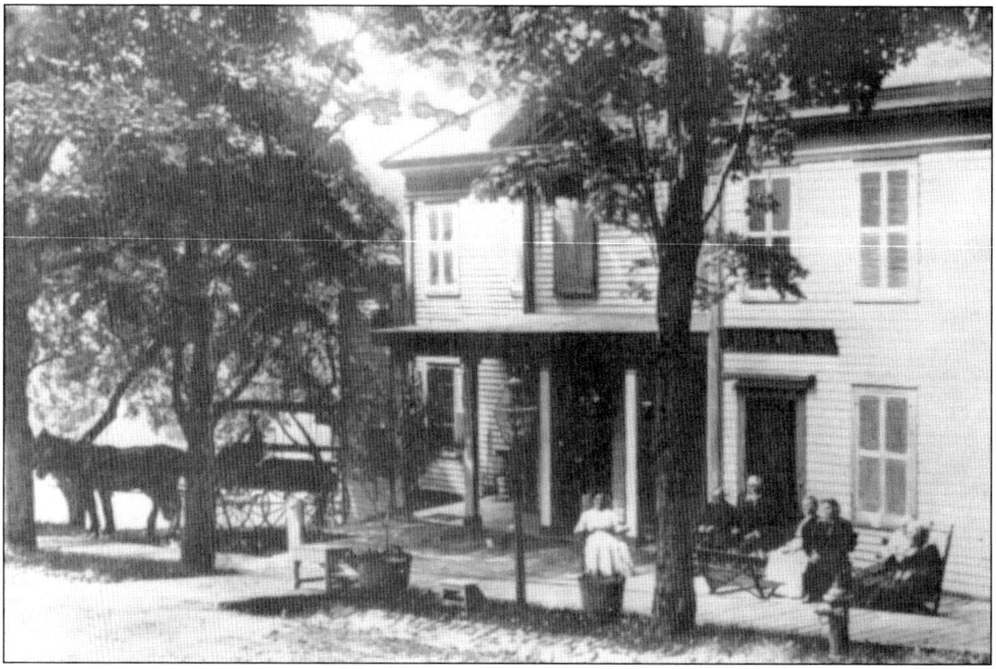

The Curry House, named for an Irish proprietor, is shown here in 1908. The home later became part of the estate of the Mayers, a New York City Jewish family who summered in Sharon Springs. Since the 1990s, owners Dan and Dave Wood have completely remodeled the building to create Edgefield, a bed-and-breakfast that has inspired others to buy and revamp old structures.

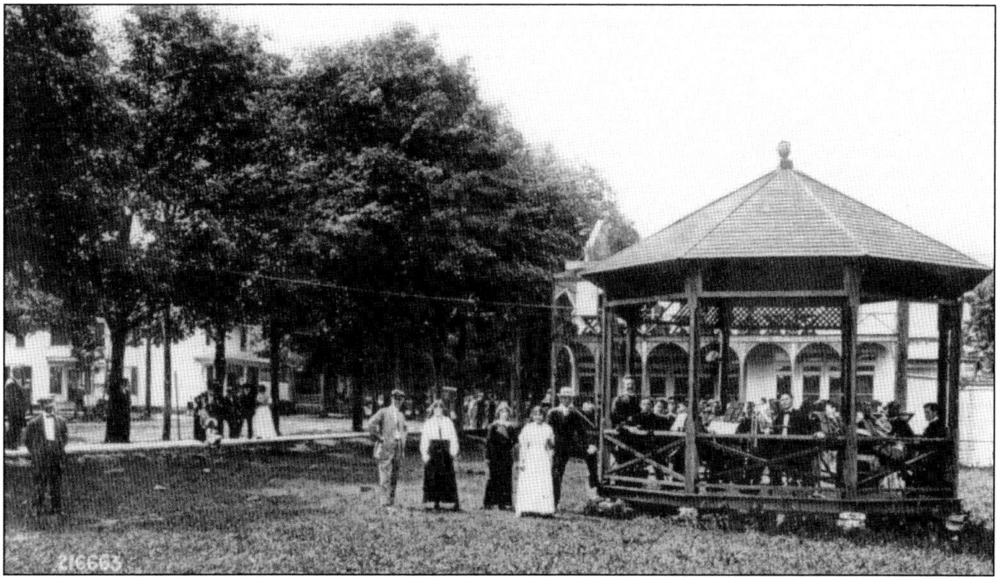

A popular pastime during any era, band concerts were once held in this stunning pavilion, seen here around 1890. During the 20th century, concerts were often held on the porch of the Imperial Bathhouse. Although this wooden structure is long gone, a similar open-air concert platform in Chalybeate Park replaced it in 2014.

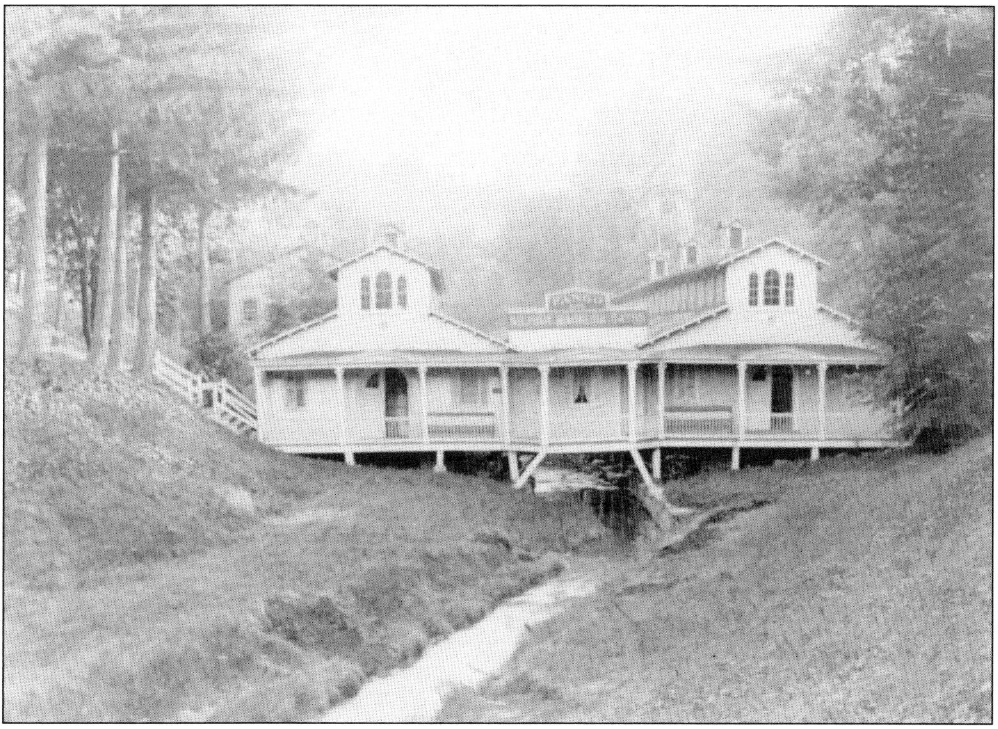

Fango Bathhouse, one of the early bathhouses, was built of wood and straddled Brimstone Creek. There were 24 bathing rooms in Fango; the price of a bath in 1847 was 25¢. Unfortunately, when the great Congress Hall fire occurred in 1875, this bathhouse was also destroyed. The Lower Bathhouse, a brick structure, was built a short distance away.

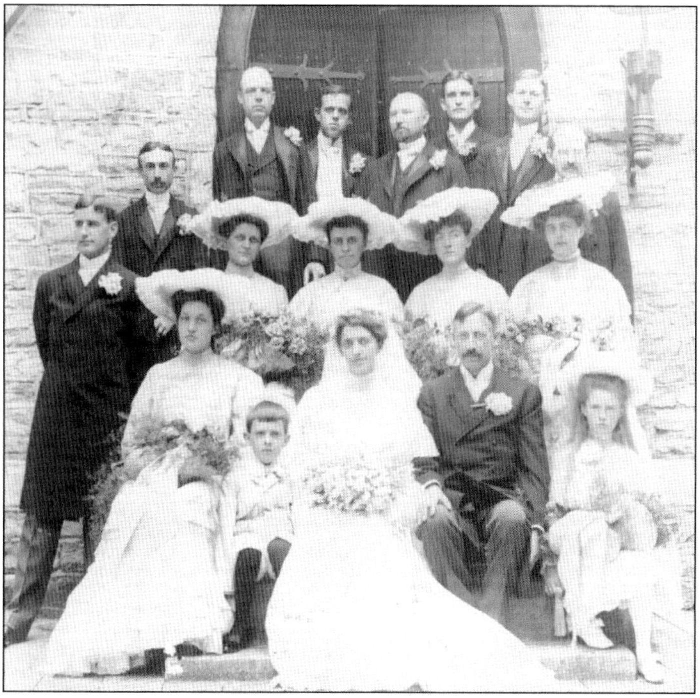

A 1906 wedding party poses on the steps of Trinity Episcopal Church. The men are attired in elegant morning coats, and the women sport fashionable hats and gloves. During the spa era, wealthy families vacationing in Sharon Springs felt safe introducing their daughters to the sons of other well-to-do parents. Often, one season's engagements led to weddings in the next. This once fashionable church has been refurbished as a private home by Doug Wagner.

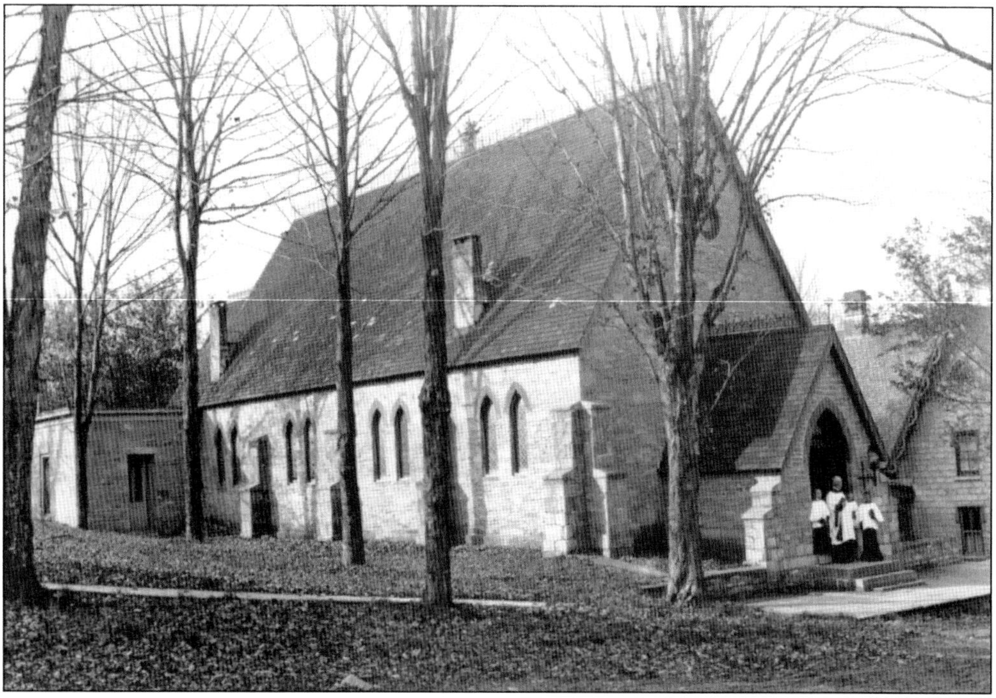

Because of the large numbers of Episcopalians among the elite summer visitors, Trinity Church was constructed in 1856 of locally quarried limestone. The church's steeply pitched roof, pointed arches, trefoil windows, and stone construction make it an excellent example of the Gothic Revival style. Until 1859, services were offered only in the summer months. Under the leadership of Rev. Edmund Cooper, however, the church embraced local residents as well.

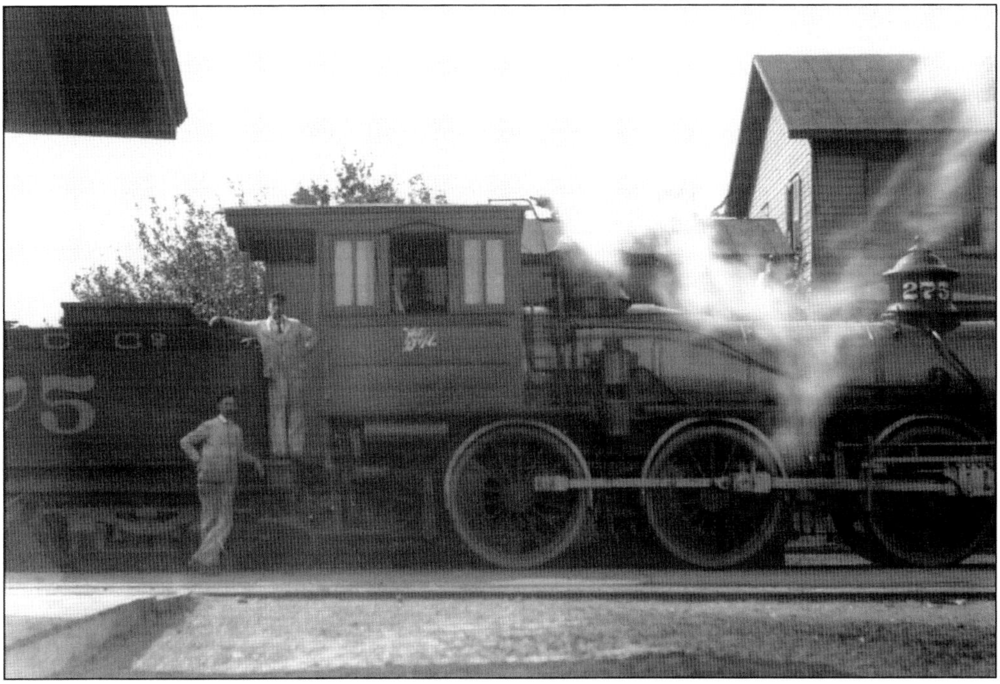

Train service came to Sharon Springs on June 16, 1870. It cost $600,000 to extend the line from Cobleskill through Sharon and on to Cherry Valley. This 1898 photograph shows a typical engine from that era. Although passenger service was short-lived, it proved to be a popular means of travel to Sharon. Local residents also enjoyed traveling to and from Cobleskill and Cherry Valley via rail.

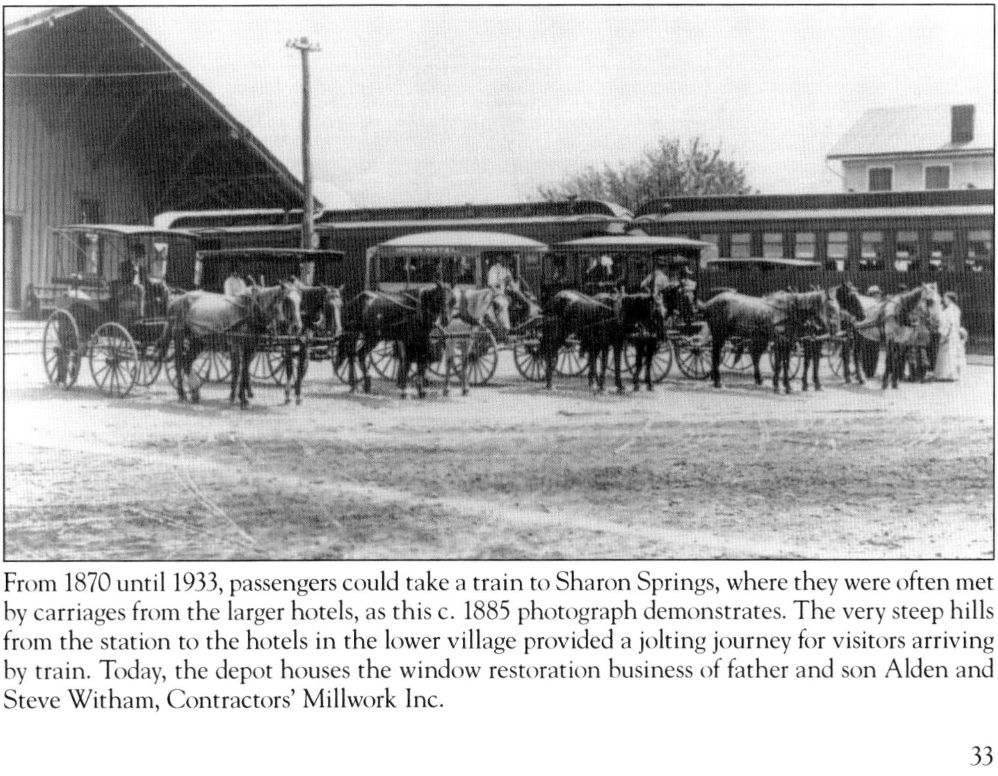

From 1870 until 1933, passengers could take a train to Sharon Springs, where they were often met by carriages from the larger hotels, as this c. 1885 photograph demonstrates. The very steep hills from the station to the hotels in the lower village provided a jolting journey for visitors arriving by train. Today, the depot houses the window restoration business of father and son Alden and Steve Witham, Contractors' Millwork Inc.

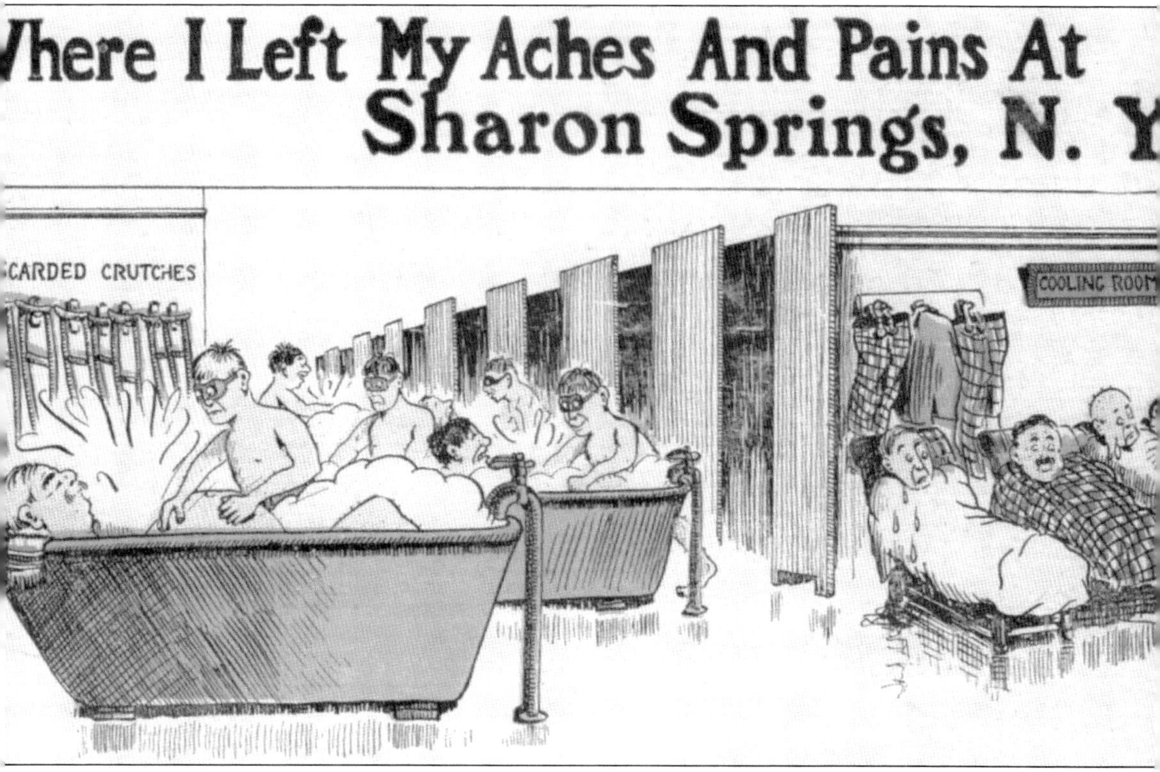

Visitors to the spa could choose from a variety of amusing postcards to send to friends back home. This one implies that bathing in the sulphuric waters, while perhaps curing a disability, was a rather wet and possibly gruesome experience. It was perhaps mostly disagreeable for the bathing attendants, seen here wearing goggles to keep the splashing water out of their eyes. There is no record of bathing facilities being shared by many bathers, as the postcard suggests. Other cards announced that spa visitors were able to shed extra pounds merely by partaking of the waters. Another proclaims, "Everybody is Cured at Sharon Springs."

Three

Hops

The cultivation of hops was the first specialized agricultural industry in New Netherlands (the Dutch name for what became New York State), having been introduced by the Dutch in 1629. Beer, which is made from hops, was an important part of early settlers' diets. By 1828, cultivation of hops had spread to Schoharie County, where the rich soil has the correct acidity for hops. In 1839, the state of New York led the country in hop production, and Central New York was the primary growing area.

Local farming families in the late 19th and early 20th centuries enjoyed an unusually prosperous time, due to the success of their hop fields, which attracted the interest of New York City brewing families. A *New York Times* article in 1890 chronicles a trip by 12 riders of the New York Riding Club through upstate and stopping at the Pavilion Hotel. Among the riders were two sons of one of the city's largest brewing families, George and Charles Clausen. Soon after, the family purchased the former Eldredge estate along Route 20.

The Schaefers, of Schaefer Brewing, were also attracted to the fashionable resort, purchasing the former Bang estate for their summer home and to oversee their investments in the profitable hops industry. The booming industry ushered in an era of good times, punctuated by the hop-picking season, which brought young men and women from Albany, New York City, and other urban centers to Sharon Springs and surrounding communities. This was yet another opportunity for local men and women to socialize with people whose life stories were different. The hops season culminated each year with the Harvest Hop; sheet music exists titled "The Sharon Springs Hop."

Unfortunately, the hops boom was erratic and short-lived. Competition from more fertile hop fields in California, Oregon, and Washington reduced the profits for the farmers in Schoharie County by the first decade of the 20th century. Then, two more events shattered hops production in Sharon: the blue mold disaster and the onset of Prohibition.

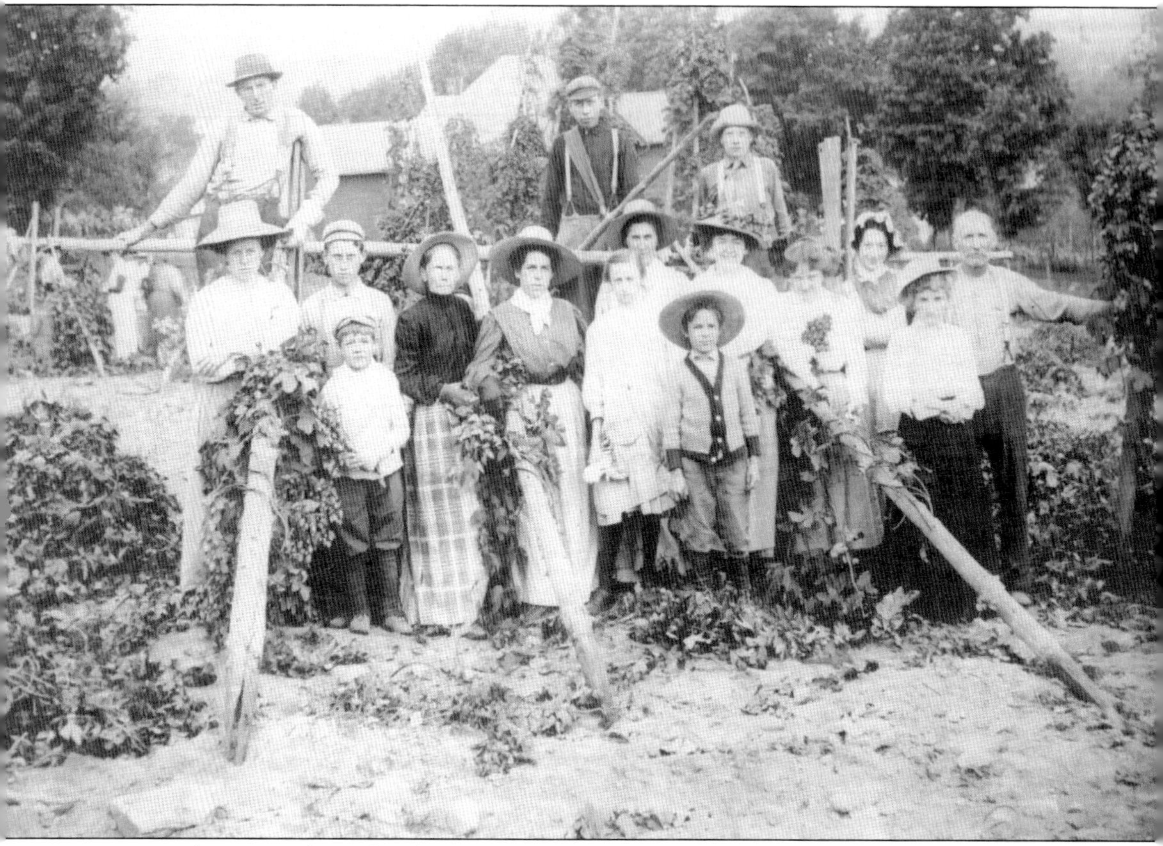

Hops picking was often a family affair; husbands, wives, and children would travel from the city to live on a farm during hops season. This c. 1890 photograph, taken on the Bowmaker family farm, shows a group of pickers with the hop poles and flowers. Because prices were set before the crop matured, hop cultivation could prove to be a risky investment. Most farmers in Sharon cultivated hops as one of many crops; for example, the Bowmakers in a typical year would devote 7.5 acres to hopyards, out of an average total farm area of 93 acres. During picking season, children worked along with their parents as a vacation from the heat of the city, a mutually beneficial arrangement. A picker could become woozy, as the hop flower produced soporific fumes; in fact, dried hops were often sewn into pillowcases to induce sleep.

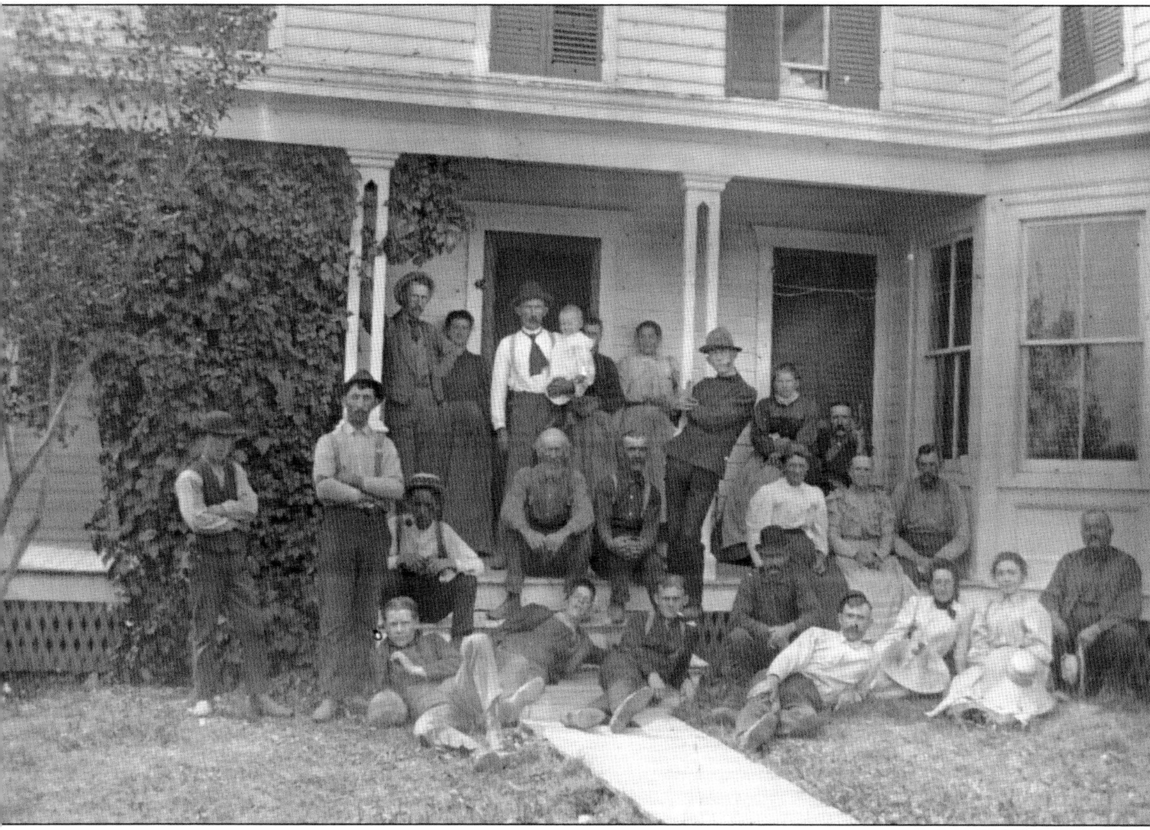

The VanSchaick family home is shown in the 1890s during hop-picking season. Often, families had dormitories built in their homes to house itinerant workers. Here, family members are photographed with their workers. It was an initial costly investment for farmers to add rooms to house the additional workforce. The harvest began in late August and usually lasted two to four weeks, during which time the workers were housed and fed at the owner's expense. One farmer spoke of hop growing as the source of a "farmer's fortune," with enough surplus cash to build a nicer house and barn (in a good year).

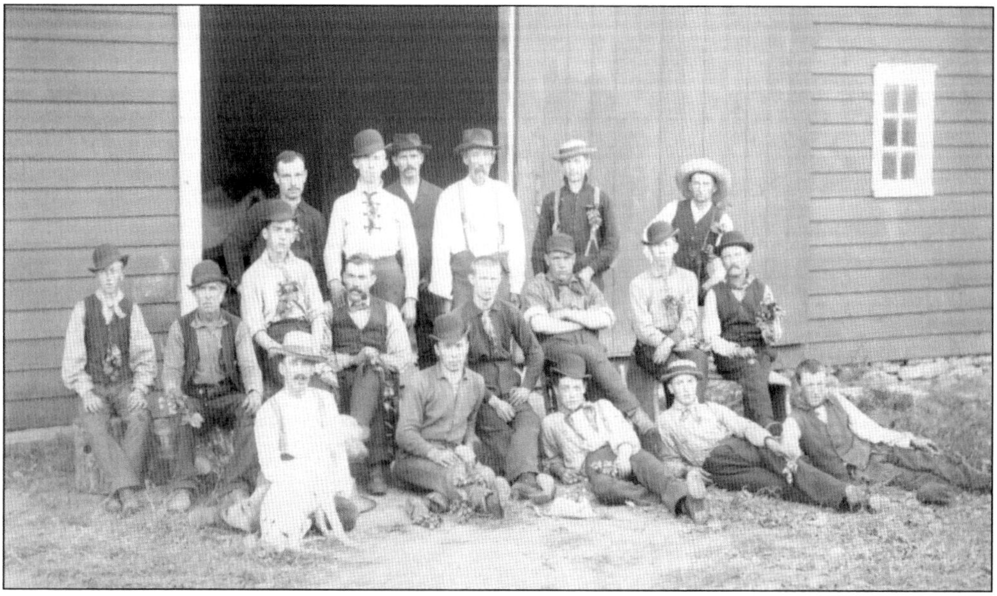

This 1890s photograph of hops pickers at Lena Snyder's home shows a group of young migrant workers. There were many reports of brawls occurring when local youths clashed with outsiders, especially after rounds of drinking. One dreadful night, a clash occurred at the village's Bucket of Blood Tavern, owned by the Finklestein family. During the fight, pitting local rowdies against outsiders, the racket was so loud, it was heard a mile away. The melee resulted in the death of one of the migrant workers.

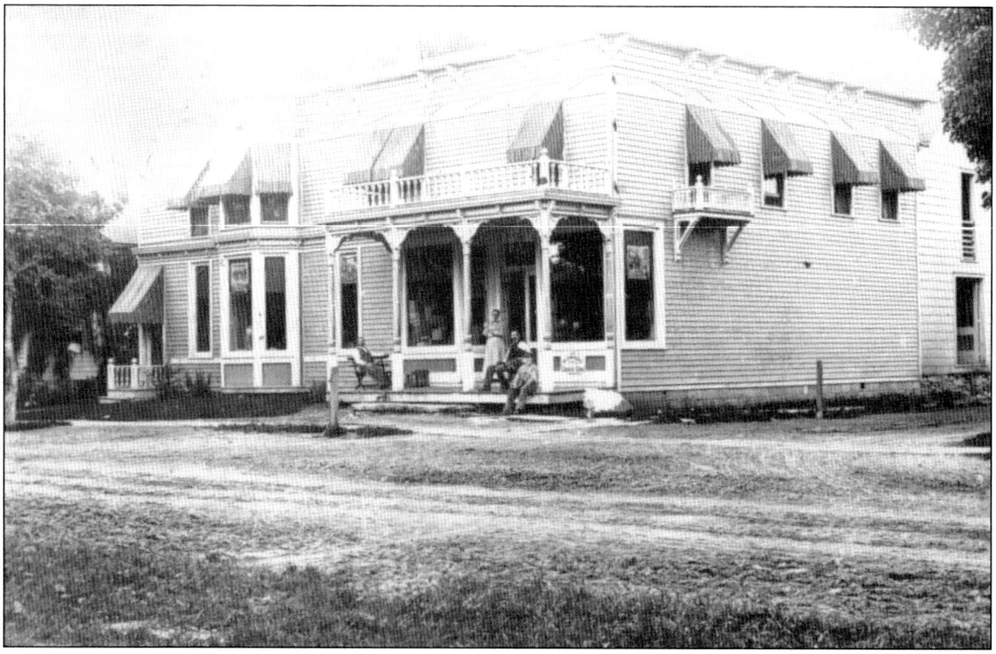

Hyney's store, shown here in 1877, was located along the Great Western Turnpike. The store carried sundries and groceries for the farming families. In later years, the building housed Schockley's Drug Store, with its popular soda fountain. Today, this iconic building is home to Chartwell Studios, the art studio of Peter Cozzolino, sculptor, and the late Marguerite MacFarlane, muralist.

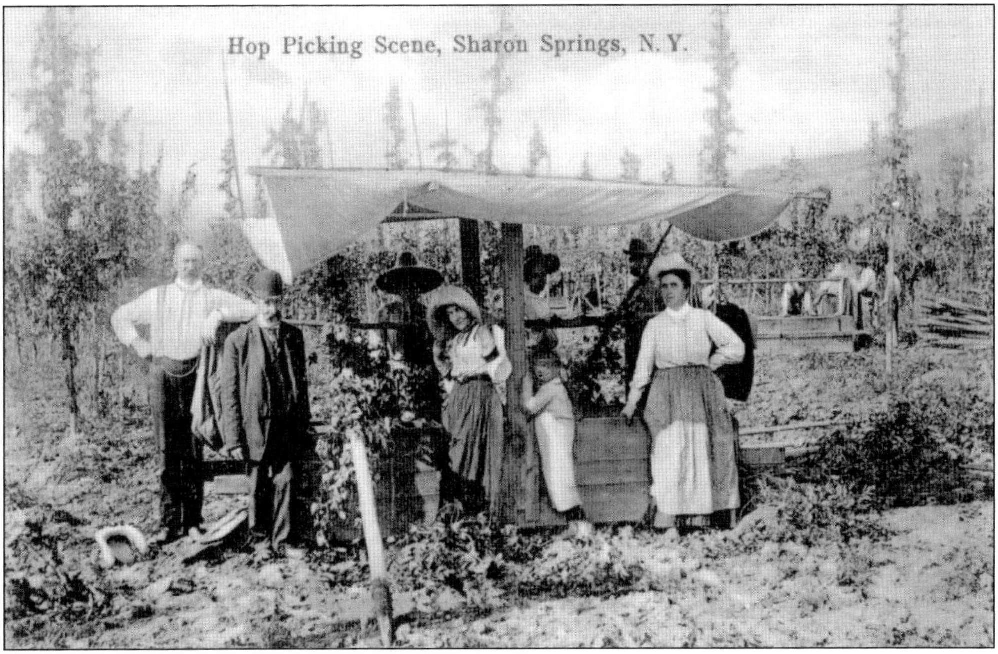

This iconic postcard romanticizes hops picking. Poems, paintings, stories, and songs like the "Sharon Hop" recall the glory days of hops growing, when farmers enjoyed a boost in income and towns sparkled with activity during the picking season. A popular refrain from the time was as follows: "'Hop picking is coming!' the boys shout in glee. 'What jolly good times we are going to see!'"

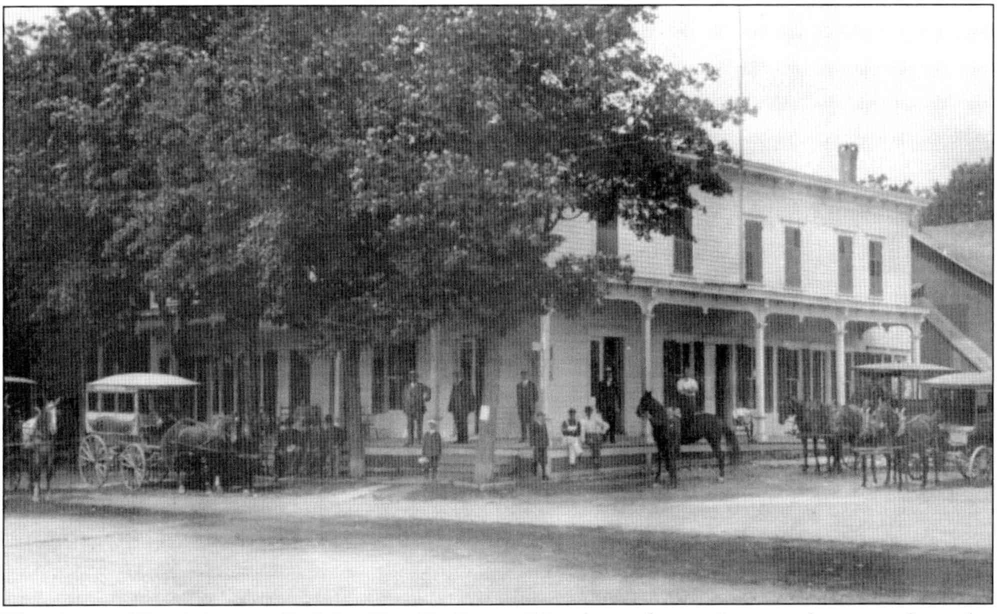

The Austin Hotel, later called the Hop Exchange Hotel, was located across the street from the depot. A place where buyers could meet hop growers, it was also a popular social hub, sponsoring dances and other social activities, like card games. Many people recalled fun times, especially during the hop-picking season.

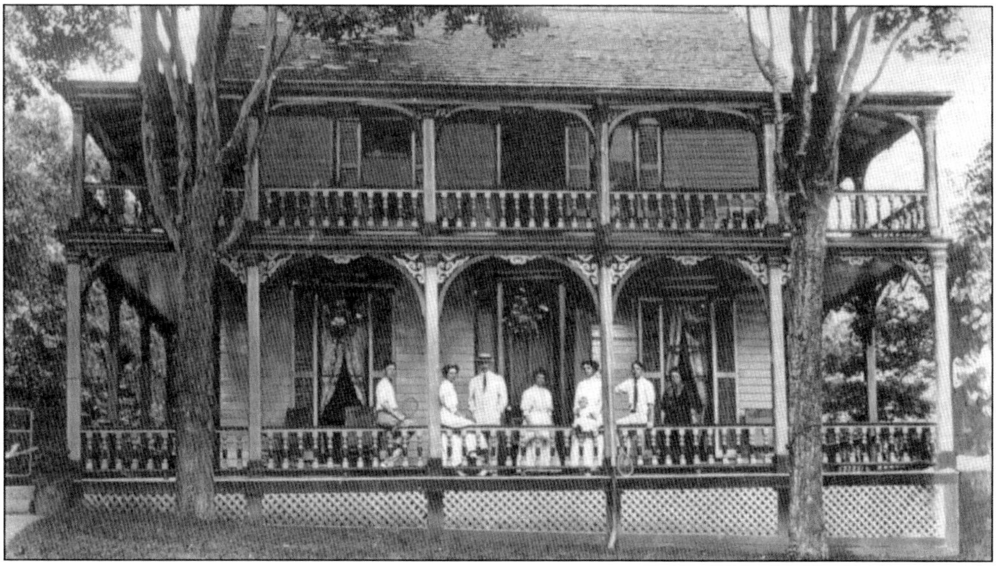

The Schaeffer brewing family purchased a summer cottage in Sharon Springs, the former H.L. Bang home in the lower village near the Ravine Falls and bathhouses. In this 1886 photograph, the Schaeffer family prepares for a tennis match. The Schaeffer/VomSaal families were stalwart supporters of the community, underwriting projects like the Sharon Springs Free Library.

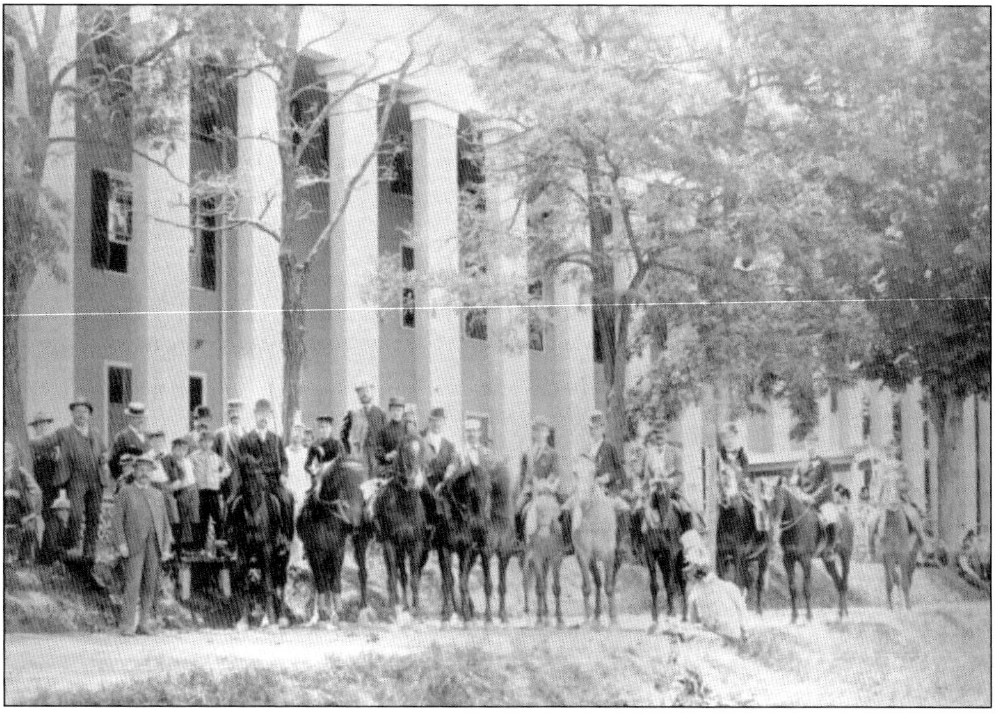

In 1888, the *New York Times* reported on a group of horsemen from New York City who traveled through upstate, stopping at the Pavilion. Among the riders were George and Henry Clausen, sons of Henry Clausen Sr., chairman of the Clausen Beer Brewing Company. Then, two years later, the Clausens purchased the Eldredge Estate in Sharon Springs in order to vacation near their hops fields.

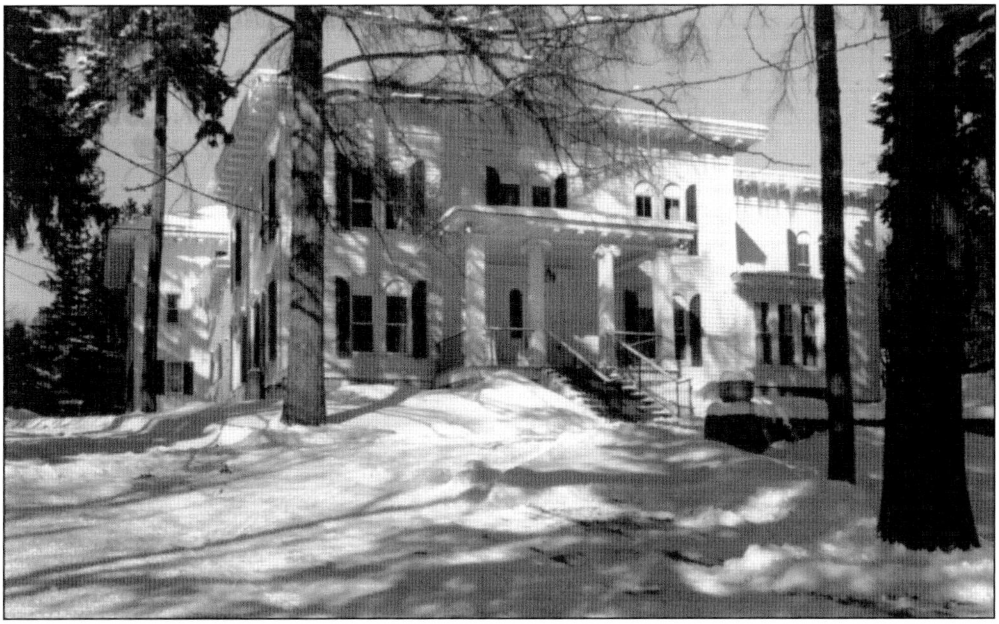

Originally the home of the Eldredge family, this elegant residence became Henry Clausen's summer cottage after his purchase of the estate in 1890. The home was considered significant enough to be included in William Roscoe's book *History of Schoharie County, New York*, published in 1882. After Henry Clausen's death in 1893, his only daughter, Marie Clausen Schmidt, inherited the property and sold the manor to her brother, Harry Clausen.

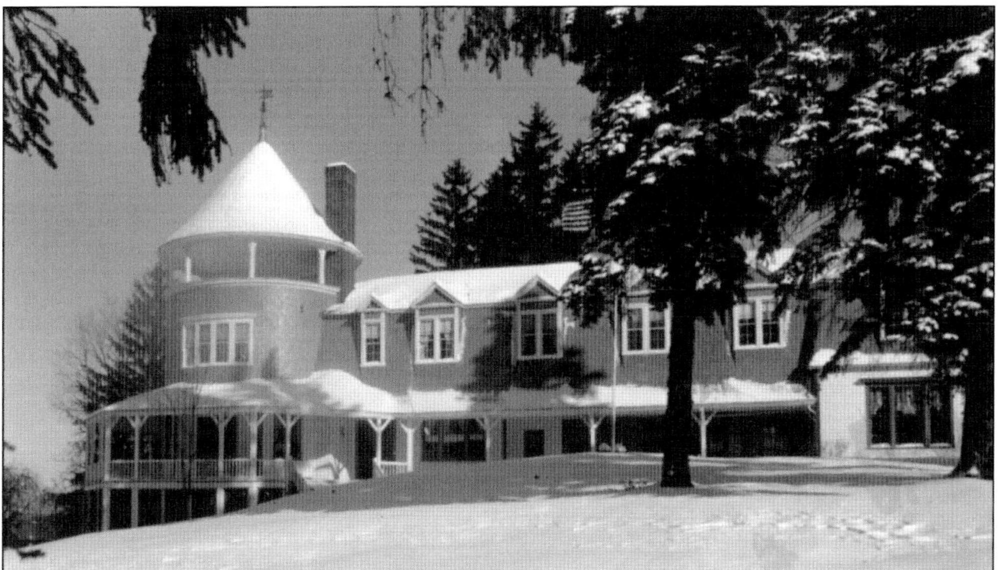

After purchasing the Eldredge estate in 1890, Henry Clausen built the Casino, a place to entertain his male friends, mostly brewing associates or Tammany Hall politicians. This two-story gentlemen's quarters has six bedrooms with semiprivate baths, a bowling alley, gymnasium, gambling facilities, and a magnificent panoramic view of the Mohawk Valley rivaling that of the Pavilion. After Henry's death, his sons George and Harry shared possession of the Casino.

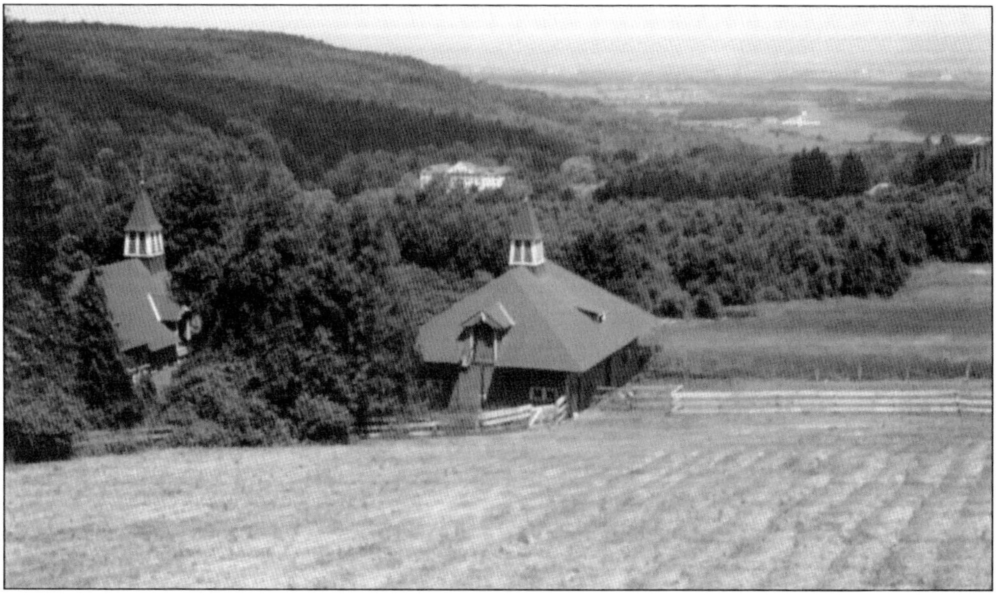

This view looks north of the Clausen Casino, showing the barns and fields overlooking the Mohawk Valley. In the distance, the Adler Hotel (white building) is visible. In the 1980s and 1990s, Tim and Kathy Spofford operated a bed-and-breakfast on the property and raised llamas in the barns. Tim, a descendant of the Clausen family, is the son of Homer and Rosamond Spofford, owners of the White Sulphur Springs Co. (Photograph by A. Zinder.)

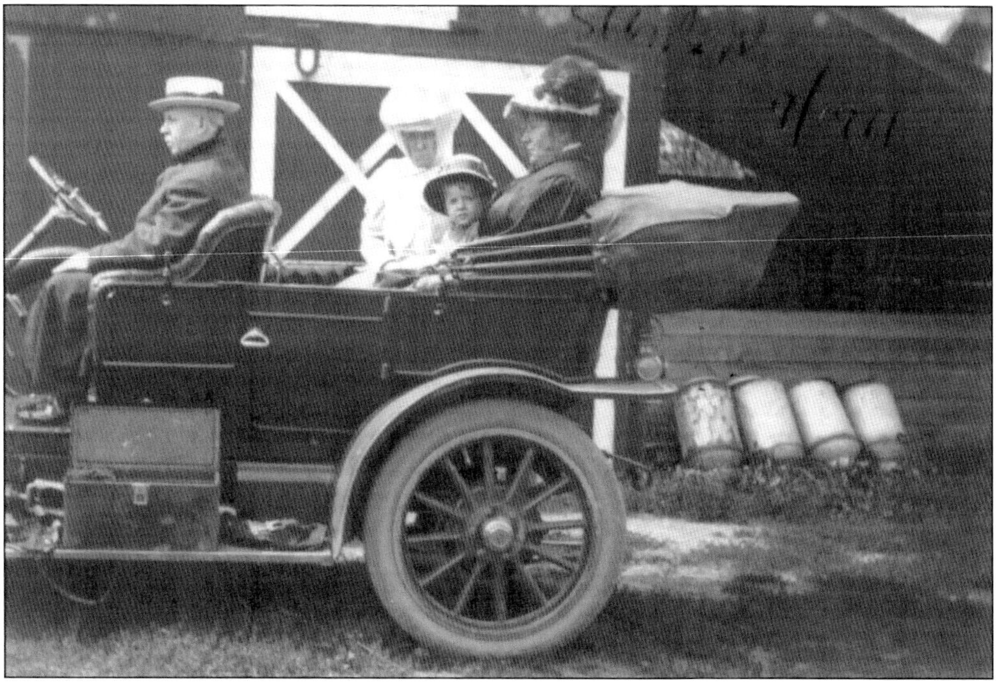

Charles Clausen is shown out for a drive in 1911 with his wife, Marie (far right), a young girl, and her nurse. Charles was the "black sheep" of the Clausen family, because he married without his parents' permission. He purchased his own estate in the lower village, away from the main Clausen estate, and continued to summer here.

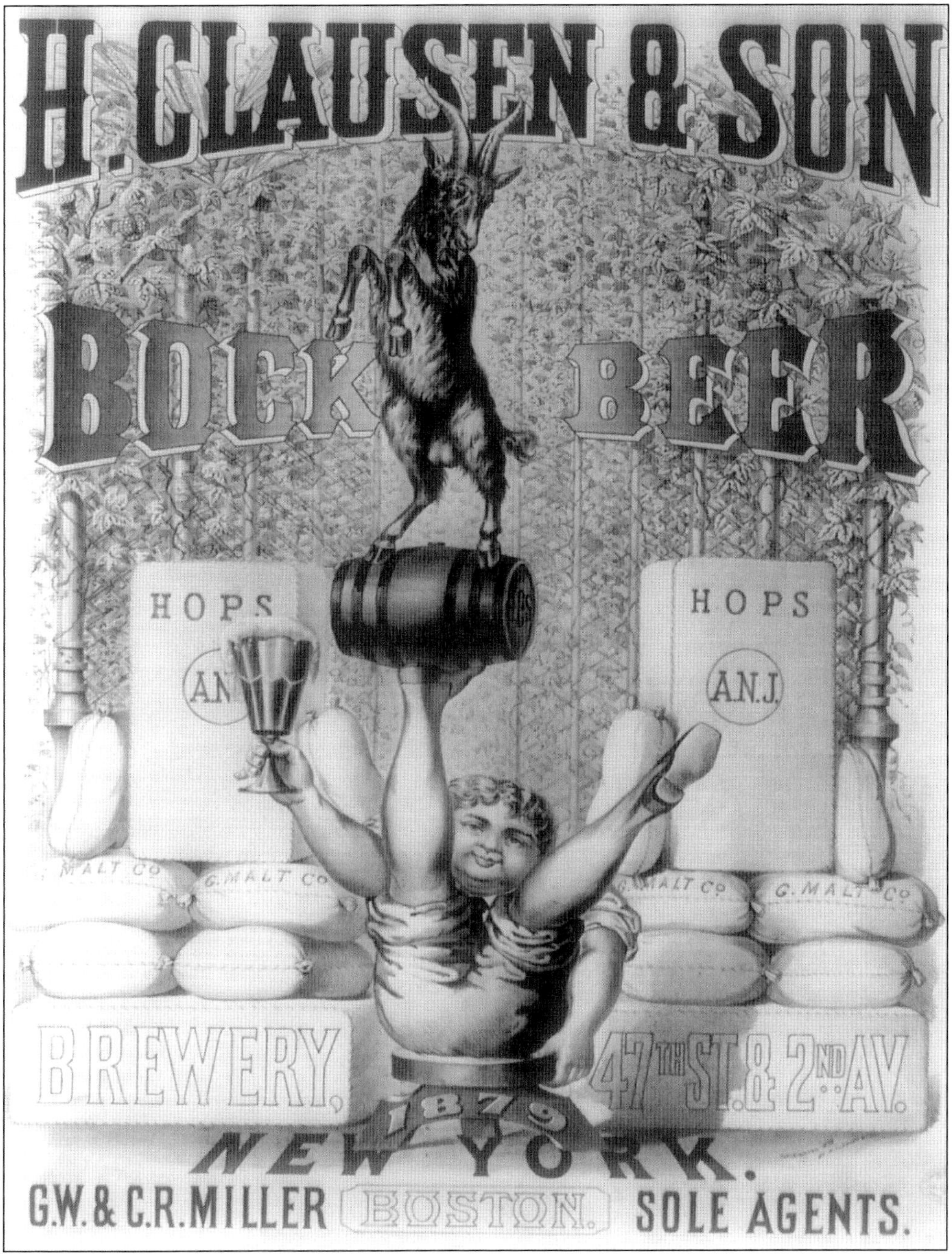

This 1880s advertisement promotes Clausen beer. By 1879, the Clausen Brewery produced 89,992 barrels of beer per year, making it the ninth-largest brewery in the United States. The founder, Henry Clausen Sr., the son of a German immigrant brewer, achieved much success financially and politically. At age 34, he became an alderman in the city of New York and was vice president of the German Up-Town Savings Bank, as well as vice president of the Brewers' Fire Insurance Company. By 1890, Clausen had been elected to the state assembly, spent several years as president of the United States Brewers' Congress, the New York City Brewers' Association, and the Plattdeutsch Volksfest Verein. During Prohibition, the Clausen Brewery went out of business.

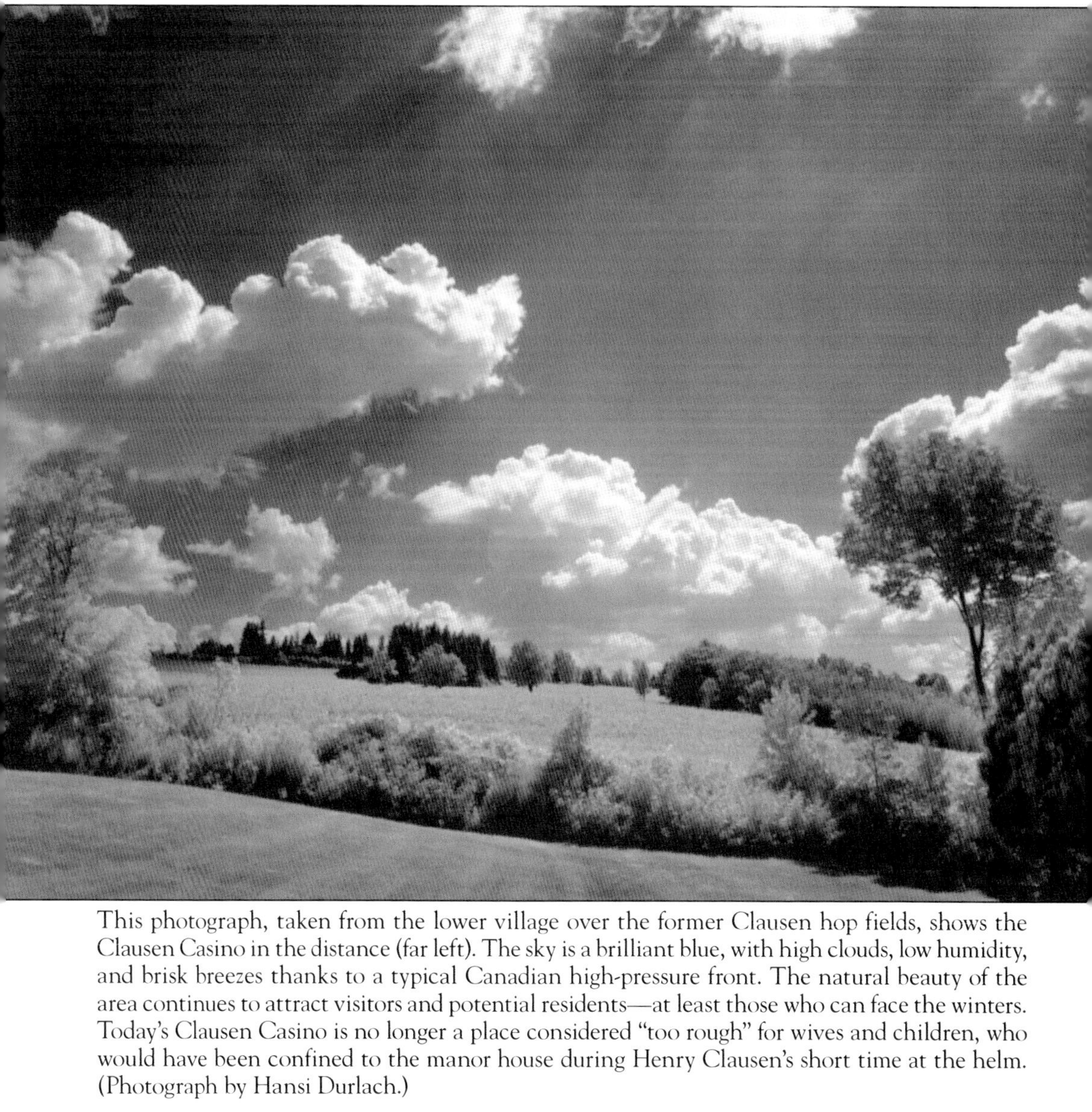

This photograph, taken from the lower village over the former Clausen hop fields, shows the Clausen Casino in the distance (far left). The sky is a brilliant blue, with high clouds, low humidity, and brisk breezes thanks to a typical Canadian high-pressure front. The natural beauty of the area continues to attract visitors and potential residents—at least those who can face the winters. Today's Clausen Casino is no longer a place considered "too rough" for wives and children, who would have been confined to the manor house during Henry Clausen's short time at the helm. (Photograph by Hansi Durlach.)

Four

THE JEWISH ERA

By the late 19th century, many in the wealthier set started to abandon Sharon Springs for their cottages in Newport, Rhode Island, or the flashier spas with horse racing and gambling, like Saratoga. In the 1870s, Saratoga and other vacation spots in New York State announced that Jewish guests would not be allowed to register in their hotels. Since wealthy Jewish friends of the Vanderbilt set had been vacationing in Sharon Springs for years, they continued to be welcomed here.

Initially, there was little change in the character of the resort, as the Jewish clientele were mainly "uptown Jews" of wealth who enjoyed the existing hotels. In 1927, the Adler was built as the first truly kosher hotel, with two kitchens, an attached mineral spa, and a gracious lobby and ballroom. When less-affluent Jewish visitors arrived seeking more affordable accommodations, the boardinghouse culture emerged. With the Depression years, even this revival was threatened, as many people could no longer afford vacations.

After World War II, the West German government paid for Holocaust survivors to receive treatment at the White Sulphur Springs Co. In one year, 75 percent of the Adler's and 90 percent of the Park View's guests were supported by West German reparations. These survivors brought their families to stay in Sharon Springs, creating a unique culture and ushering in a new paradigm in cultural interactions for visitors and townsfolk alike.

In the late 1960s, yet another group arrived when the Satmar Hasidic rebbe and Holocaust survivor Joel Teitelbaum made the village a destination for his followers each summer. The Satmar held themselves apart, spoke Yiddish, and rejected modern and secular culture, all of which created tension with other Jewish visitors and the village's permanent residents.

In 1987, a *National Geographic* staff reporter, observing the Satmar in the village, wrote, "We saw a fragment of Poland that no longer exists . . . here for the first time in our lives we saw a town, as if it had been transported through time from prewar Poland. On wooden porches, around tables lit by bare bulbs, sat bearded men in hats studying the sacred texts, heatedly discussing verses from the Talmud." Many local residents felt they could travel to a foreign country simply by walking down the main hill into their village.

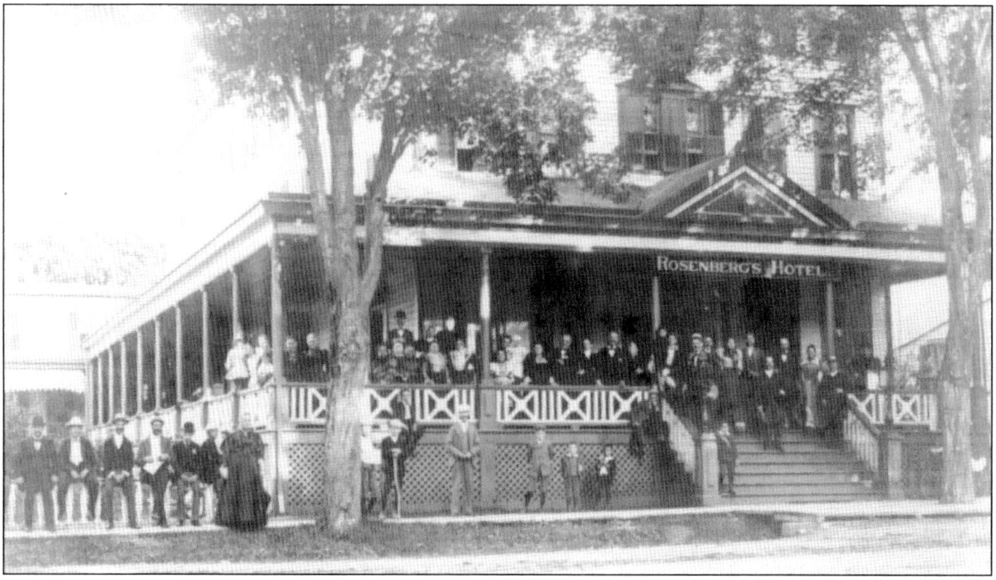

Built in 1880, the Rosenberg House, seen here in 1890, claimed to be the preeminent hostelry of the "American Carlsbad." Serving German American kosher cuisine, with tea dances and evening dances, it was a popular destination. Located on Main Street, the small hotel was in the center of activity and a favored spot for assimilated Jewish families. During Prohibition, the village served as a way station for Jewish bootleggers on the way from Canada to New York City.

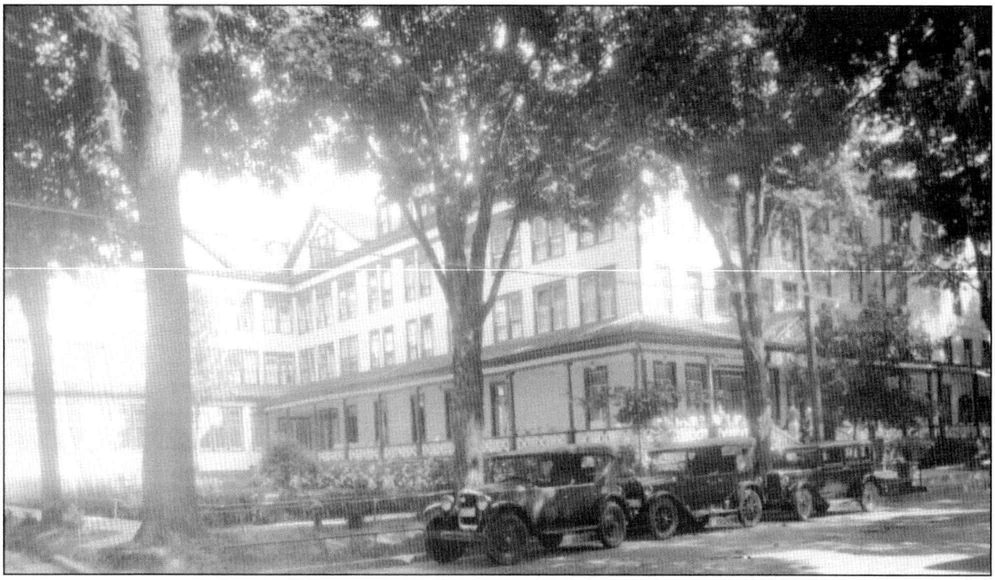

The Roseboro Hotel was one of the most elegant of the kosher hotels in the 20th century. The hotel was created in 1905, when the Howland House and the Rosenberg merged. Many local residents fondly remember working at the Roseboro for the Wasserman family. The hotel, seen here in 1930, closed in 1968. In the 1990s, it enjoyed a brief renaissance when Dennis Giacomo and Dawn Belloise began a restoration. In September 2014, Ron Ketelsen purchased the hotel and immediately began extensive renovations to host the 2014 Victorian Holiday over the weekend of December 5–7 featuring a "Parade of Trees" in the ballroom. Ketelsen's future plans include restaurants, B&B facilities, a Titanic museum, and more..

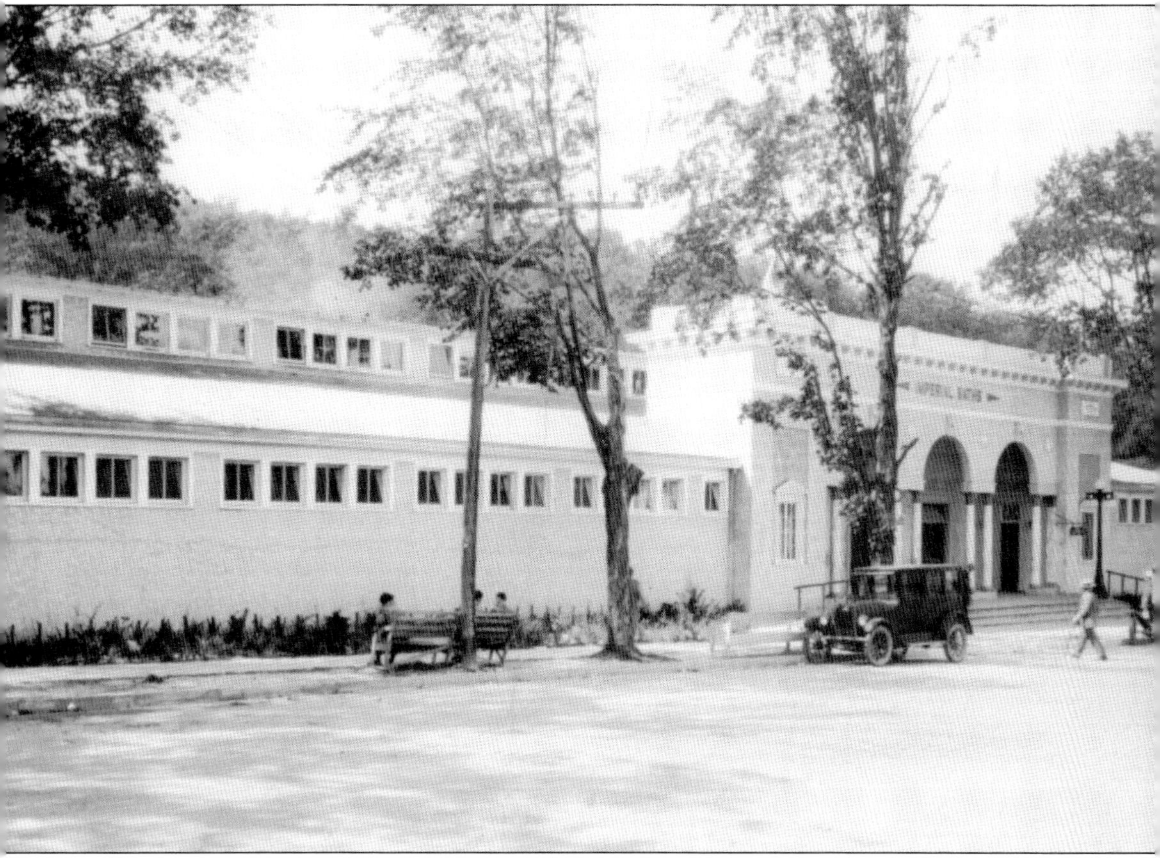

This 1927 photograph shows the new Imperial Bathhouse on Main Street. With its double Corinthian columns and Beaux-Arts entrance, the facility could offer 5,000 treatments daily. It was the largest of five bathhouses in Sharon Springs. Advertisements at the time promised "all the benefits of distant European Spas." The Gardner family traveled frequently to spas in Europe to study the treatments available there before introducing new techniques at the bathhouses in Sharon. "Direct Inhalation, Pulverization, Douches, Gas and Dry Inhalation" were advertised for treatment of "Nasal Catarrh and Diseases of the Respiratory Organs." The mineral waters from Sharon were awarded a diploma and a silver medal at the Paris Exposition in 1900 and at the St. Louis World's Fair in 1904.

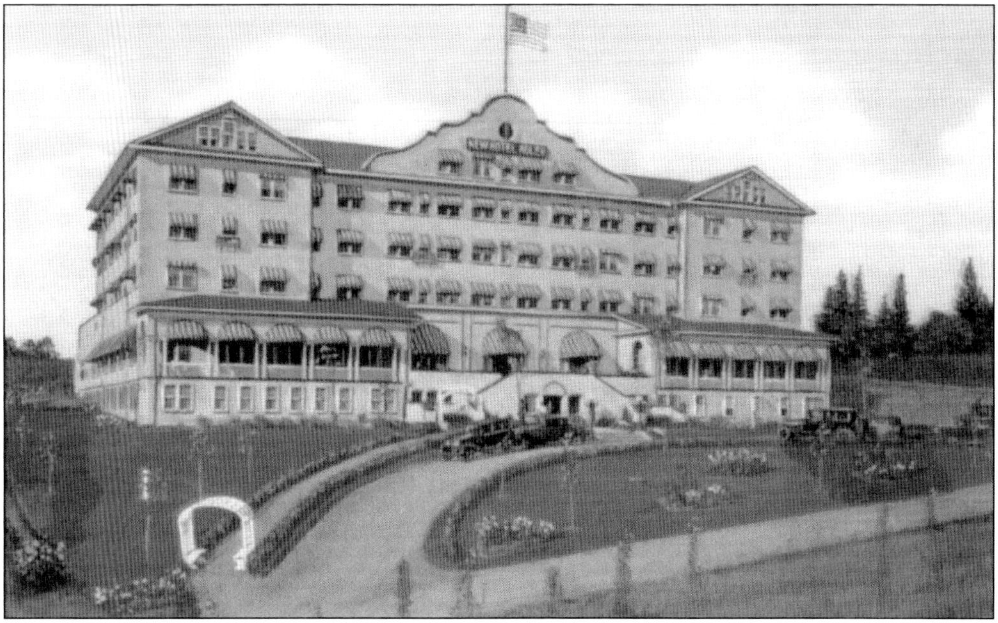

Built in 1928, the Adler Hotel was the last large hotel erected in Sharon. It had 150 rooms, its own bathhouse, theater, ballroom, and kosher kitchen with resident rabbi to ensure the quality of the kosher food. This Spanish Colonial Revival hotel enjoyed decades of success, but it is now closed and decaying.

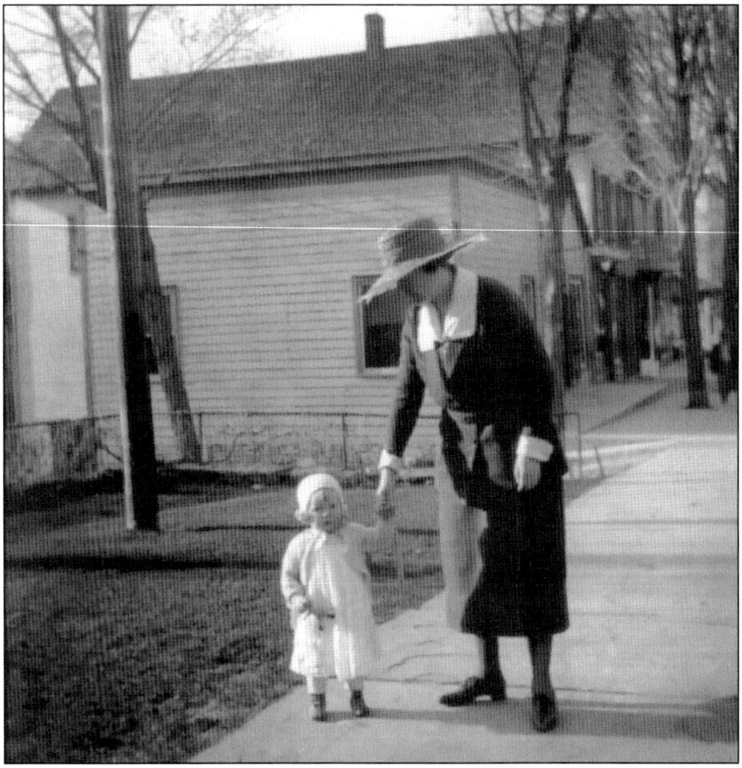

The area around the Chalybeate Temple was transformed in the 1940s into "Berman's Little Village," comprising several boardinghouses, a restaurant, and a garden area. Even the temple was enclosed as housing for a rabbi. Local residents remember walking past the boardinghouses on Friday nights when observant Jewish women, who did not work on the Sabbath, would beseech them to turn off the gas or electricity in their rooms.

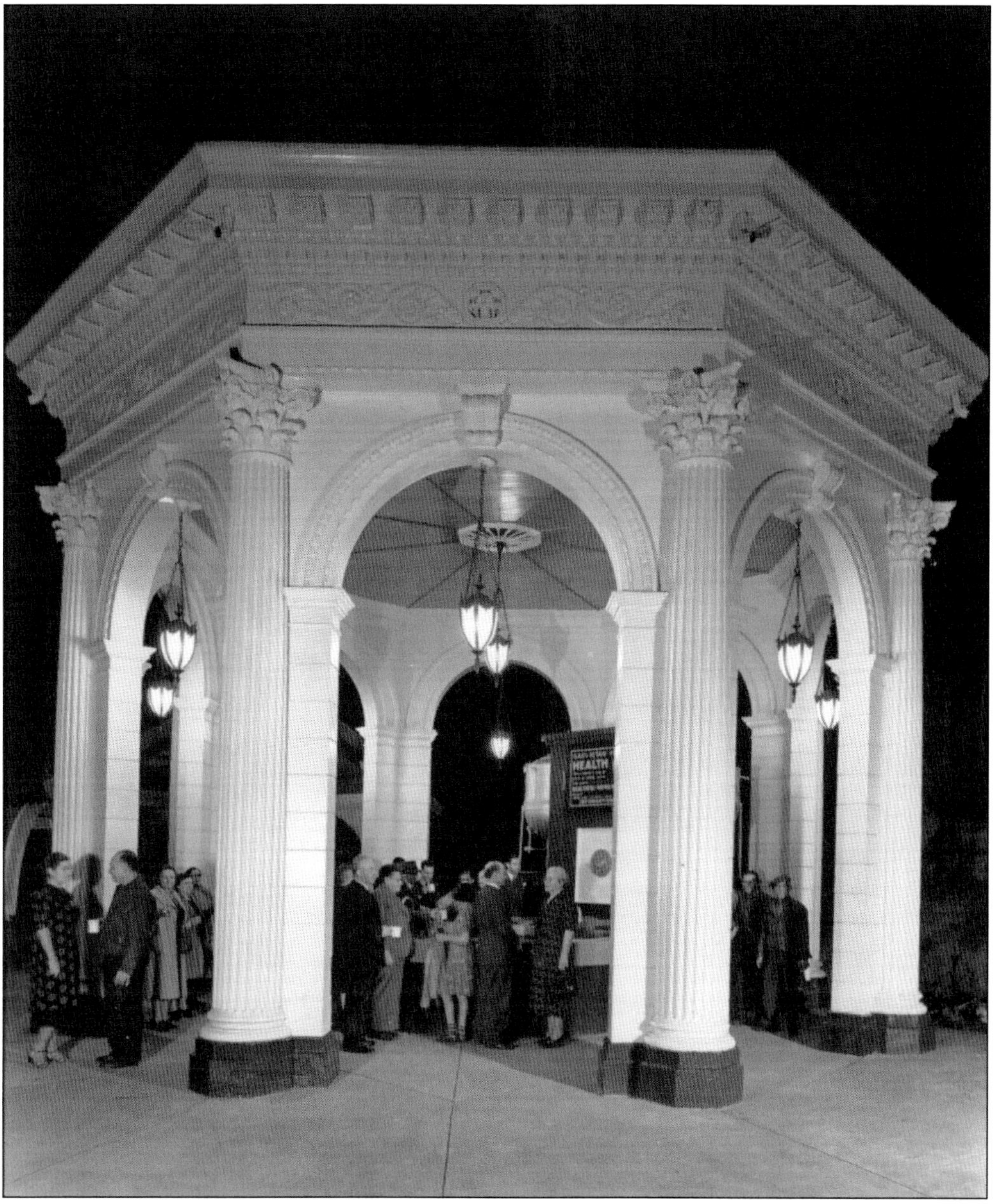

Visitors gather at the Sulphur Temple on a summer evening in 1950 to partake of the waters. The park surrounding the temple was a favorite spot for visitors and residents alike in the summer months. Sulphur water was believed to help with intestinal disorders, especially constipation. After weeks of bathing in the mineral waters as well as drinking the waters, the odor of sulphur would permeate the skin. This Classical Greek–inspired temple has for years been the symbol of the village. Due to its recent abandonment, however, its future is uncertain.

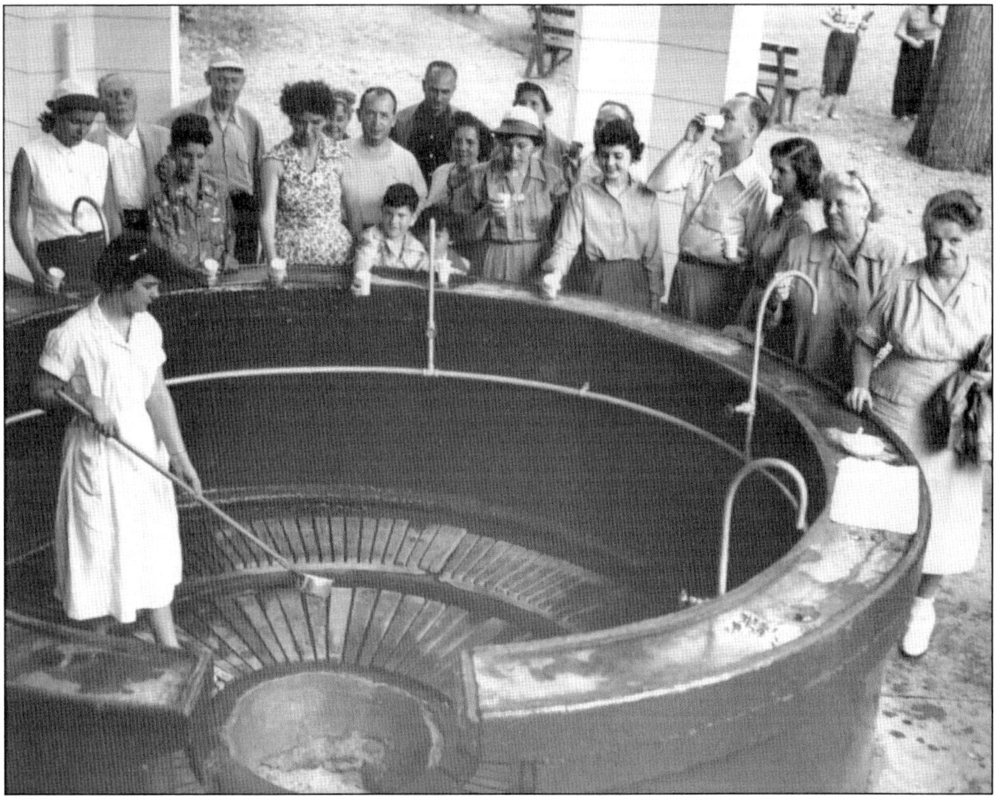

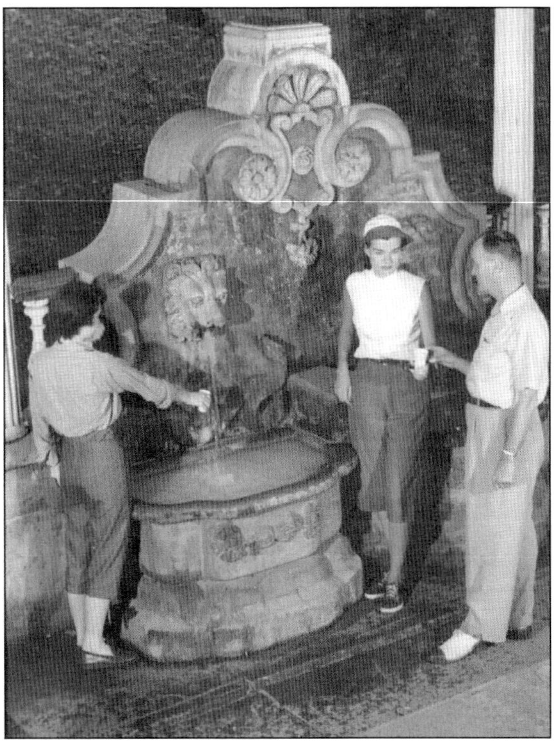

Tourists wait for drinks of sulphur water inside the Sulphur Temple in 1950. When tourism was flourishing (the peak year was 1946), attendants would scoop the water into individual cups for those brave enough to drink the strong mineral water. Several people described it as having a flavor reminiscent of the scent of rotten eggs.

As this 1950 photograph shows, the Magnesia Temple continued to be an attraction for visitors to the spa, and the Stone Lion Head Fountains were still in situ. Magnesia water was recommended for various internal/digestive disorders. The taste, while a bit chalky, is less overwhelming than sulphur water.

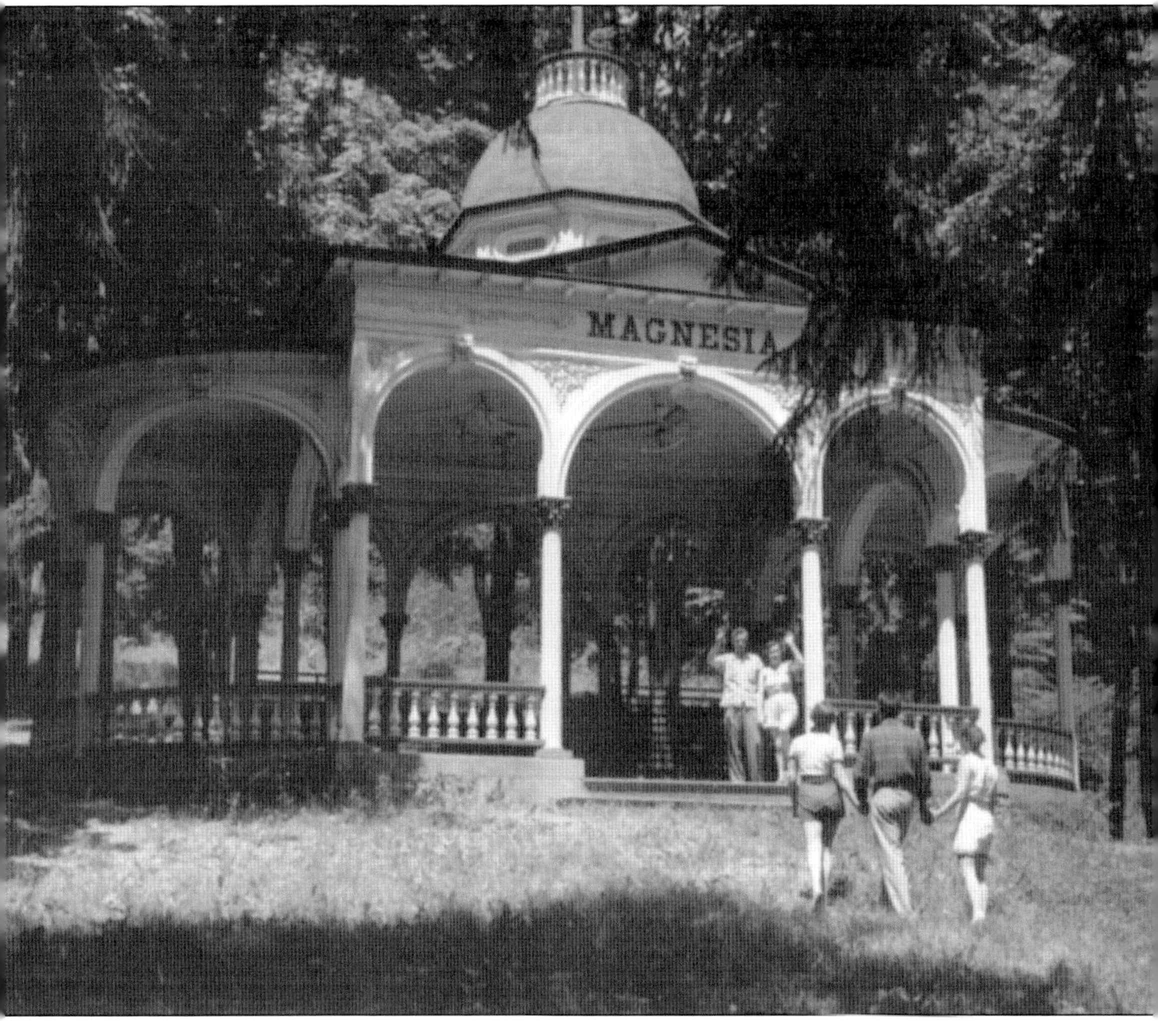

A 1950 publicity photograph shows young people enjoying a stroll through the park and stopping at the Magnesia Temple. Although the temple and surrounding property were privately owned by the VomSaal/Schaeffer family (not connected to the White Sulphur Company), they continued to maintain the temple and keep it open to the public. This ended in the 1970s, after the property passed into other hands.

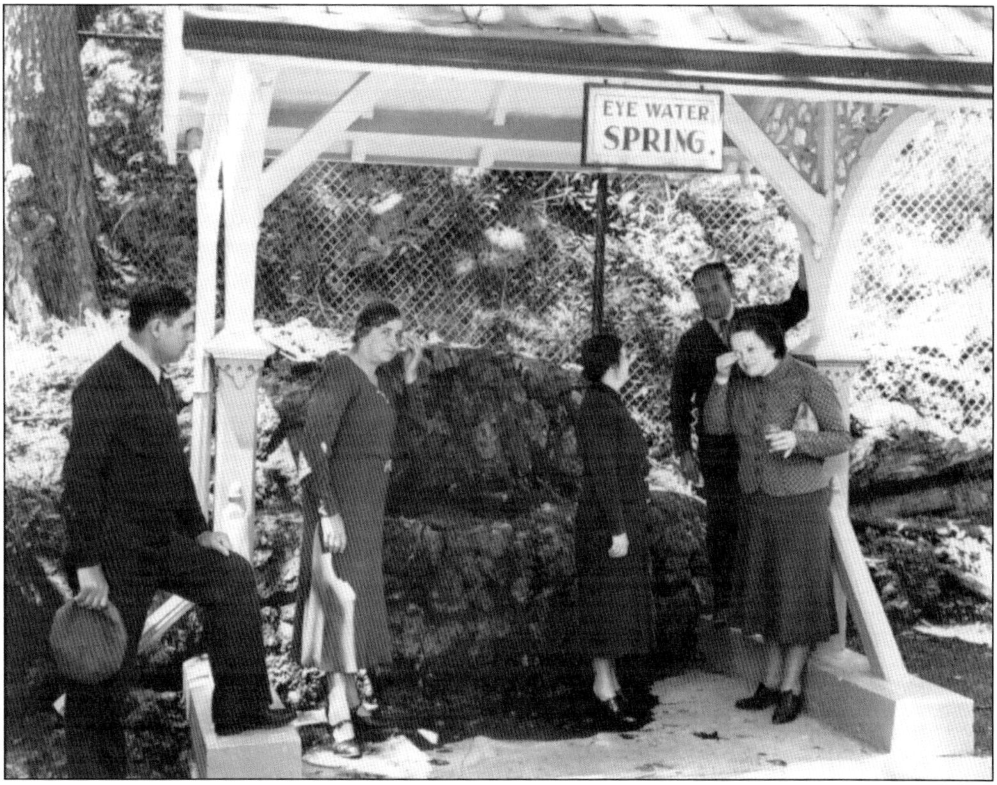

The Eye Water Spring, next to the Sulphur Temple, has been used for centuries to treat eye inflammations. These visitors in 1939 enjoy the beneficial water, which feels like satin or silk when applied to the skin. Saline is one of the chief ingredients; the entire basin where the springs are found was once a great sea.

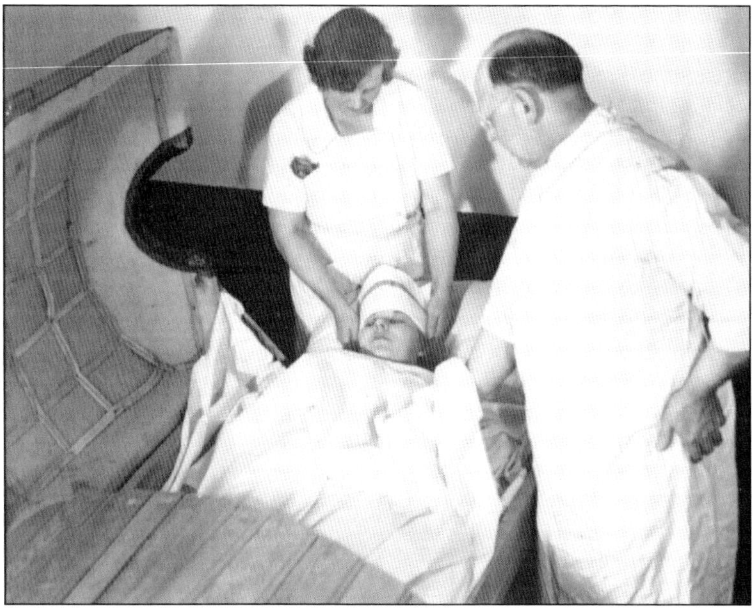

Dr. Leland White (right) and Vera Bogardus attend to Jeanette Lehman MacBride in 1939. The Gardner family, owners of the baths, visited European health spas and brought treatment options back to Sharon Springs. This contraption is reminiscent of the iron lung, used in the treatment of polio.

This late-1940s publicity photograph shows a typical room in the Imperial Bath men's section, including sulphur bath and massage table. The bath temperature was kept between 98 and 100 degrees Fahrenheit, with a massage to follow when prescribed. Although the photograph shows two patrons, in actuality, only one patient occupied a room at a time.

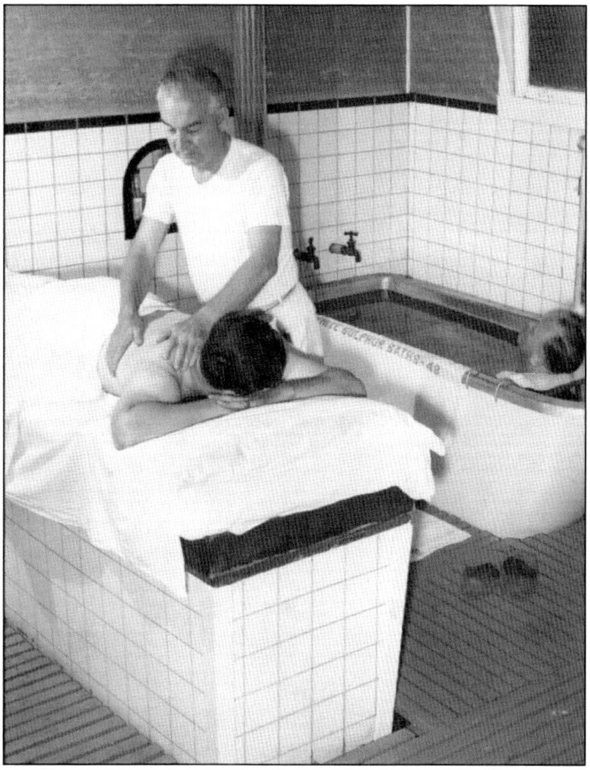

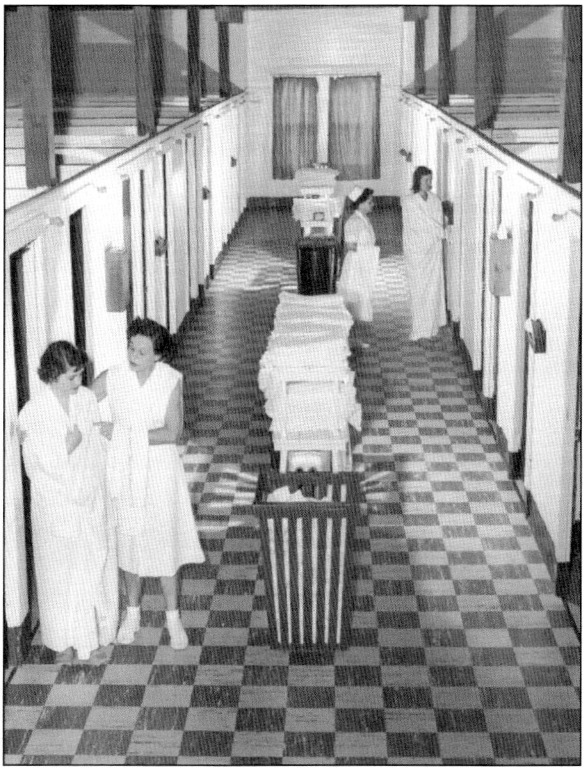

Attendants and patients are seen in the women's treatment area of the Imperial Baths. A doctor usually prescribed a half hour of soaking, followed by an hour of rest. Doctors also prescribed the number of glasses of different waters to drink and called for walks through the streets, from spring to spring, to allow patients to breathe the healthful air. The combination of treatments generally made visitors feel better.

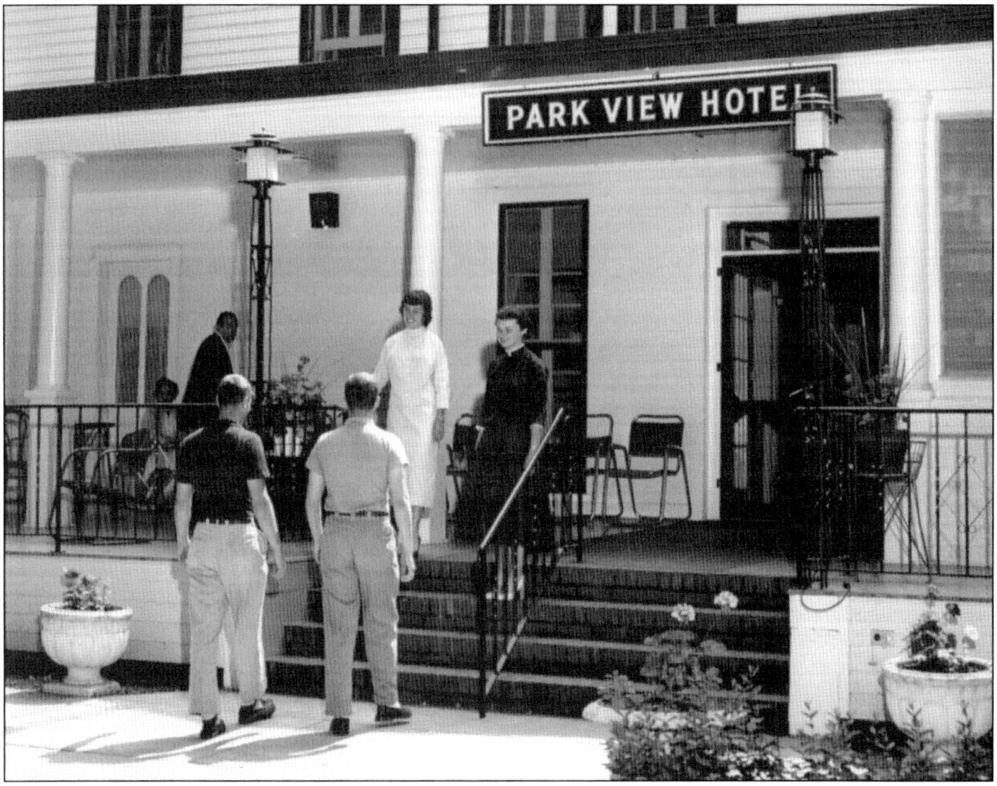

After 1911, the Park View Hotel was owned and operated by the Engle family, and they continued in this role through much of the 20th century. While the Engles practiced Judaism, they were not Orthodox, opening their hotel to people of many faiths. This hotel did not offer a kosher kitchen. The Park View Hotel was reduced to ashes in 1996 after an arsonist set fire to it.

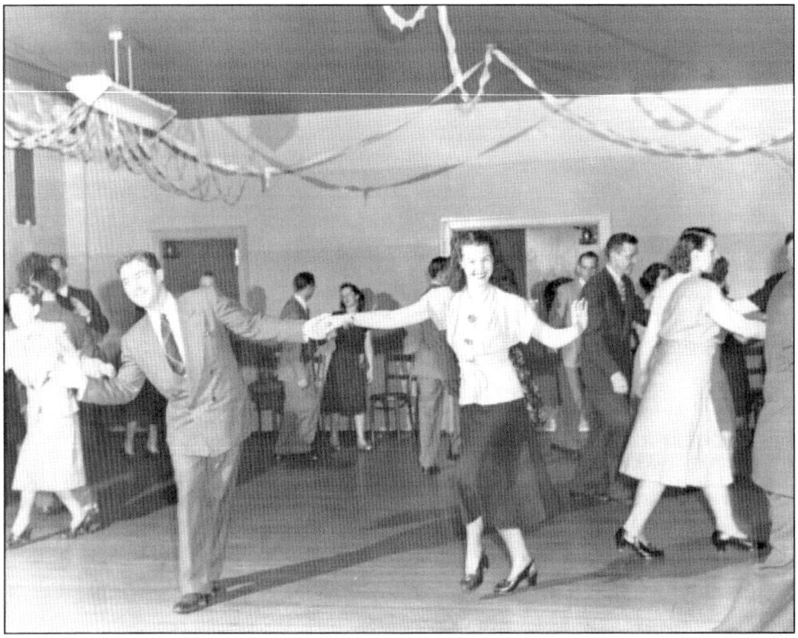

As part of an effort to attract more affluent clientele to the resort, a dance was held at the Park View Hotel in 1949, where this publicity photograph was taken. Dennis and Charlotte Engle, the owners of the Park View at that time, were active in promoting Sharon Springs.

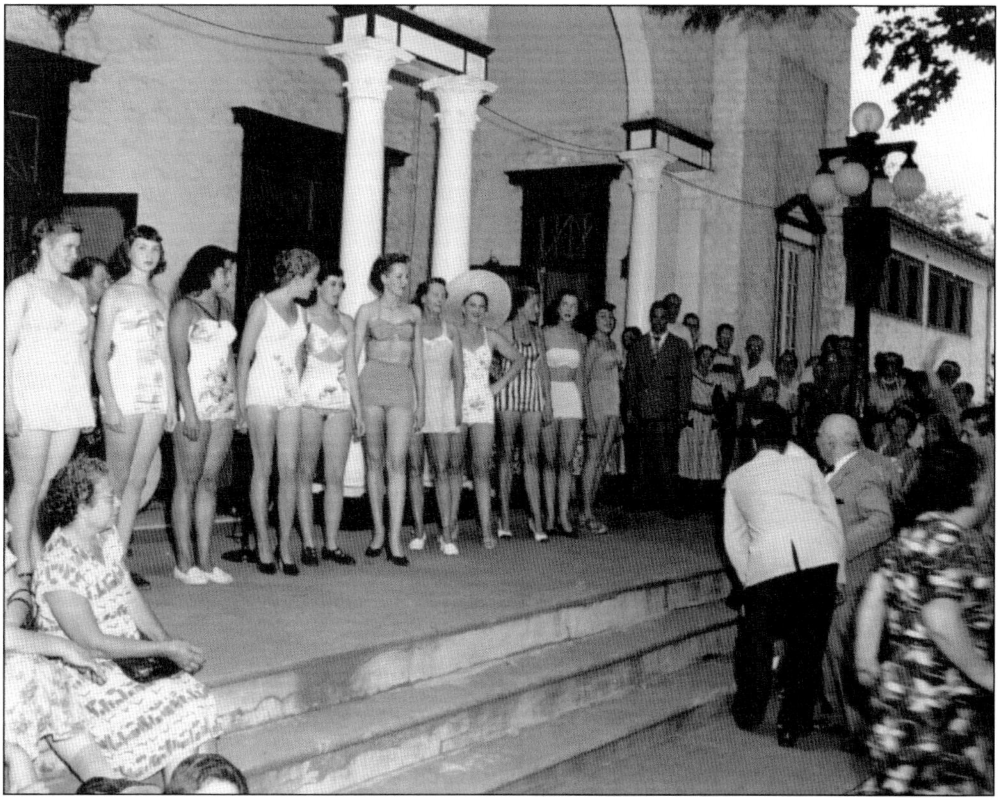

In 1949, in a well-financed publicity effort, a Miss Health contest was held on the steps of the Imperial Bathhouse. Contestants came from many states to compete for the coveted title. This photograph shows the swimsuit contest.

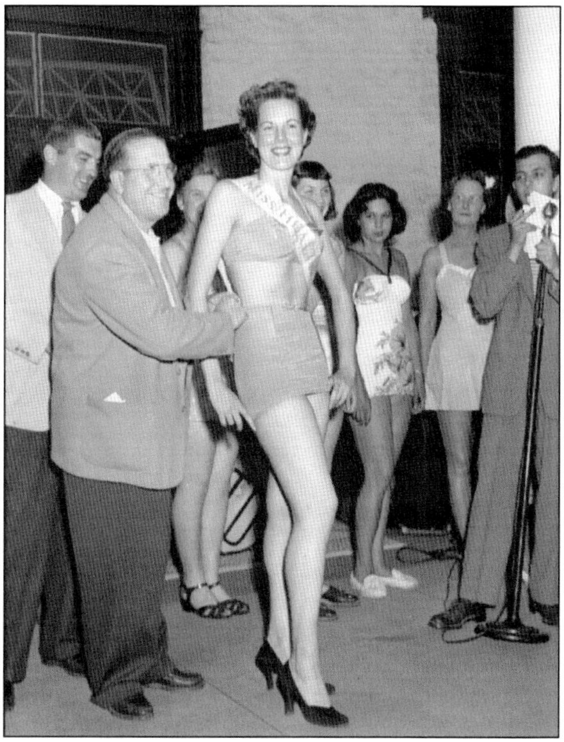

Lucille Papp from North Carolina was crowned Miss Health. She is seen here with Homer Spofford (far left), owner of White Sulphur Baths, and Dennis Engle (second from left), owner of the Park View Hotel. Both men were active in the Board of Trade for Sharon Springs and worked to bring more tourism to the spa.

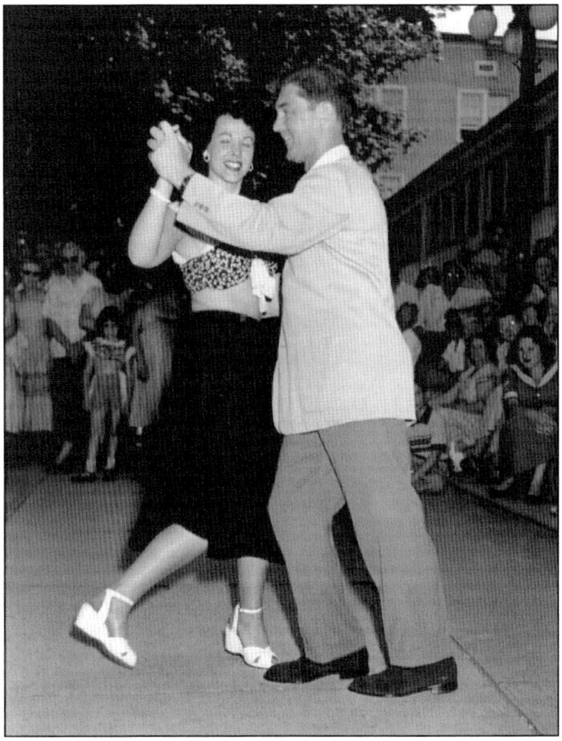

In addition to the beauty contest, this 1949 street dance was part of the campaign to attract younger, more-affluent visitors to the spa. On summer evenings in the 1940s, 1950s, and 1960s, the area in front of the Imperial Baths on Main Street was blocked off for concerts and dances.

In the summer of 1950, these acting students from the University of Miami put on an evening's entertainment in the park as part of a New York State tourism grant. This was one of many activities offered in the park, including band concerts, plays, and ice-cream socials.

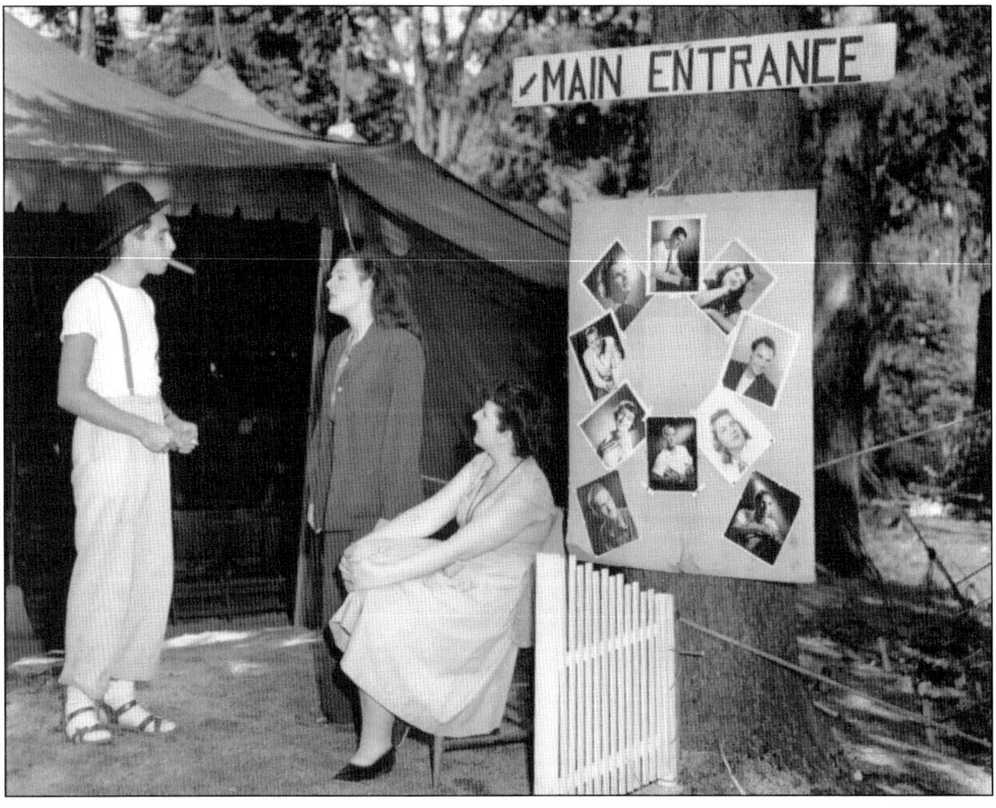

Visitors arriving by Greyhound bus at the Board of Trade could choose accommodations from a list of more than 50 hotels and boardinghouses, as seen here. The secretary of the Board of Trade would then telephone proprietors to check on availability and make reservations.

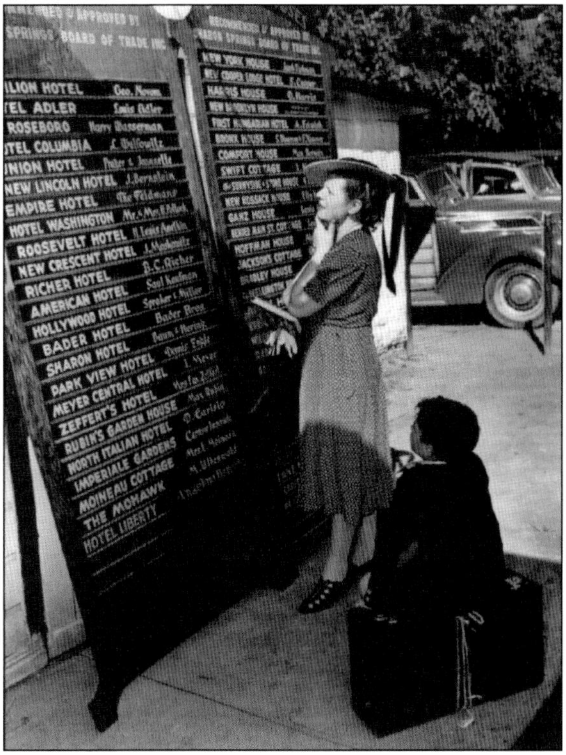

Through much of the 20th century, the Sharon Springs Board of Trade was situated at the north end of Main Street. The Greyhound bus made daily trips to and from New York City. Taxi service was also available to and from New York City or to connect to the train station in Albany.

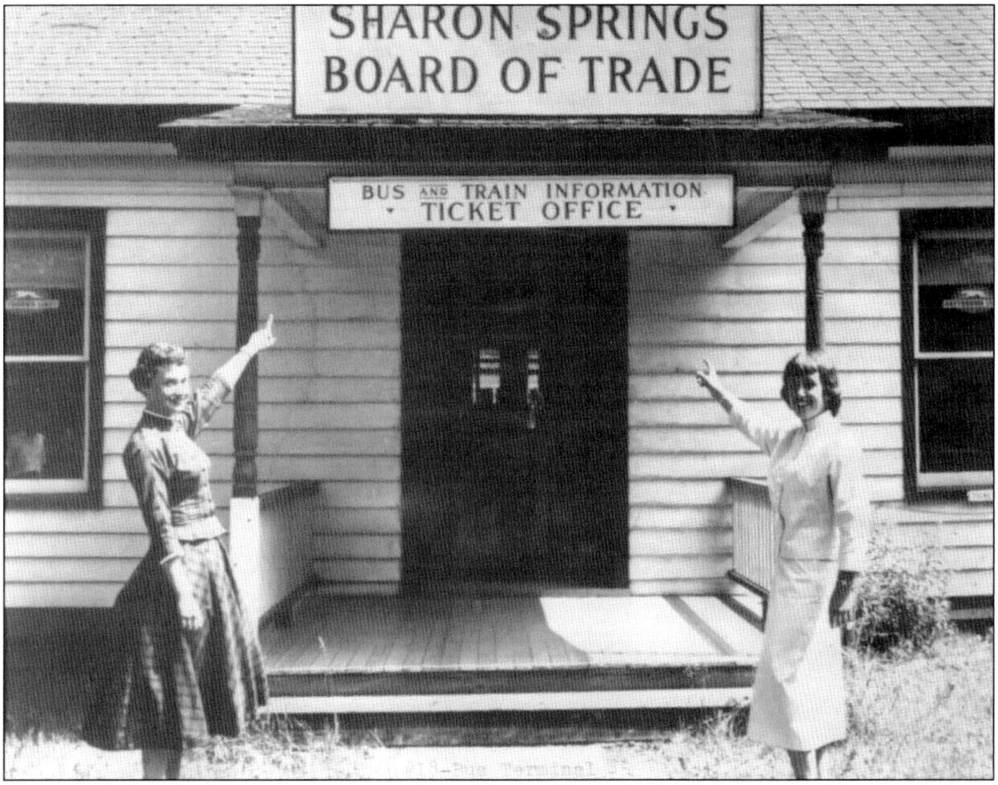

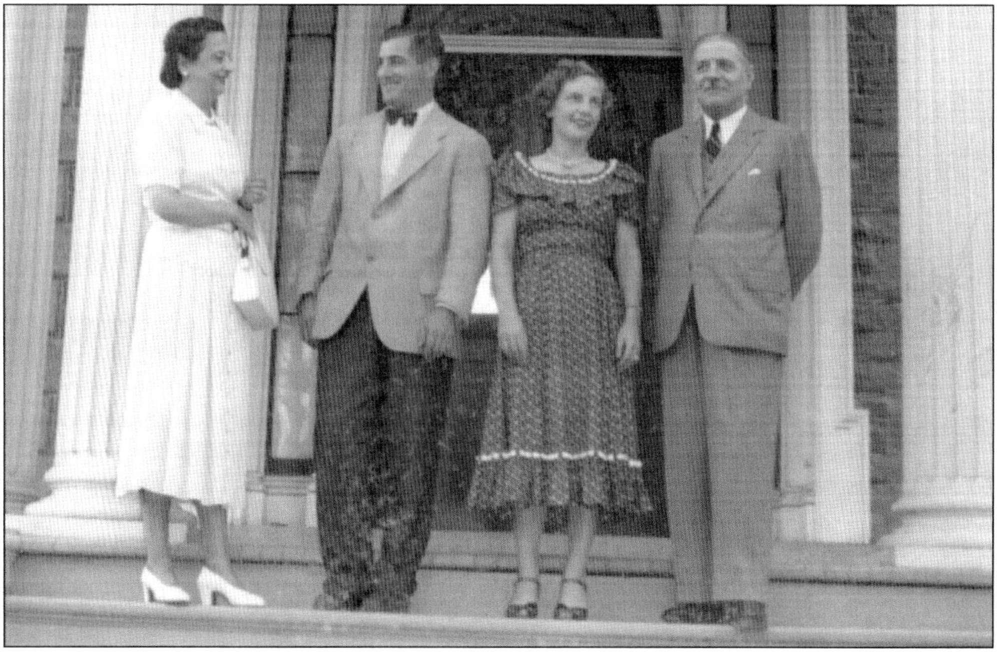

Because of the spa, many dignitaries have visited Sharon. Here, Homer and Rosamond Spofford (center) entertain the Philippine ambassador and his wife on the steps of the Stone House. The Spoffords purchased the White Sulphur Baths and Stone House Mansion from the Gardner family in 1941, and they operated the baths until selling them to the Yarkony family in the 1970s.

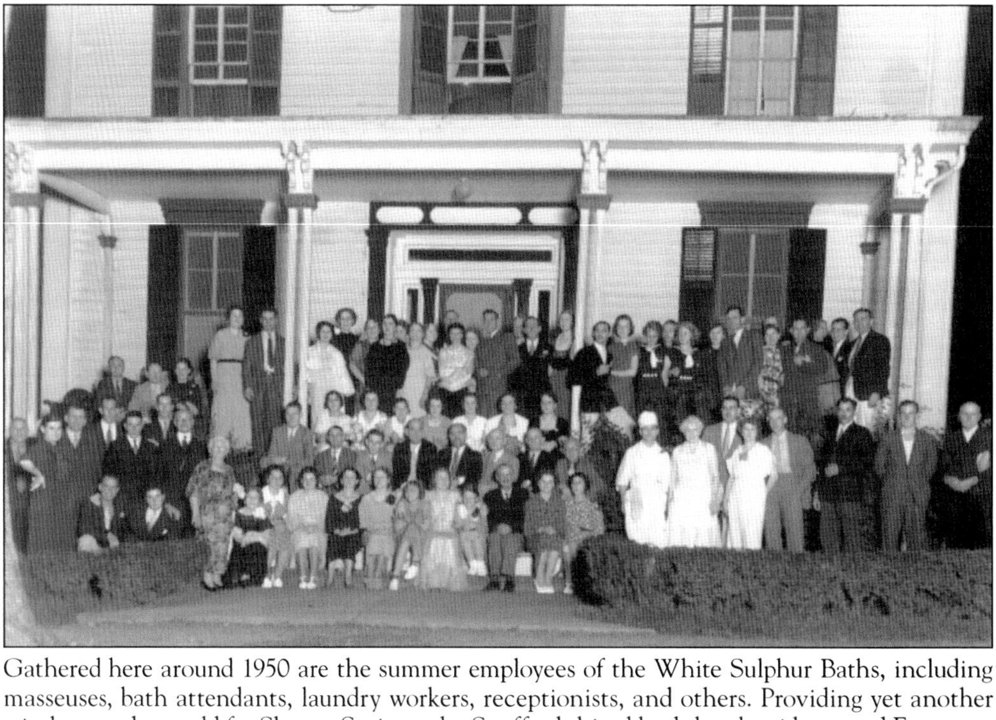

Gathered here around 1950 are the summer employees of the White Sulphur Baths, including masseuses, bath attendants, laundry workers, receptionists, and others. Providing yet another window on the world for Sharon Springs, the Spoffords hired both local residents and European employees, including refugees from the Hungarian uprising of 1956.

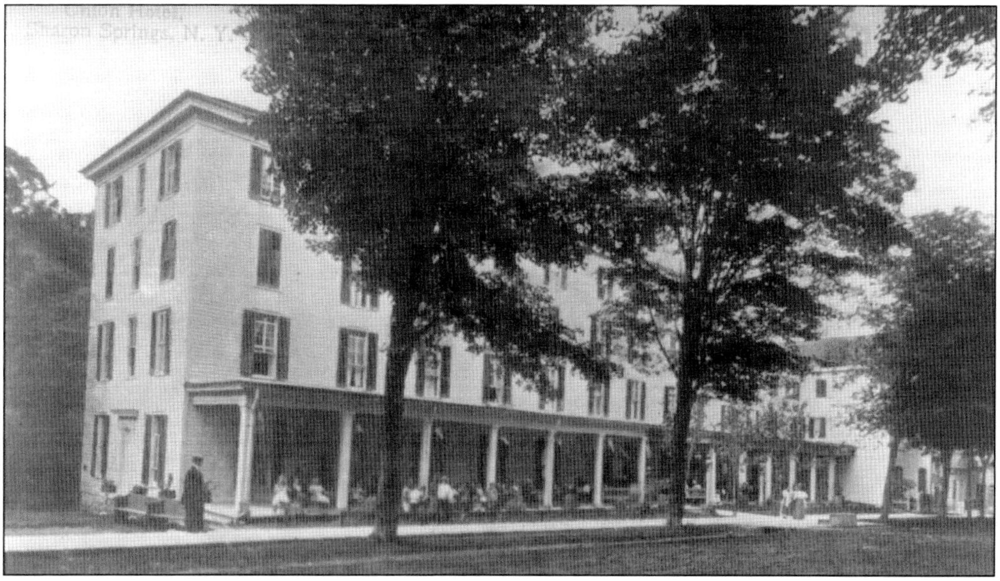

Built in 1865, the Union Hotel, seen here in 1926, was a full-service hotel with billiard room, barbershop, stables, and a chalybeate spring on the grounds. The hotel was locally famous for the day in 1950 when Viola Empie's brakes failed as she was driving down steep Washington Street. Her car plowed straight through the hotel, narrowly missing guests playing bridge in the lobby and hitting a new car parked in back for safety. Luckily, no one was hurt.

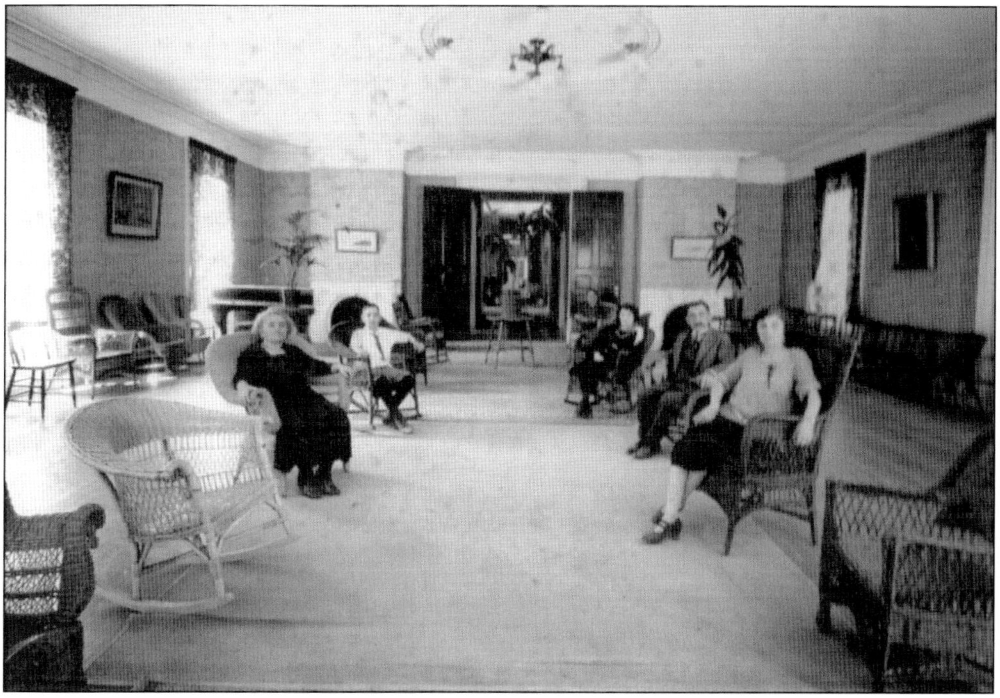

The Union Hotel lobby is seen here in the 1940s. Guests must have been surprised to see a car barrel through the room! In its heyday, the hotel employed a resident physician to assist guests in planning their treatments. After years of deterioration, the hotel was torn down in 1970. An empty lot remains today, across the street from the Roseboro.

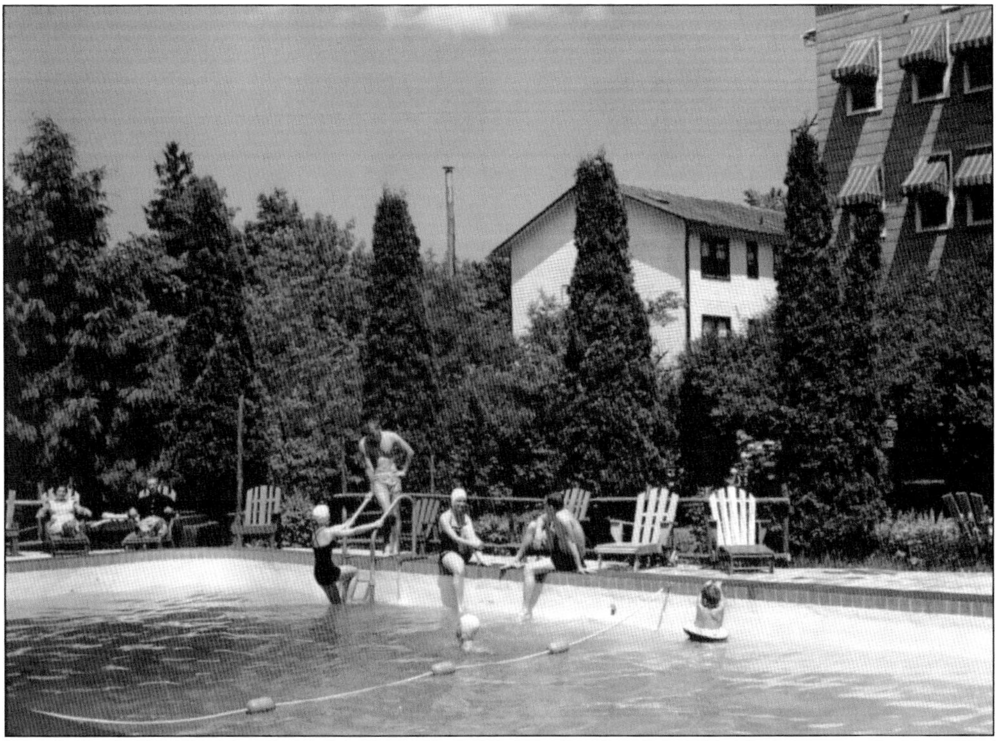

This 1950 photograph of the Columbia Hotel pool depicts a popular kosher hotel of the era. Amenities included nightly piano music, some rooms with private baths, the swimming pool, and easy access to the Imperial Baths. Many bar mitzvahs were celebrated at the hotel in the summer.

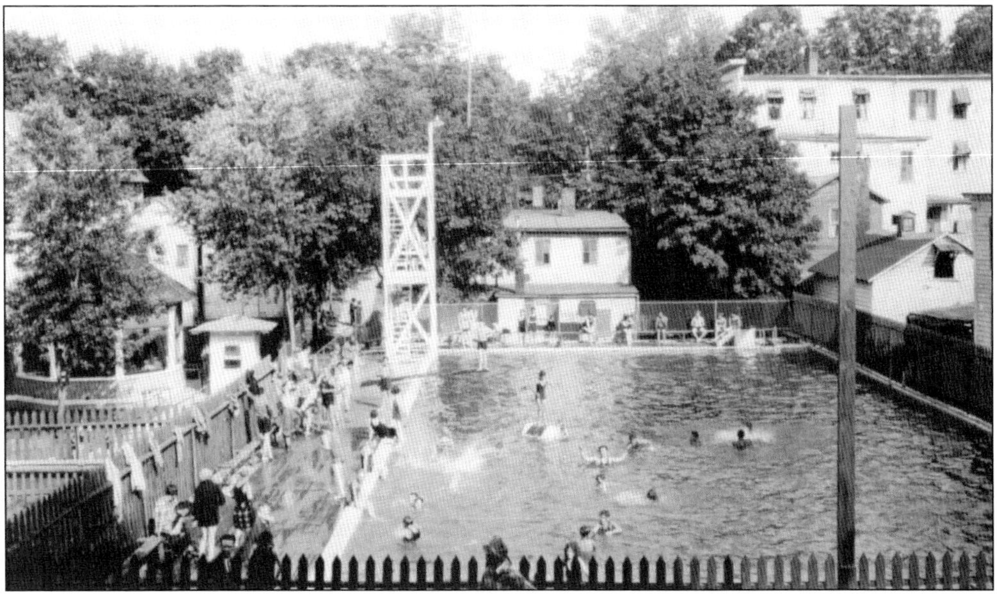

Part of a complex of buildings, Smith's pool, with its changing room, was built in 1926 near the Chalybeate Temple. In the 1940s, entrance to the pool area cost 10¢ for children. The pool closed shortly after World War II, and the area around the chalybeate spring became Berman's Little Village.

The Fisherman family poses in 1949. They are, from left to right, Carl, Edna, Nancy, and Michael. The family summered in Sharon every year. Michael Fisherman was a musician at several hotels, and, as teenagers, the children worked in the hotels and bathhouse. In 1948, the family bought and modernized a former one-room school in the countryside as their residence. The family continues to be well loved by their neighbors, most of whom are year-round farmers. (Courtesy of Nancy Fisherman Goodman.)

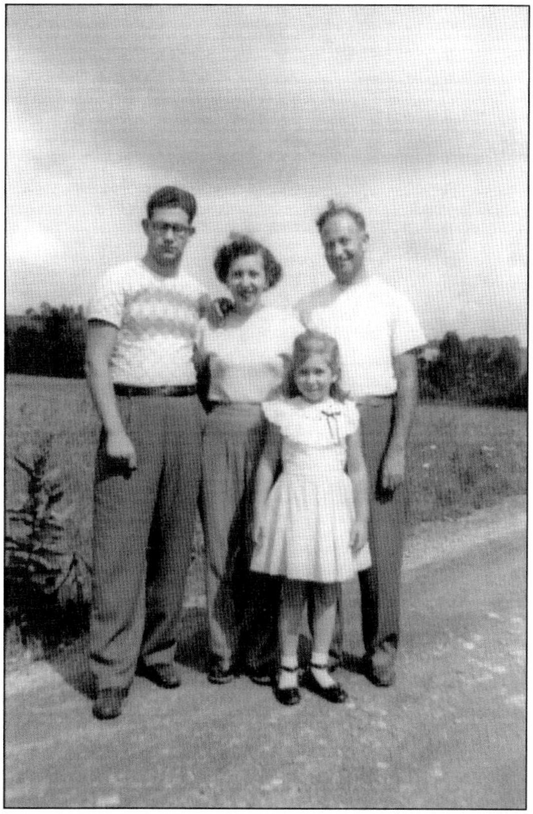

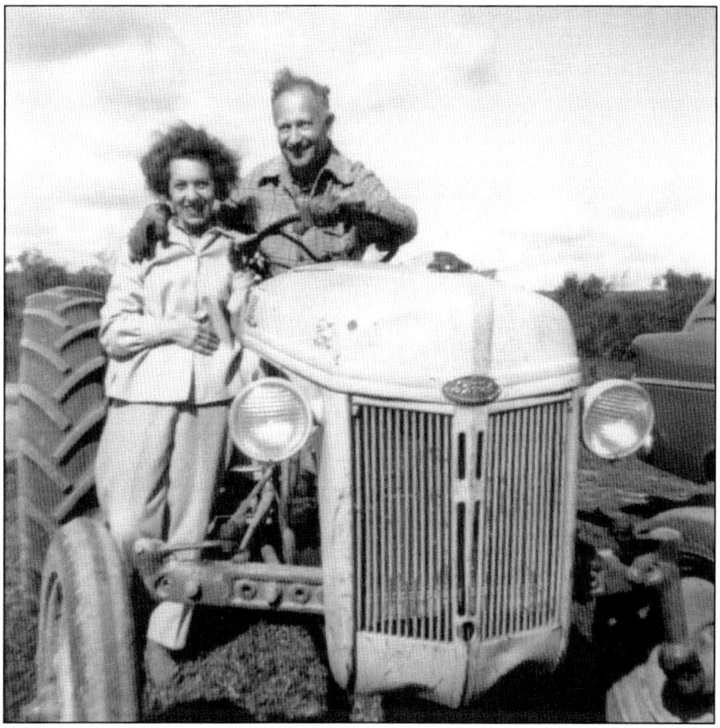

Living next door to the Lynk farm, the Fishermans occasionally helped out with chores—a unique experience for this city family in the summers. When Michael Fisherman arrived each summer, his first words were, "Ah! I love this country air!" Here, Edna and Michael Fisherman pose with the Lynks' tractor in 1949. (Courtesy of Nancy Fisherman Goodman.)

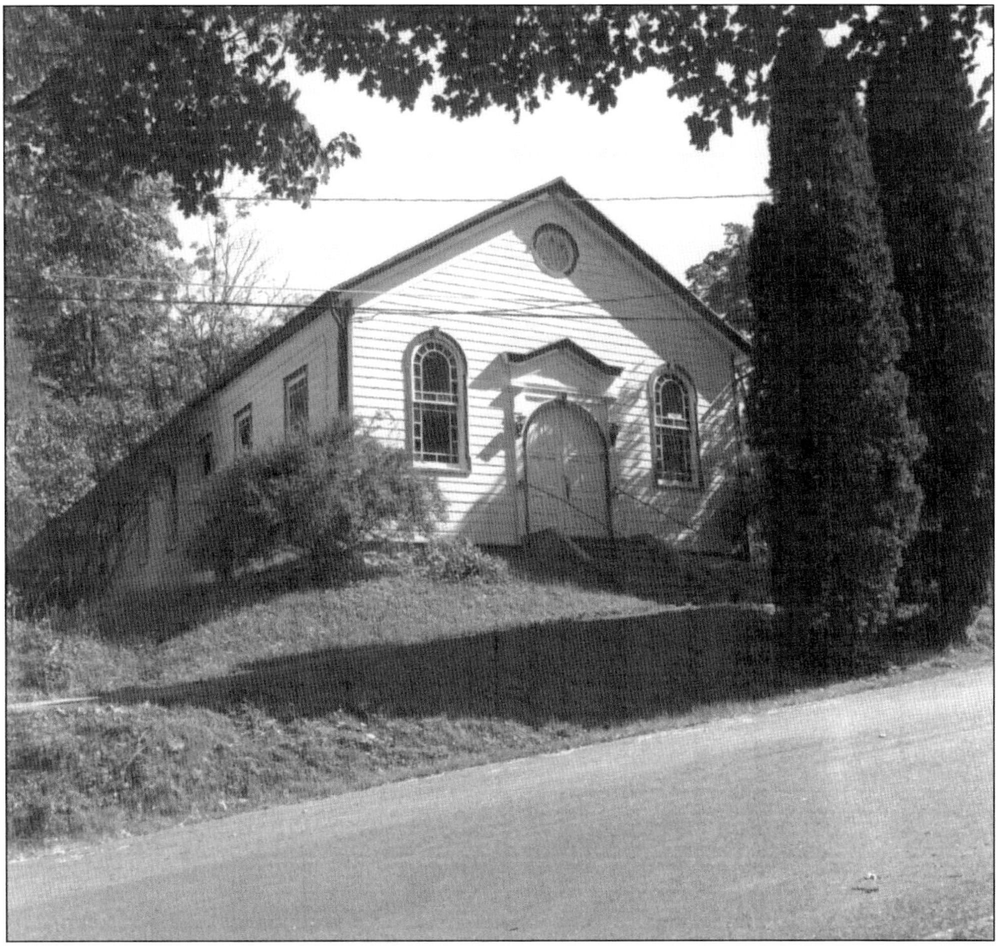

The Sharon Springs Synagogue sits prominently along Willow Street. It was built in 1904 after a fundraising effort led by Rabbi Dr. Bernard Drachman, whose New York congregation included Harry Houdini. Drachman has been called "a forgotten champion of Orthodoxy." Under his guidance, Sharon Springs became a second home to many Jewish families. In 1915, there were eight services by Rabbi Spiegel, with an average attendance of 150. Services were so popular that a daily Hebrew service was offered in the summer. The synagogue remained active until the baths were closed in 2005. (Photograph by Leila Durkin.)

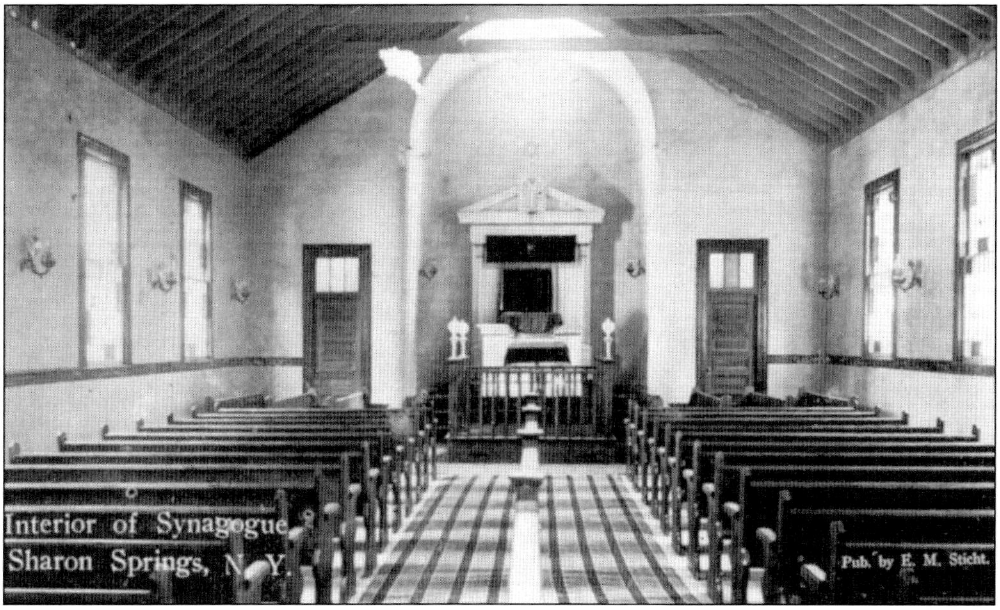

Originally an Orthodox synagogue, its earlier congregations were somewhat relaxed, with men and women sitting together, reflecting a vacation experience. The early congregations were active in fundraising efforts for Jewish causes and led the effort to establish the Joint Relief Committee for the Jewish War Sufferers in World War I.

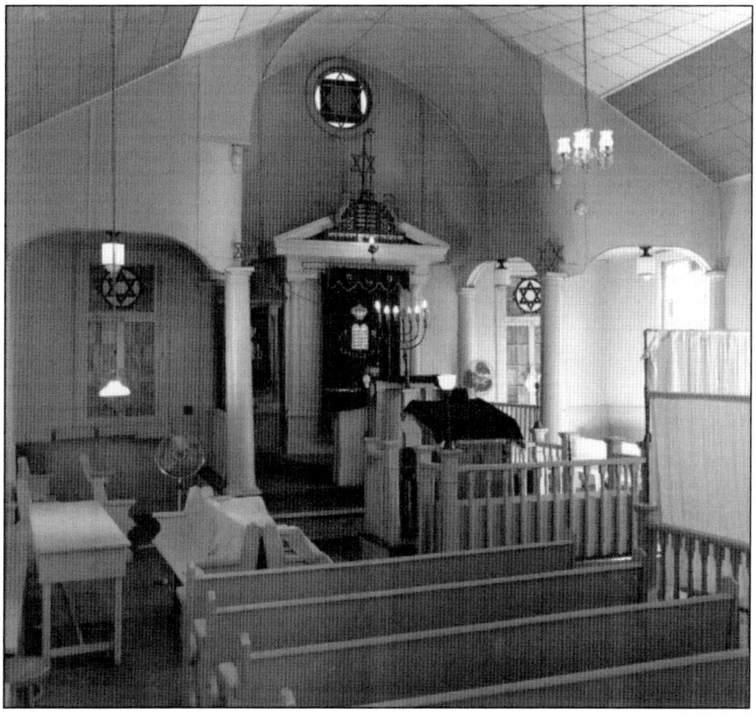

Once the Satmar Hasidim became the dominant Jewish summer population, the synagogue was altered, with a divider setting off the women's section. Other changes included a cleansing of the kitchen to make it more acceptably kosher to the Satmar, the most orthodox of all Jewish sects. (Photograph by Leila Durkin.)

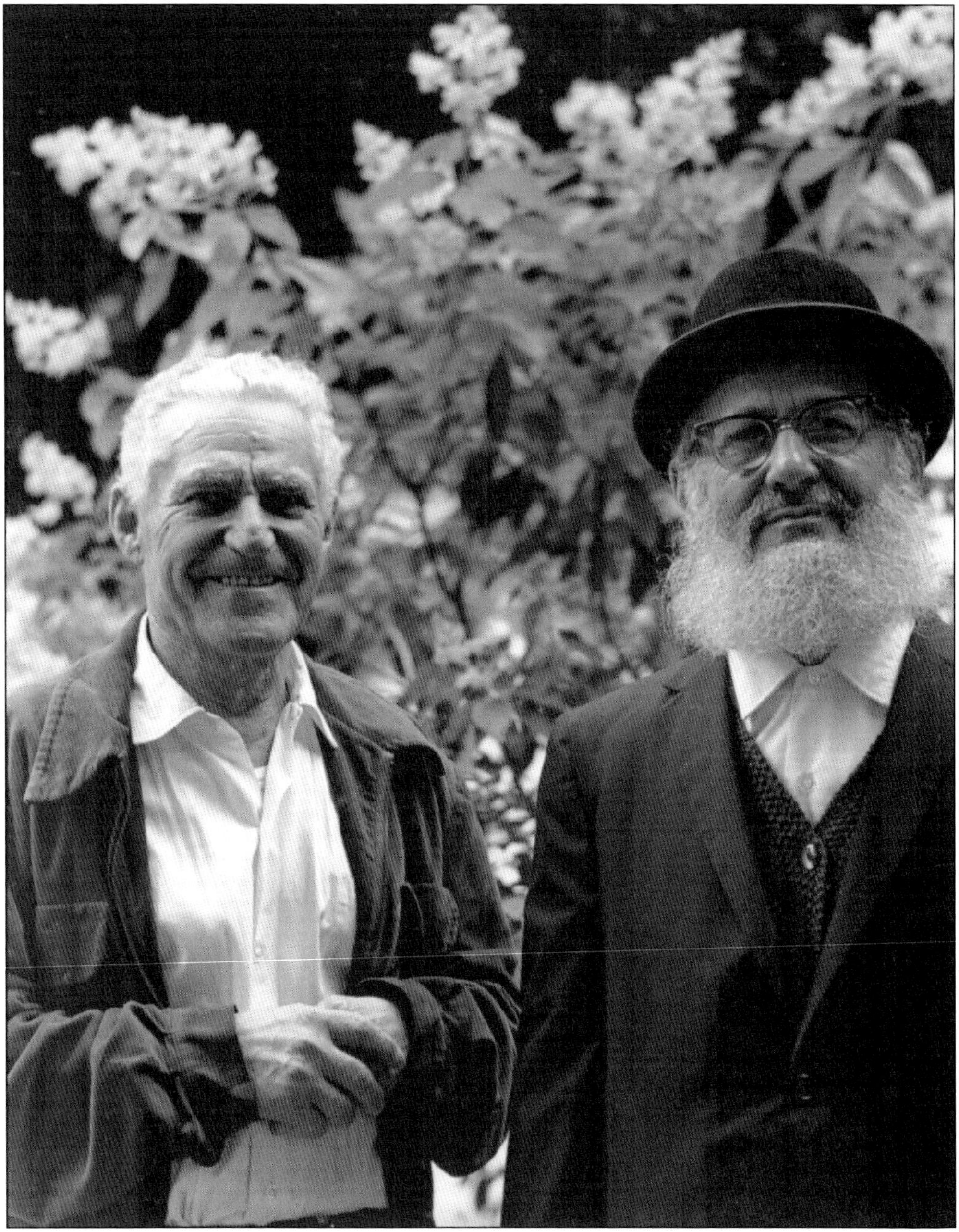

Some Hasidim were less orthodox than the Satmar and mixed freely with residents and other visitors, as this late-1970s photograph attests. The mixing of cultures created a unique atmosphere—sometimes tolerant, but other times reactive. Yiddish was heard throughout the village, klezmer bands played at hotels, and the United Jewish Appeal held concerts in the parks to raise funds. (Photograph by Hansi Durlach.)

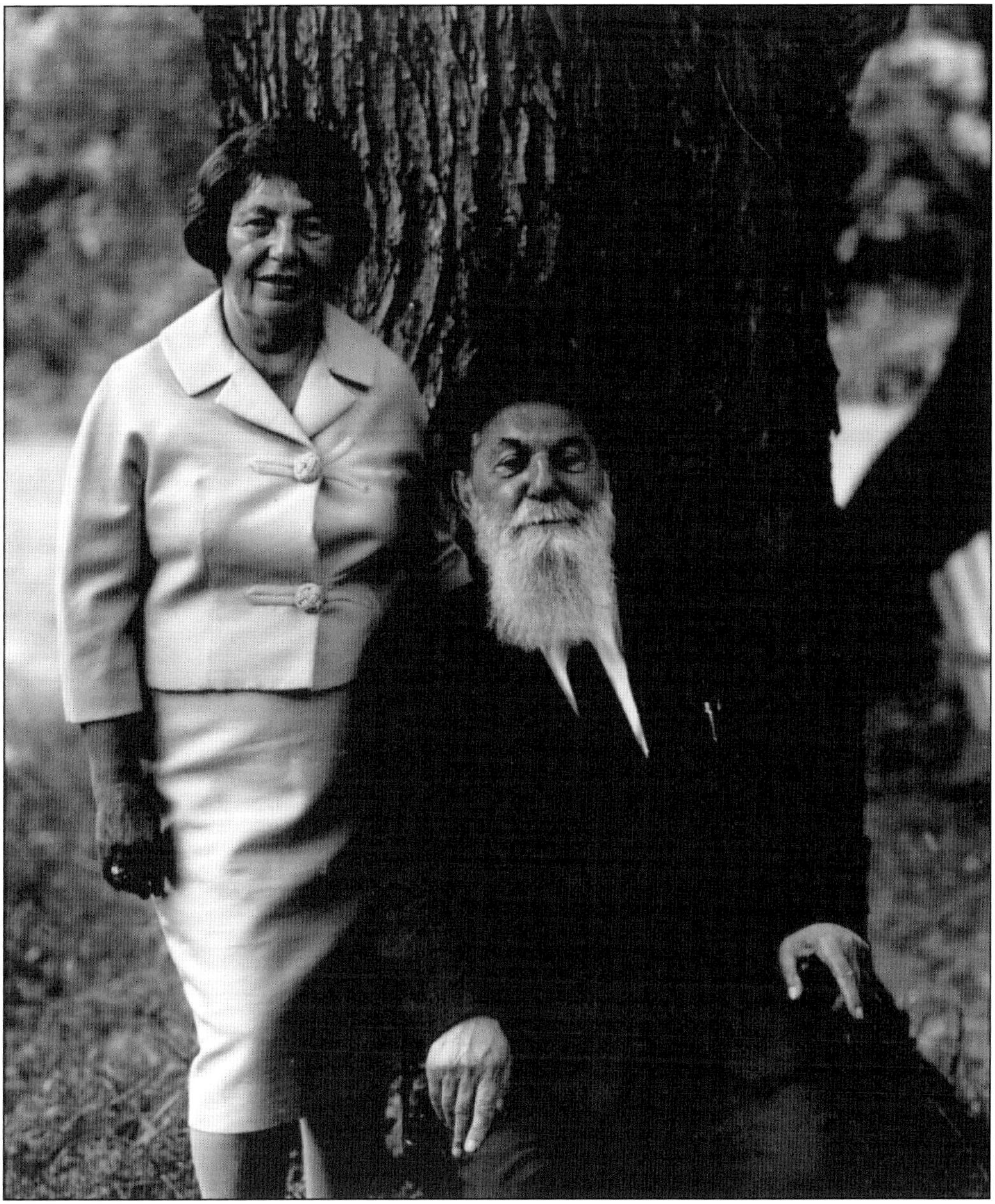

Rabbi and Mrs. Basch are shown at the Brustman House in 1950. Many Jewish families became summer residents, extending their stay through Rosh Hashanah in September. Several of their obituaries even mentioned their fondness for Sharon Springs. (Photograph by Hansi Durlach, courtesy of Sharon Historical Society.)

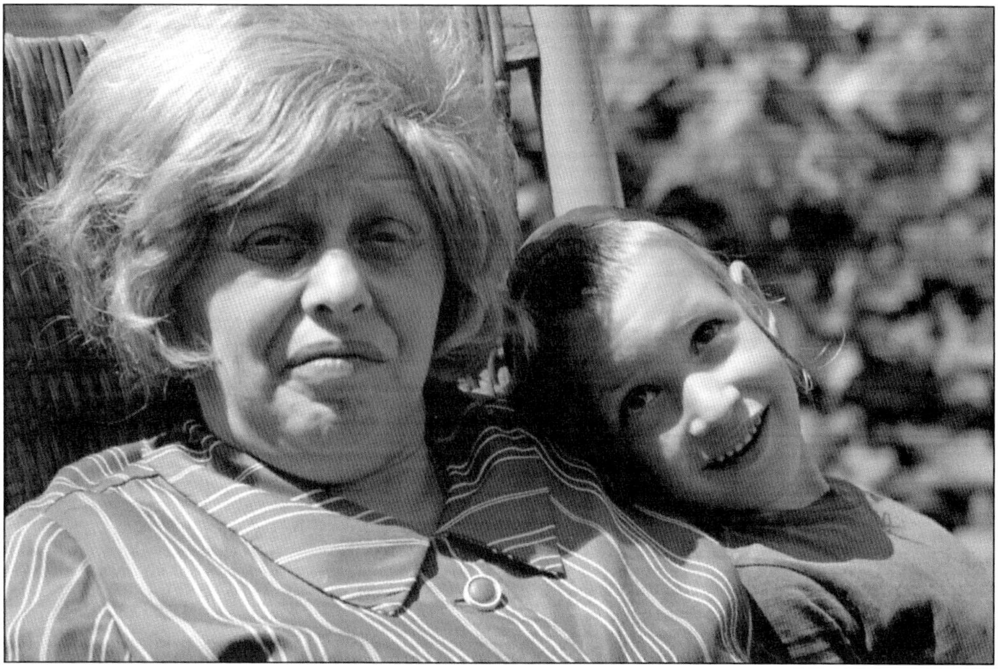

A Hasidic mother and her child are seen summering in Sharon Springs in 1980. The children were often tempted by non-Jewish as well as less-observant Jewish children to engage in activities not allowed by their religious laws. (Photograph by Hansi Durlach, courtesy of Sharon Historical Society.)

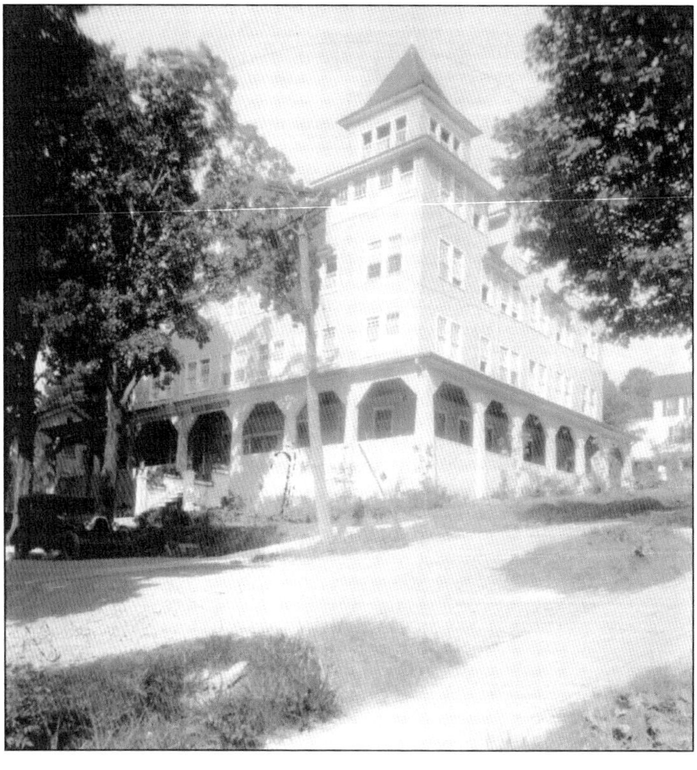

Built in 1927, the Mission-style Empire Hotel had several incarnations. Philip Feldman built it to serve as a Jewish school, but, for years, it operated as a kosher hotel. In 1967, the Satmar Hasidim opened the Talmudical Academy of America for Hasidim boys; it closed within a short time.

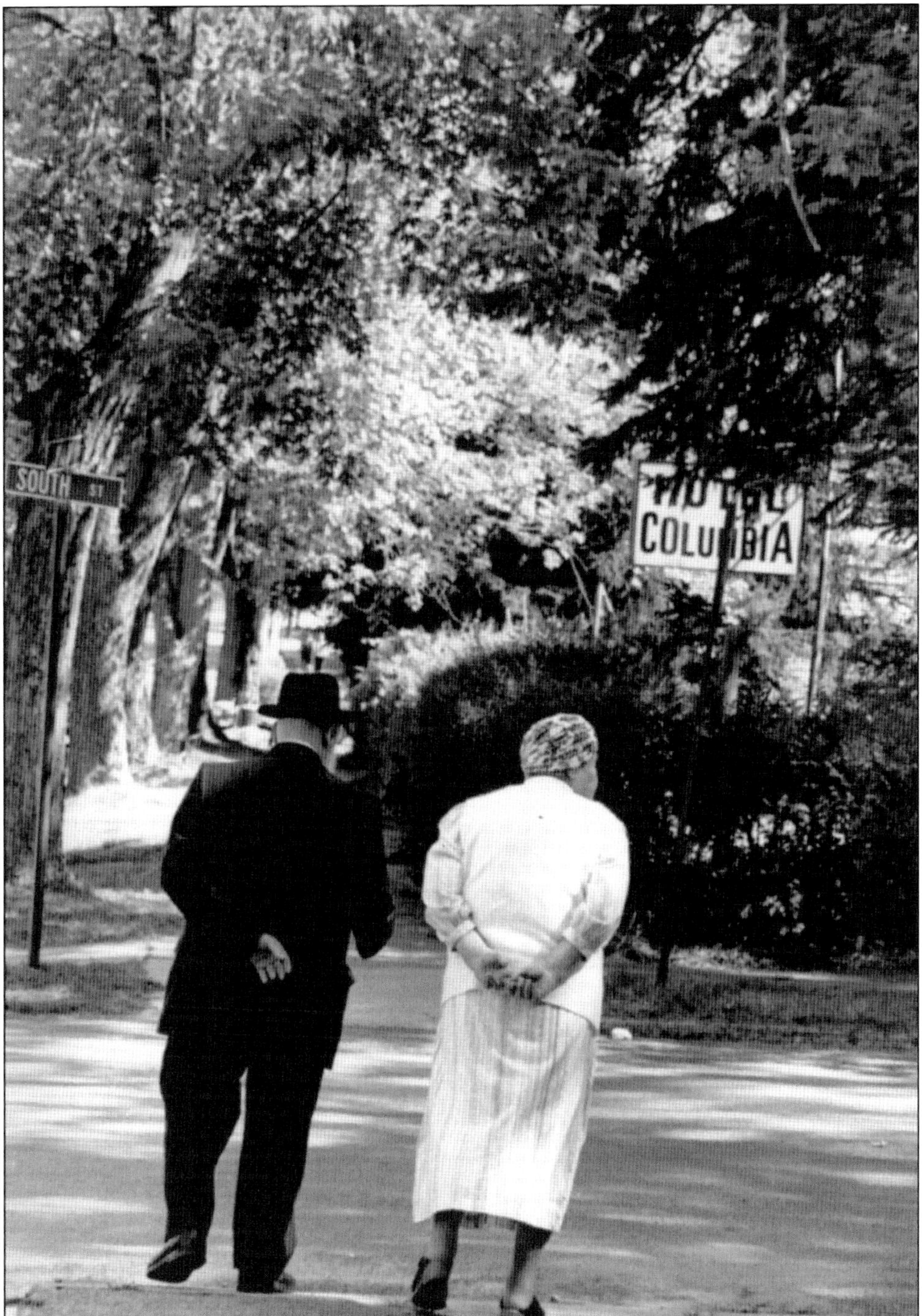

A Hasidic couple enjoys a stroll along tree-lined Main Street in Sharon Springs in 1990, near the Hotel Columbia. The men always dressed in suits and hats. Women wore conservative, below-the-knee dresses, and wigs or scarves covered their heads. With the arrival of large numbers of Hasidim, a Mitvah was built in the village for the ritual monthly bathing of women. (Photograph by Leila Durkin.)

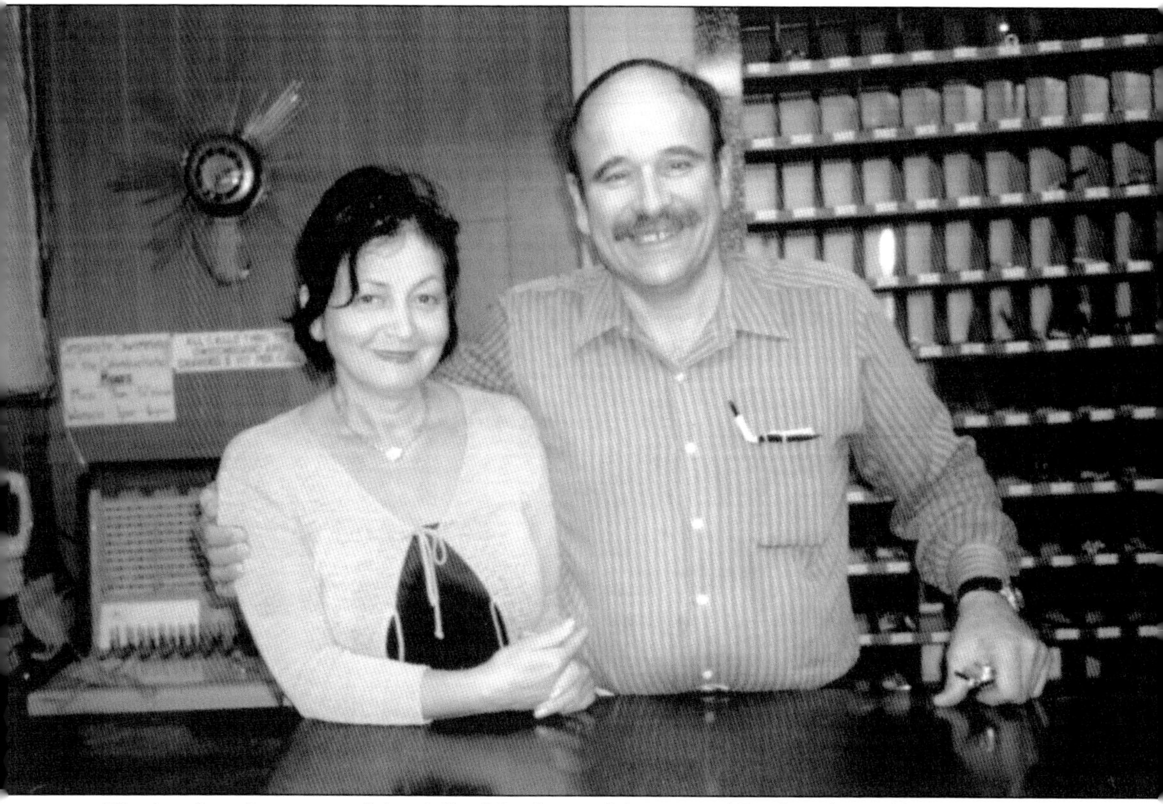

The last Jewish owners of the Adler Hotel were Miriam and Fred Yarkony (shown here). Fred's father, Mordecai, a Holocaust survivor, purchased the hotel in the 1970s and brought together many fellow survivors there. When director Steven Spielberg was doing research for *Schindler's List*, he came to the Adler to interview some of those saved by Oskar Schindler. In 2005, the Yarkony family sold the hotel and bathhouses to a group of Korean investors.

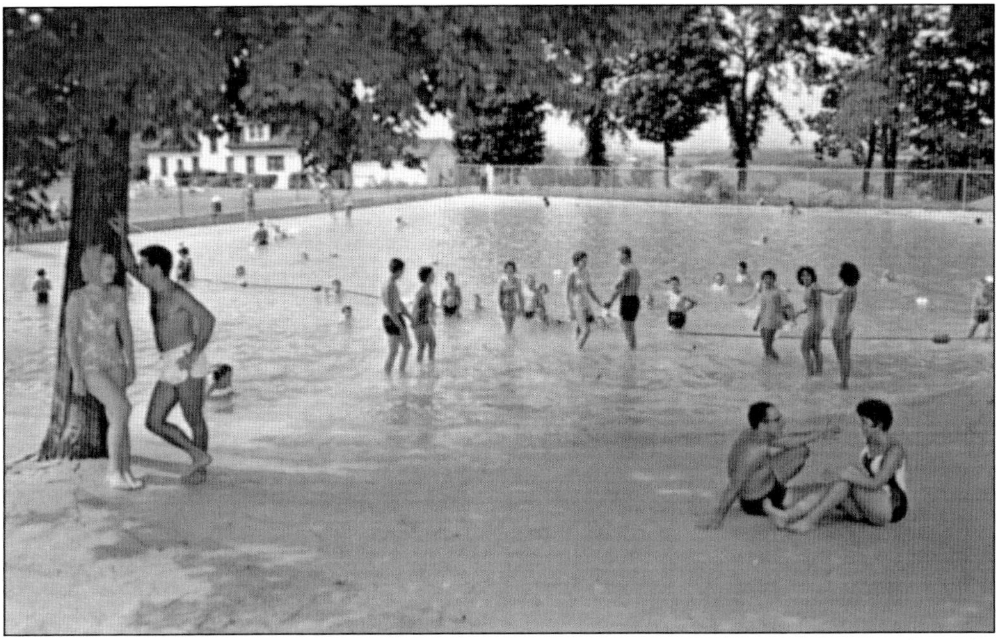

The former "mud hole" was coated with cement in 1960. This postcard photograph from the summer of 1961 shows a variety of young people enjoying the sun. The pool was a very popular spot, where townspeople met easily with summer visitors and the staff from the several hotels.

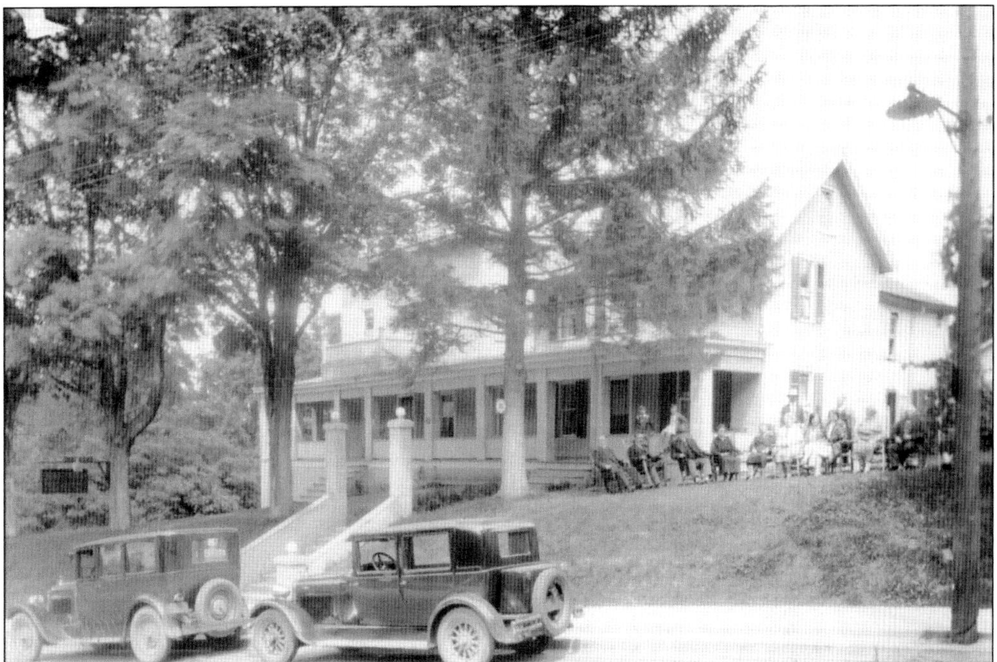

The Liberty Hotel, pictured here in the 1930s, was one of four hotels catering to Italian clientele in the 20th century. Many Italian American families who summered here were recent immigrants who brought with them fascinating foods, games, and other customs. Current residents remember hearing lively games of bocce ball played on the grounds.

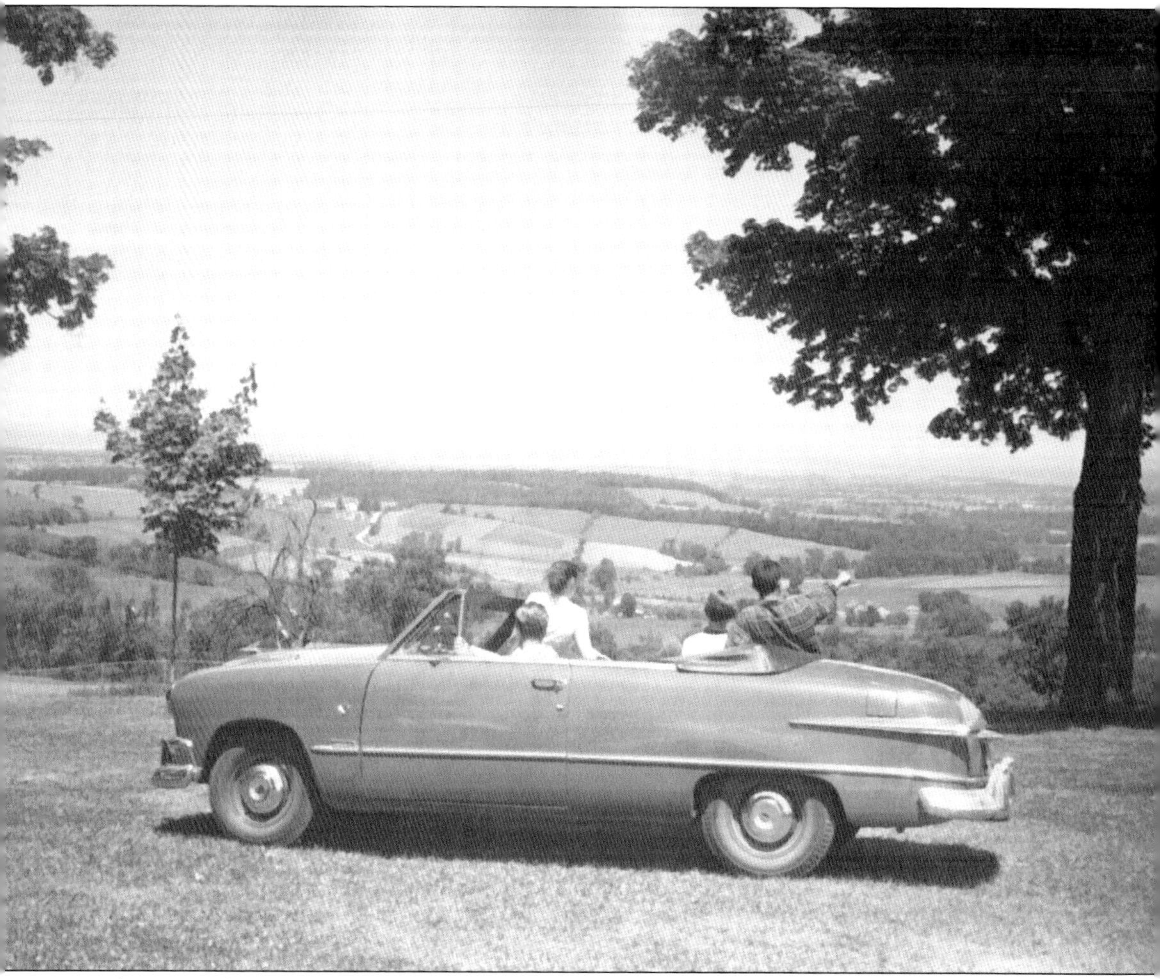

This 1950 photograph was taken from the summit where the Pavilion Hotel once stood. The summit, offering a view of the Mohawk Valley and Adirondack Mountains, continued to be a popular place to drive or walk to until the 1990s, when No Trespassing signs were posted on the property and the former golf course reverted to nature, obscuring the view.

Five

Town Life

While agricultural practices have changed over the centuries, Sharon is still a "right-to-farm" community. The school, volunteer organizations, clubs, churches, and multigenerational businesses continue to provide pride of place to the full-time residents of Sharon. Like the spa at the bottom of Main Street hill, the upper village and town have experienced economic woes, with foreclosures, abandoned buildings, and empty storefronts. Yet the community endures.

It is that sense of community, nurtured by caring teachers and other mentors, that fuels volunteer organizations, sports teams and their fans, festivals, parades, and other activities residents remember fondly.

Through the centuries, several ethnic communities have migrated to the town. With the paving of Route 20 and other roads, many Italian and Irish families arrived and found homes here, followed by immigrant families from Eastern Europe (Poland, the Ukraine, Czechoslovakia) and French Canadian neighbors, all bringing with them new customs and cuisines.

The town is comprised of several small hamlets; most of which had a discrete church at one time. The life of Sharon has been influenced by several Lutheran congregations, two Baptist churches, the Dutch Reformed Church and Methodists, a Universalist congregation, the Catholic church, an Episcopal congregation, and, in the summer, a lively synagogue. Today, only the Methodist church holds regular services in the village, while the town has a smattering of the former large collection of churches: Leesville's St. Matthew's Lutheran Chapel, the Reformed Church near Beekman Corners (formerly Dutch Reformed), and Rose of Sharon Church of God, formerly the True Church of Christ, in Sharon Hill.

With a population of fewer than 2,000 people (547 of those in the village), the area offers a rural landscape, a true escape from urban America, and many newcomers to the town and village express that reason for buying property here. The mixing of different cultures—the meeting of townspeople with Jewish, Italian, and today's gay community—has created a broader sense of inclusiveness and of one's place in a wider world than exists in most small towns.

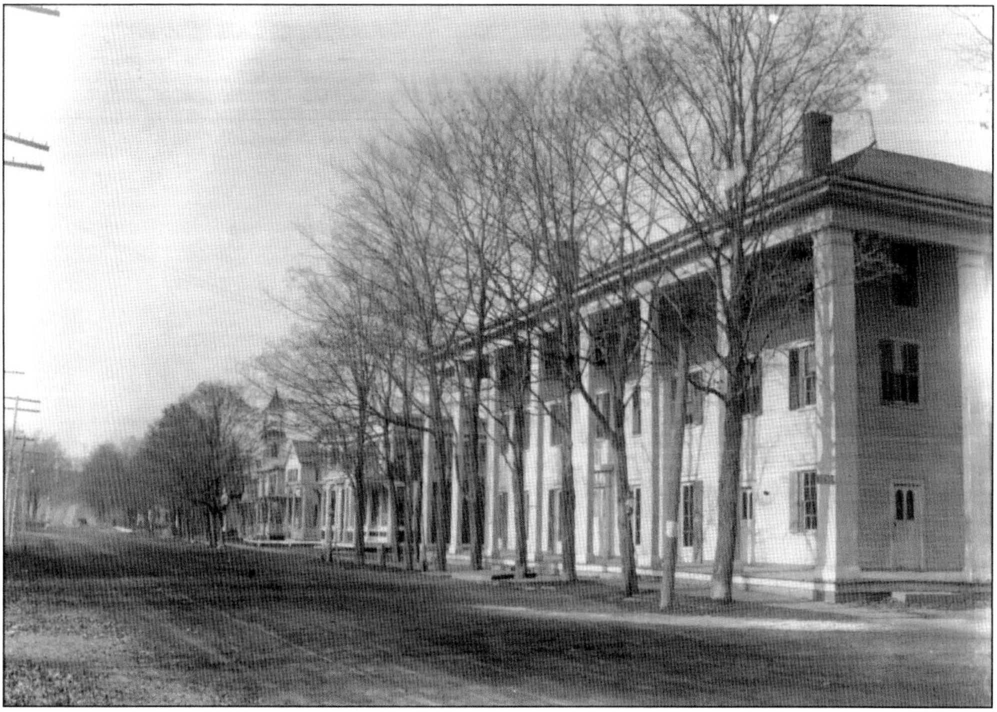

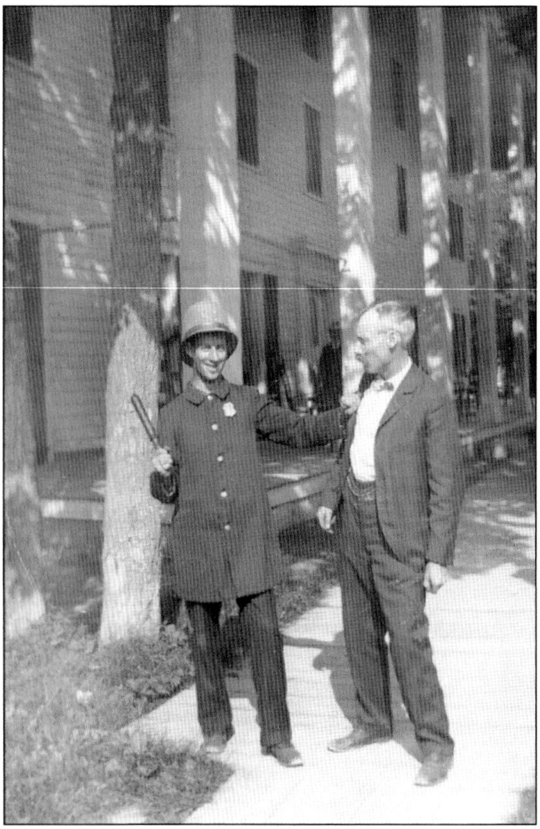

Built in 1865 using material from the demolished Grove Seminary in Carlisle, Fether's Hotel was a popular wayside inn along the Great Western Turnpike (US Highway 20 today). Sadly, this gracious structure was consumed by fire in July 1911, when sparks from a fire at the Shaul House across the street reignited during the night and were blown by the wind to the hotel. Both buildings were completely consumed.

The village's first policeman, George Nehr (left), poses with Charles Dempster in front of Fether's Hotel in 1901. With his billy club and dome-shaped helmet, Nehr resembles city policemen of the time—or today's British bobby.

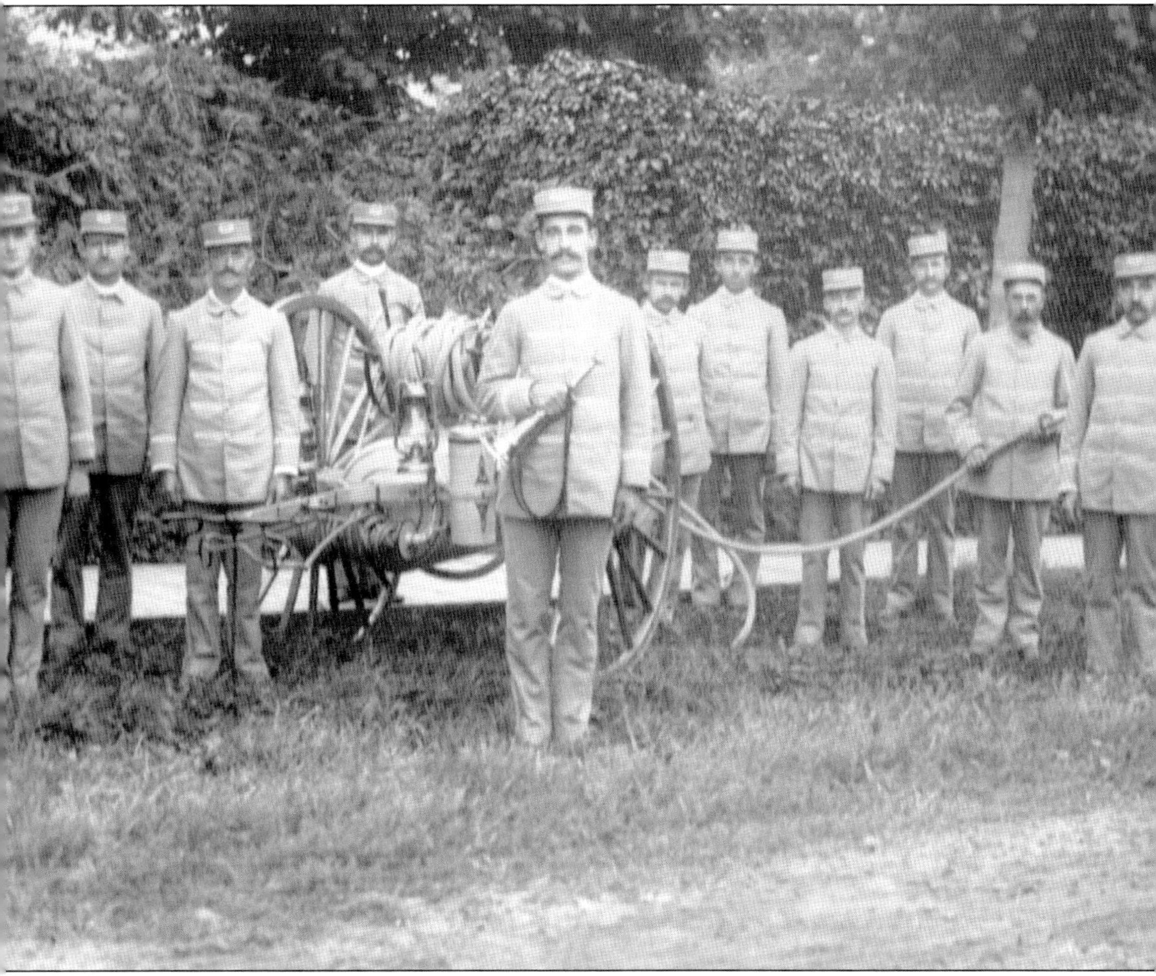

This 1886 photograph of the first volunteer fire company in Sharon Springs was taken on the lawn of Fether's Hotel. Ironically, the hotel burned to the ground in 1911 when the firemen were unable to save it. Shown here are, from left to right, Augustus Harper, James Bowmaker, Ronelle Bullock, Peter Austin, Lester Becker, Lyman Mereness, William Morrell, Julius Preston, John Lehman, Peter Lykes, and Newell Becker. Many of their descendants can still be found living in Sharon.

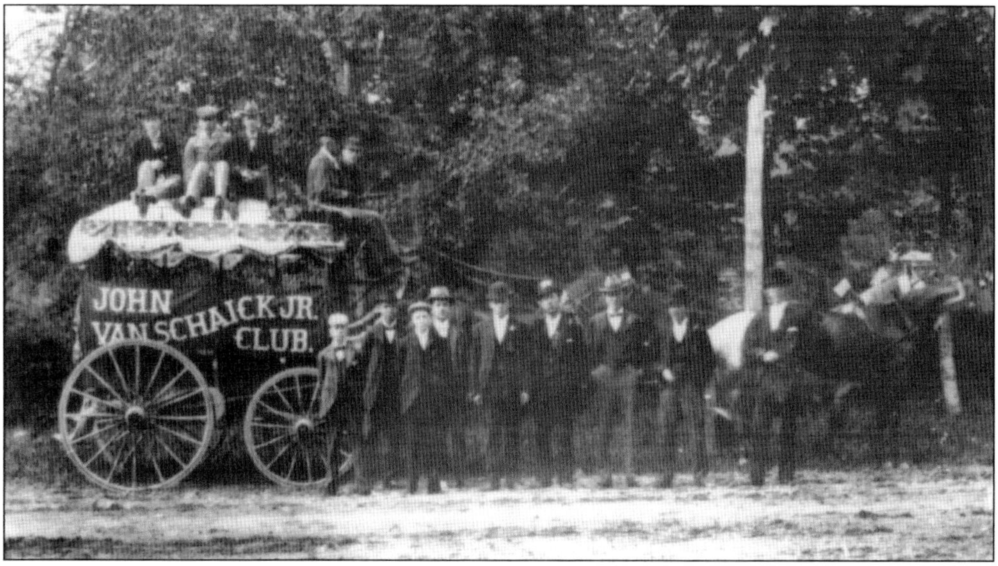

The John Van Schaick Jr. Club, seen here in the 1890s, was formed by a group of high school students to honor their teacher, Van Schaick. The club replaced the men's Lyceum Club, which had disbanded earlier that year. The 19th century ushered in many clubs for men and women—literary, athletic, and social.

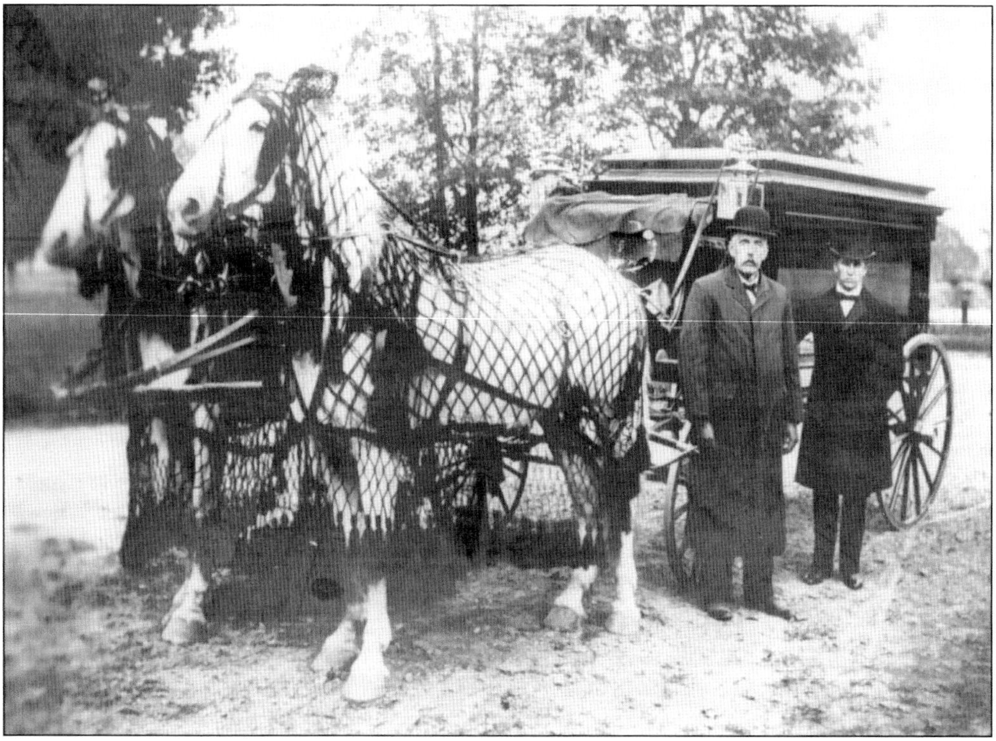

The Lappeus funeral hearse is led by two horses draped in black netting in 1906. The deceased in his or her coffin rode in style inside the glassed-in wagon. The Lappeus family operated the business for generations, and Lappeus Funeral Home continues in 2014 under its new owner, George VanGarderen.

St. Matthew's Lutheran Chapel stands at the crossroads in Leesville. It is one of the oldest continual congregations in Sharon. The church was built in 1854 at a cost of $2,000. Originally, the congregation was the Evangelical Lutheran Church of the Reformation; in 1970, the church merged with Zion Lutheran Church of Cobleskill.

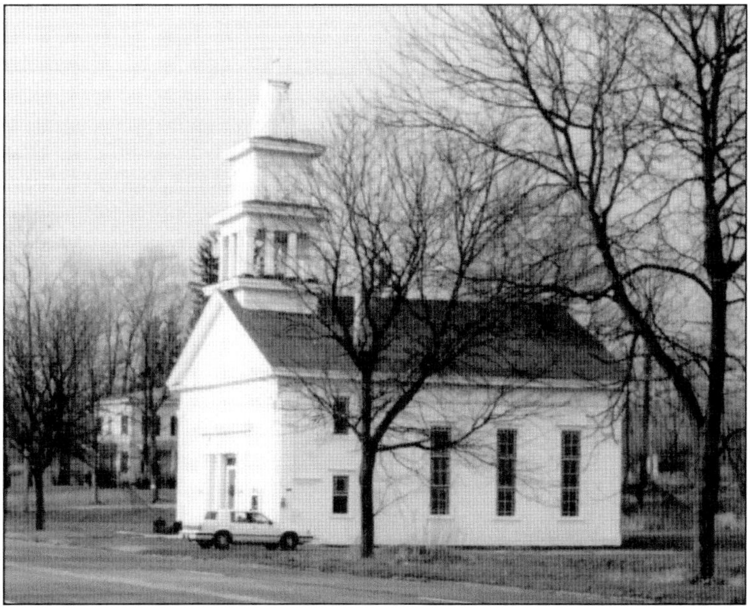

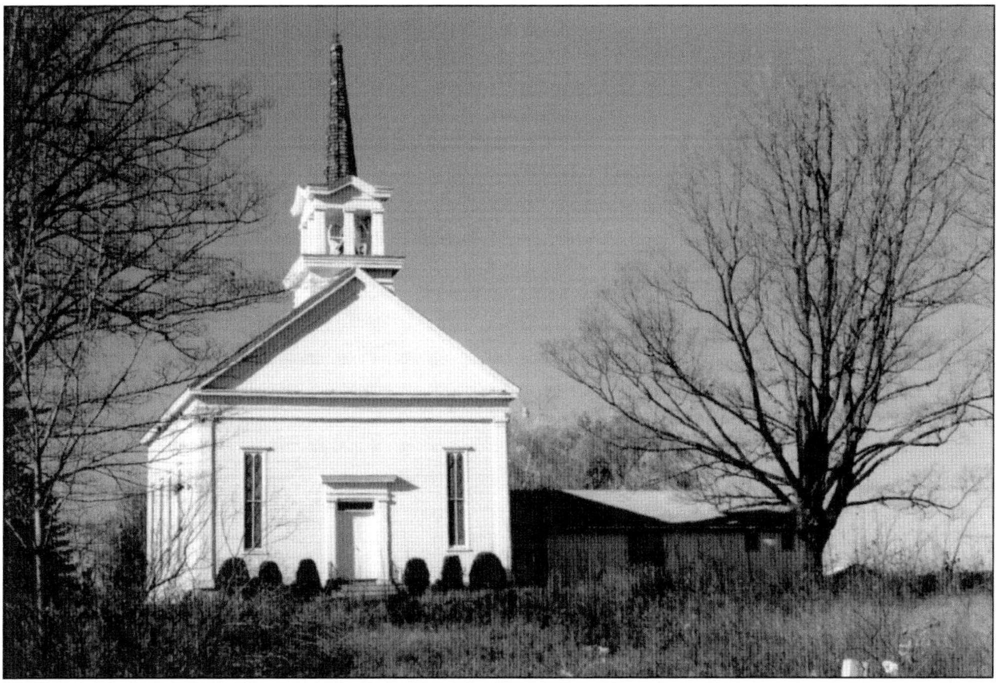

The Dutch Reformed Church (now Sharon Reformed Church), located near the Beekman mansion, was the Beekmans' family church. The frame of the church is oak, and the rafters and studding are of black walnut. A carved "S" adorns the backs of some pews, believed to stand for "slave." Several of the more prosperous families of Sharon had slaves, including William Beekman. Built in 1796, the church continues to hold services today.

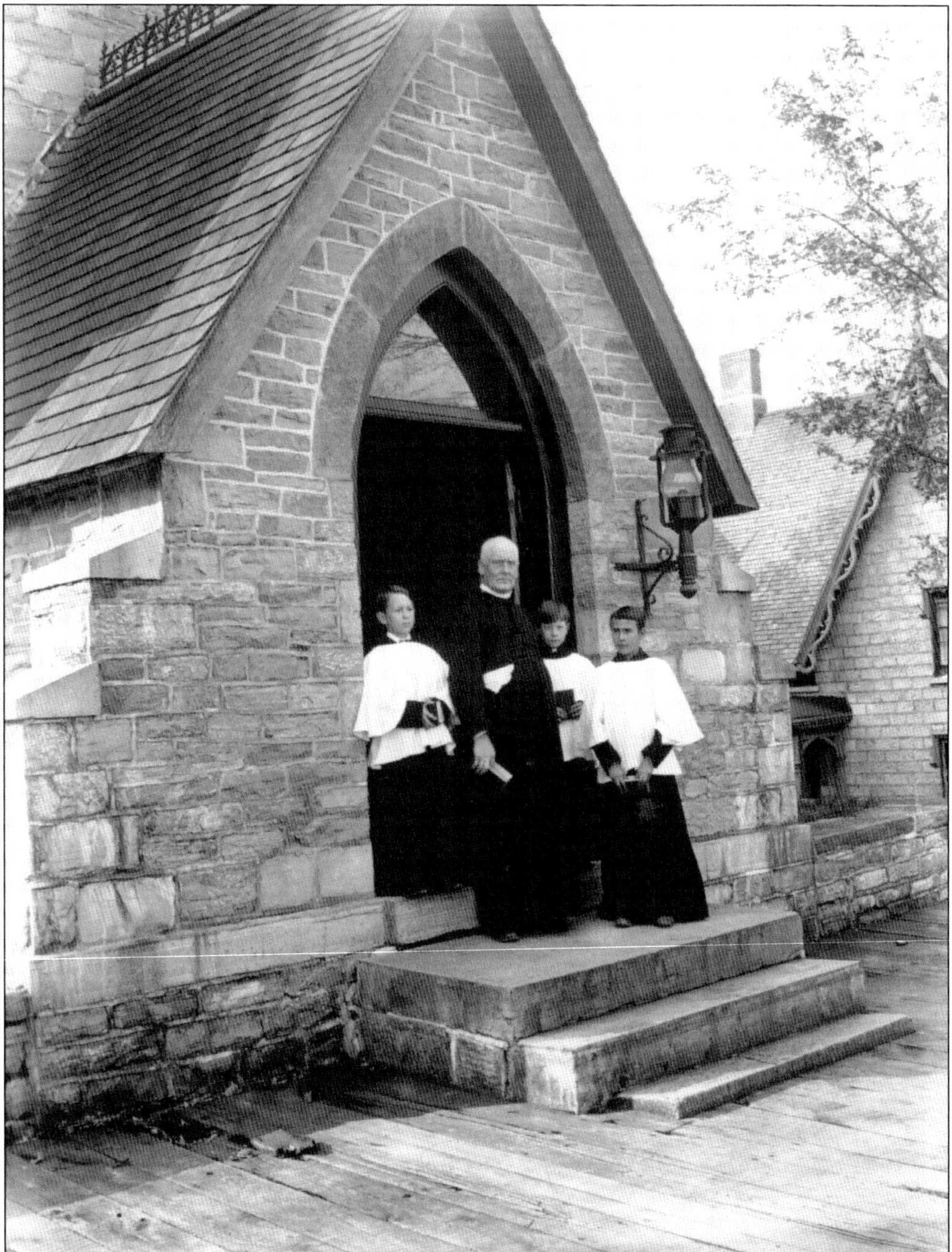

Trinity Episcopal Church was built in 1865 with financial support from the Gardner family. Rev. Edwin Armstrong, seen here in 1905 with acolytes, was pastor for many years. According to church records, Armstrong inaugurated the use of acolytes at Trinity. He helped found the Sharon Springs Free Library and was an active youth leader. When he suffered an accident that left him blind, many youth in Sharon volunteered to help him.

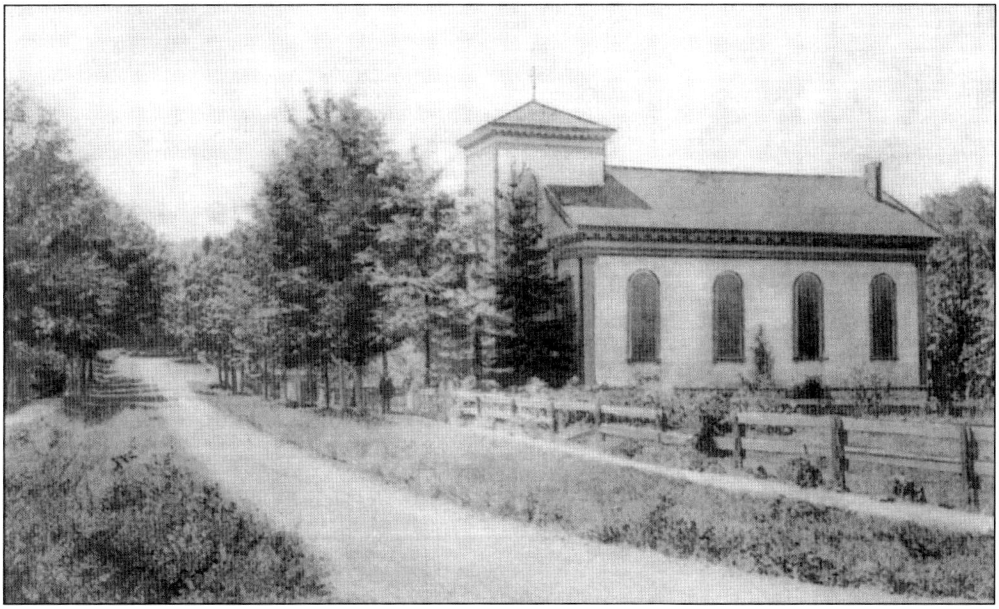

The original 19th-century Catholic church was located in the lower village on Center Street. Deemed too costly to repair in 1959, it was sold and dismantled, and its materials were used to build a Vrooman home on Route 10 South. A second church was built along Route 20, but it was closed by the diocese in 2009. It has been dismantled. In 2014, the property became the site of a Dollar General store.

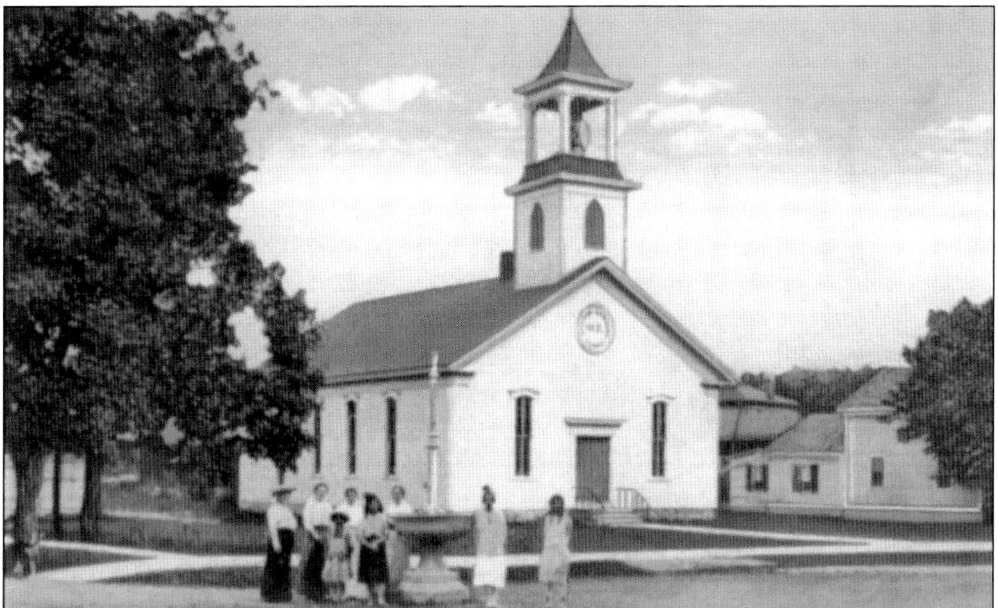

The Sharon Springs Methodist Episcopal Church, seen here in the 1890s, continues to enjoy an active congregation today. It is the only church in the village that has survived. In the 1850s, the Lutheran and Methodist congregations shared this house of worship. The Methodists gained full control in 1867.

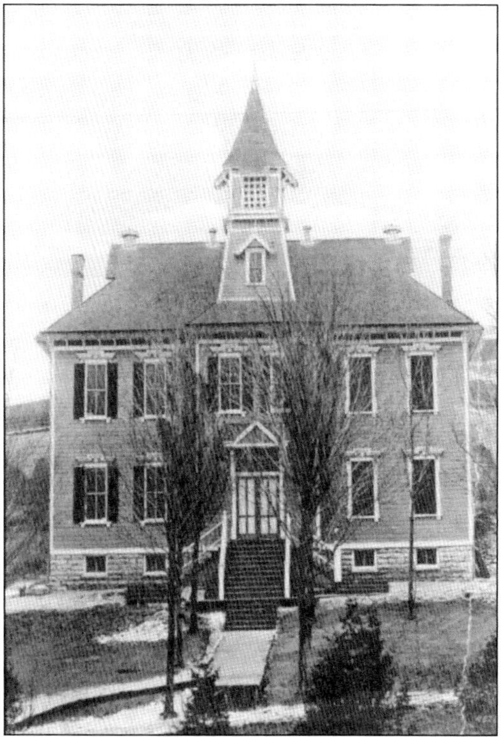

Union School opened in 1885 to accommodate students from both the Rockville and Springs districts. It stood on land halfway down the Main Street hill. It closed in 1930, when a larger central school building opened along Route 20. This "new" school, Sharon Springs Central School, continues to serve the town population today.

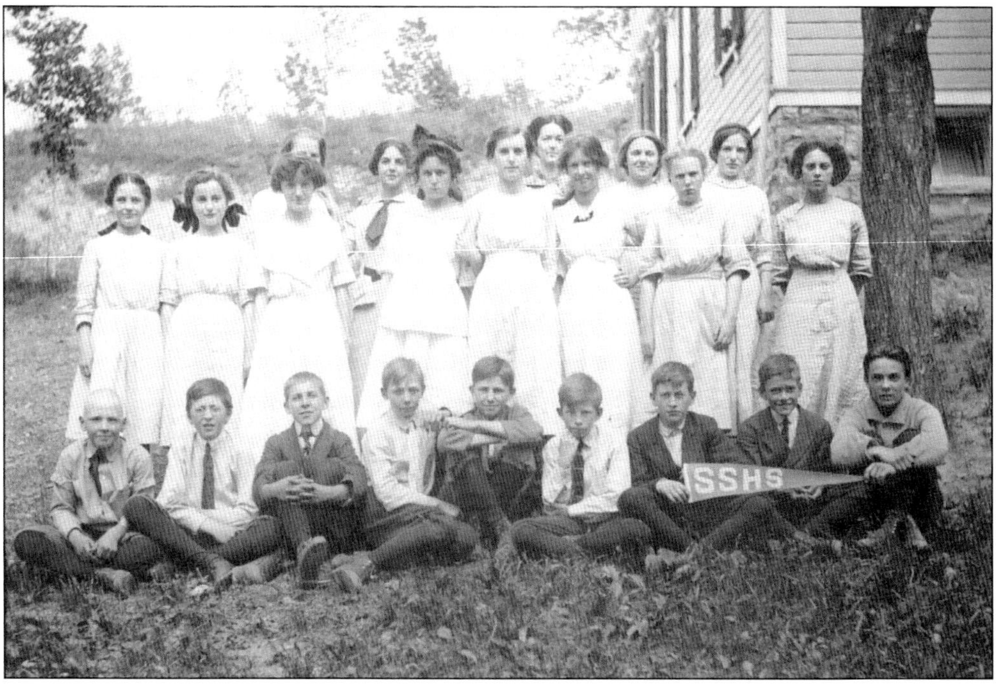

Union School students pose for a class photograph in 1913. It is interesting to note that the females outnumber the males. In the 19th and early 20th centuries, young women often graduated from school, studied a year or so at a normal school to train as teachers, and took over classrooms at a very young age.

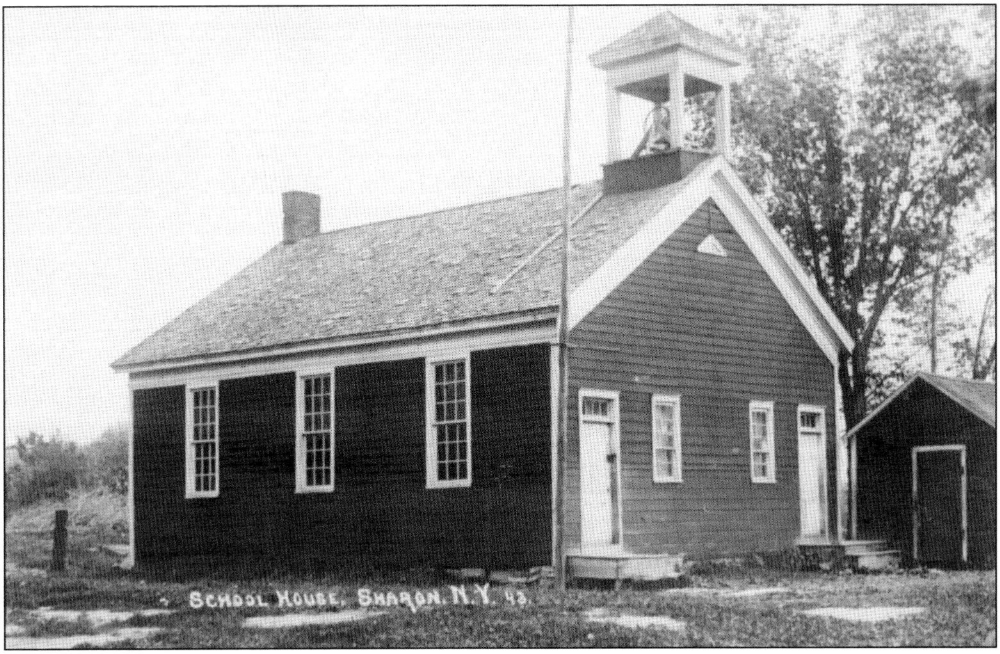

A typical one-room schoolhouse, this one was located in Sharon Hill. At onetime, there were 16 individual one-room schools in the town. Before mechanized transportation, children walked to school or occasionally traveled by horse and wagon. In the winters, the sleigh was a common mode of transportation to school. Teachers were expected to keep the firewood chopped for the stove, start the fire, and generally do much of the cleaning and maintenance, with help from the older students.

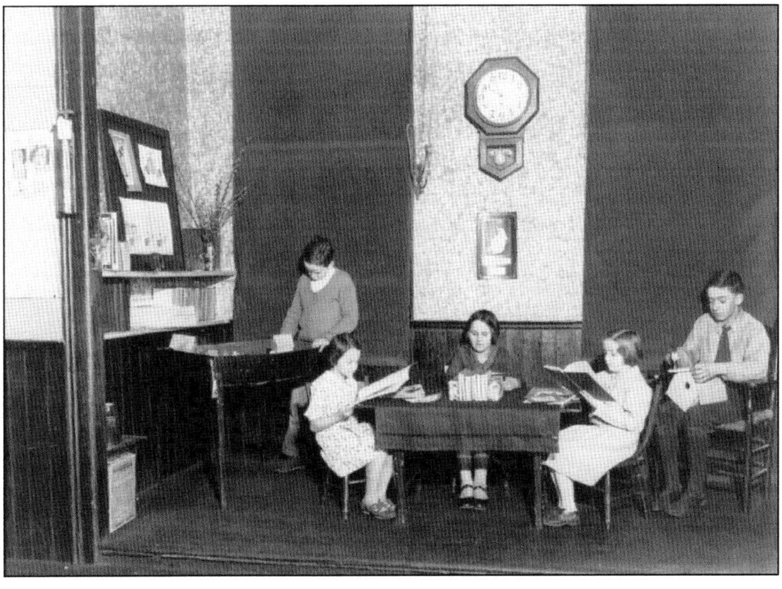

This 1933 photograph shows children studying in the one-room schoolhouse located in Sharon Center. The little school had a homey look and feel, with displays of the children's projects and books on the shelves.

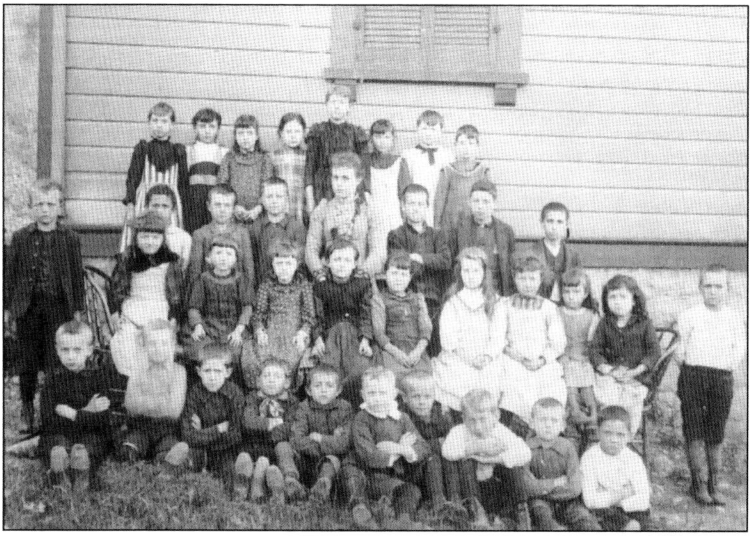

Students and their teacher pose in front of the Hollow School around 1880. The one-room school in the lower village was built in 1853, across from the Episcopal church. It was torn down in 1885, after which the students transferred to the Union School.

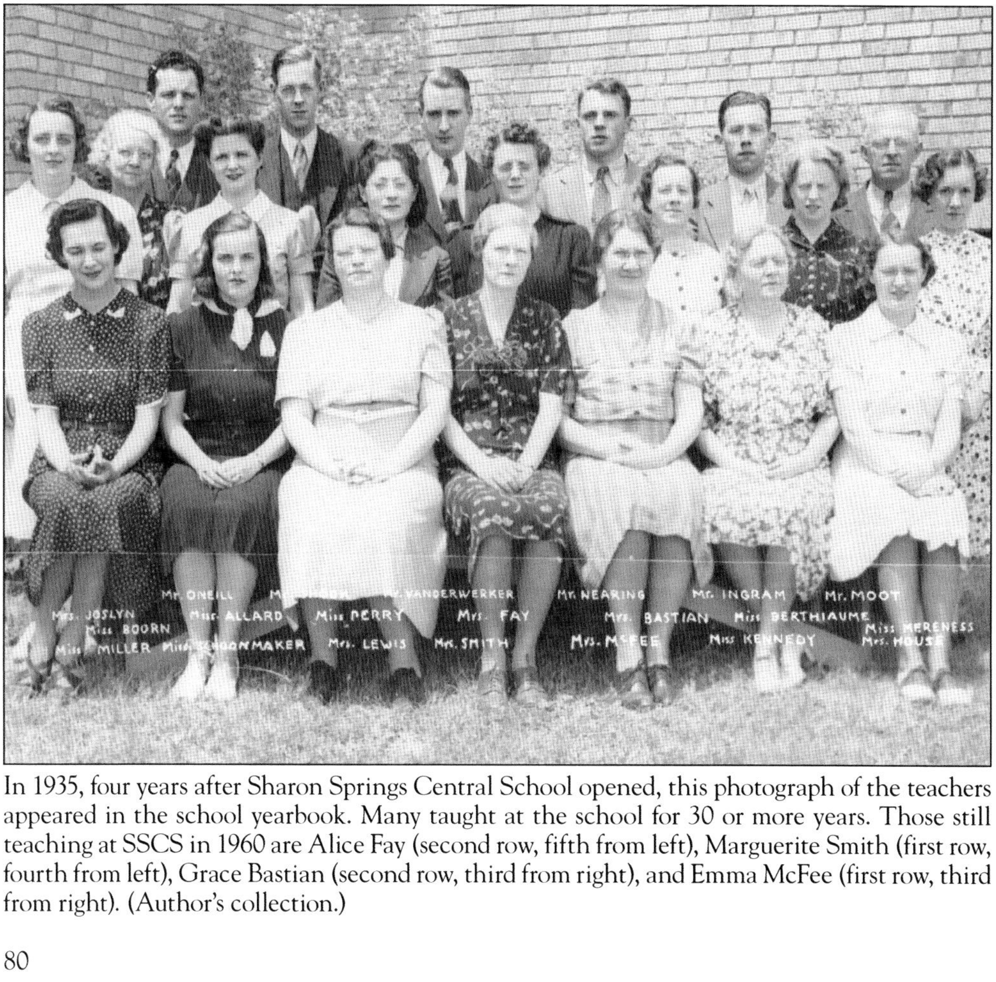

In 1935, four years after Sharon Springs Central School opened, this photograph of the teachers appeared in the school yearbook. Many taught at the school for 30 or more years. Those still teaching at SSCS in 1960 are Alice Fay (second row, fifth from left), Marguerite Smith (first row, fourth from left), Grace Bastian (second row, third from right), and Emma McFee (first row, third from right). (Author's collection.)

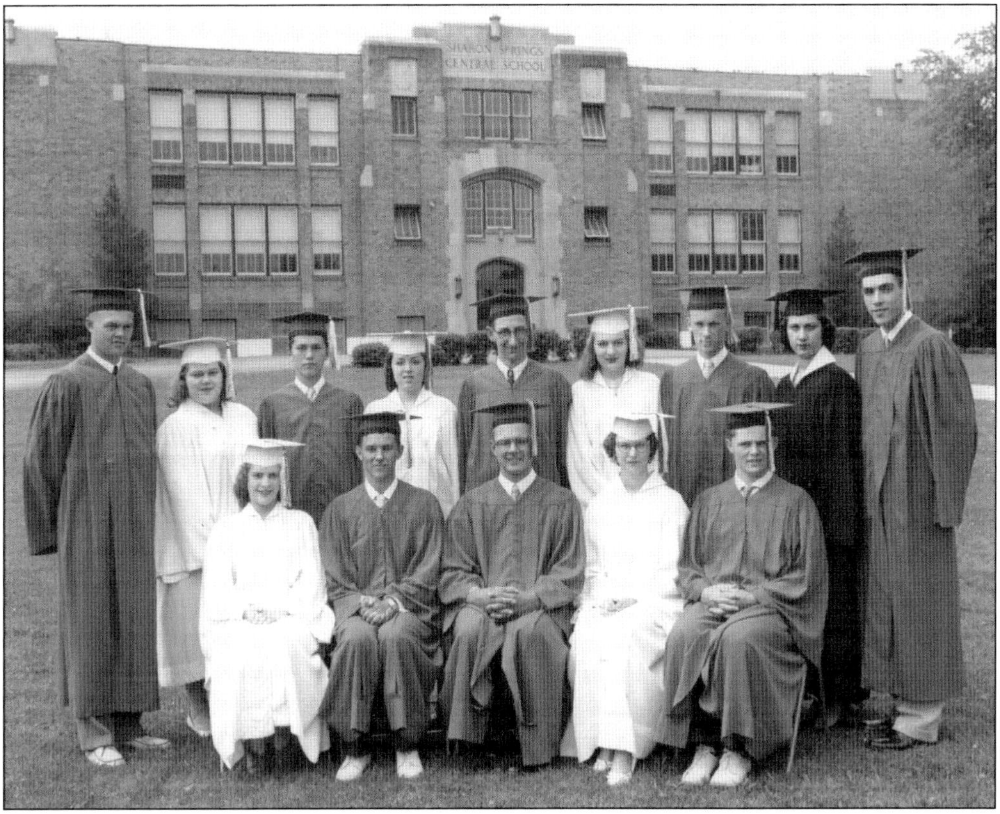

The 1958 graduating class poses in front of the school with its faculty adviser. Graduating classes vary between 16 and 35 students, small for a public high school. Here, everyone knows each other's names. Pictured here are, from left to right, (seated), Karla Doolittle, John Meka, Michael Putlack, Irene Haner, and Ellsworth Lambert; (standing) Robert Wall, Charlene Terpenning, John Miller, Patricia Neale, Gerald Nikolaus, Janice Mereness, Dale Blothenburg, Mrs. Remza Abbadessa, and Arnold Mereness. (Courtesy of Sharon Springs Central School.)

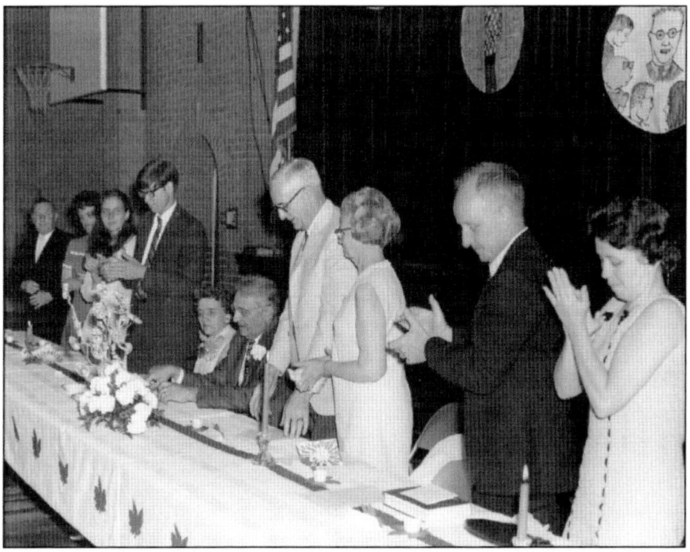

This is the retirement party for Avery DeLuca in 1970. DeLuca served Sharon Springs Central School beginning in 1939, most memorably as principal and mentor. Pictured are, from left to right, Rev. John and Jeannine Wolfe; Carol, David, Helen, and Avery DeLuca; Mr. and Mrs. Lynn Secor; and Ruben and Dorcas Comrie.

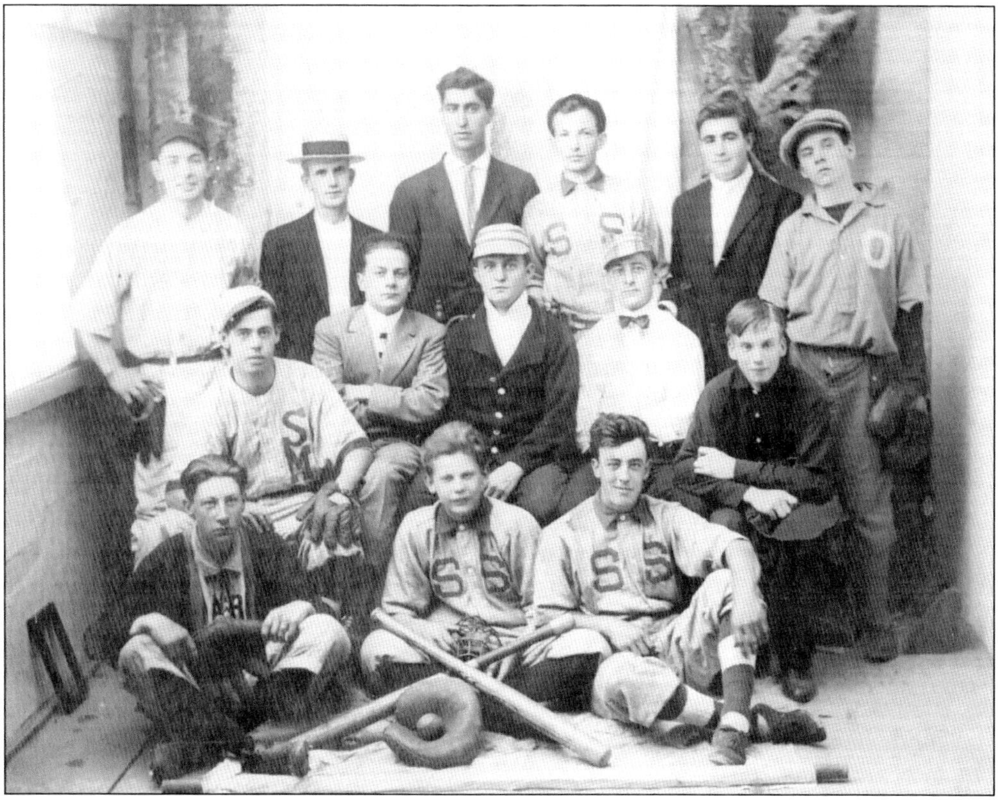

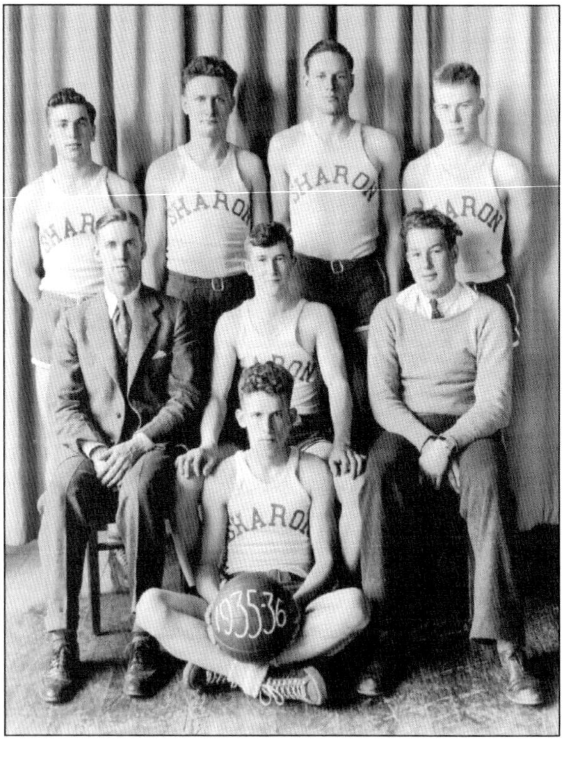

A high school baseball team poses in the 1890s. The enthusiasm for sports has continued through the years. Baseball is especially popular; Cooperstown and the National Baseball Hall of Fame are only 25 miles away.

This high school basketball team gathers for a photograph in the 1935–1936 school year. Most of these young players went on to serve in World War II, returning to Sharon Springs to raise families. Pictured here are, from left to right, George Bowmaker (holding ball); (first row) Hagan Andersen (coach), Harry Haig (captain), and Francis Hazzard; (second row) Floyd Kettler, Michael Bautochka, Alex Bautochka, and Malcolm Lynk. (Author's collection.)

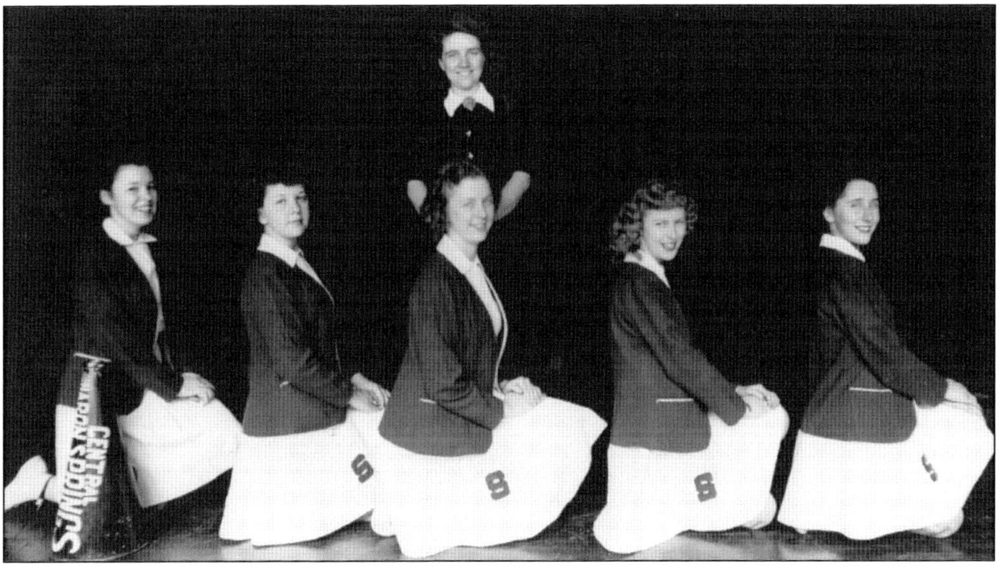

The cheerleaders and their coach, Helen DeLuca (standing) pose in 1945. Kneeling are, from left to right, Mary Ellen Snyder, Esther Grant, Marjorie Smith, Geraldine Fonda, and Wilma Greene. According to the *Clarion* yearbook of that year, 16 girls had competed for the coveted role of varsity cheerleader. Those pictured were awarded varsity letters. (Courtesy of Sharon Springs Central School Alumni.)

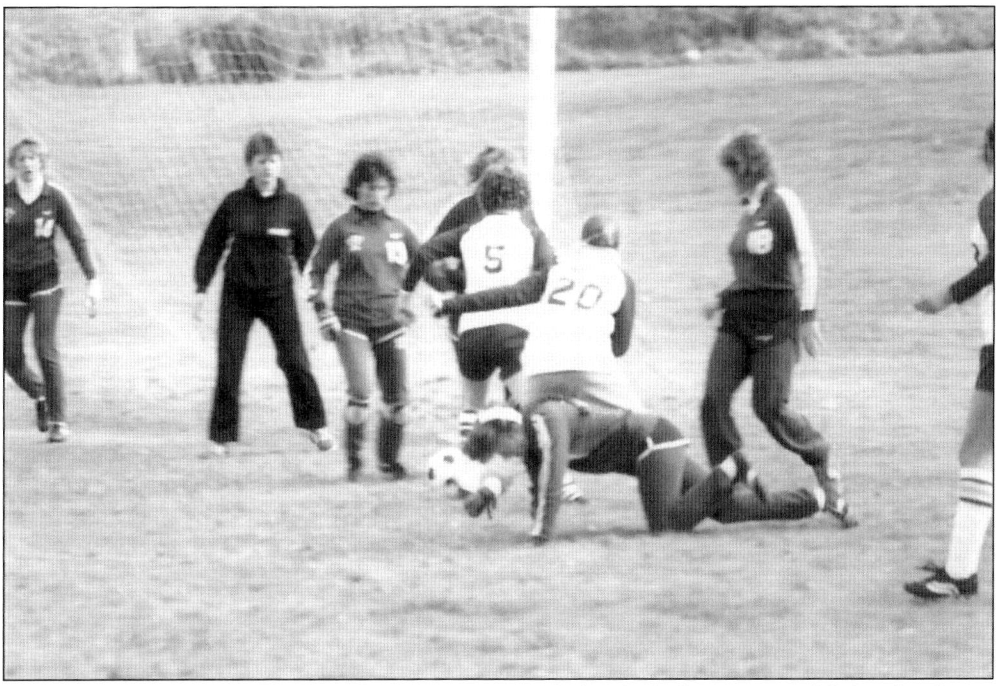

Members of the 1983 SSCS girls' soccer team scramble for the ball against Middleburgh. Shown here are Katina Manko (5) and Tara Hayner (20). Yearbooks in the 1930s included women's sports teams, but in the 1940s, 1950s, and 1960s, the only varsity-level sport for women was cheerleading. Title IX legislation in 1972 changed the sports landscape, and today, women participate in various school-sponsored sports as well as cheerleading. (Courtesy of Sandra Manko.)

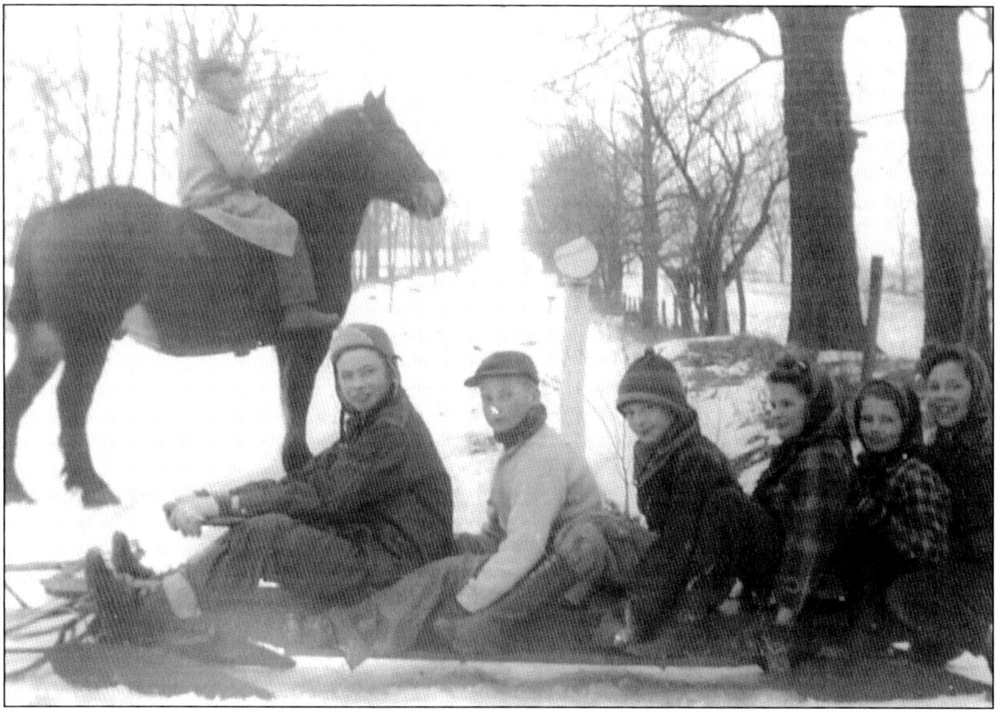

This winter scene on the Button farm around 1940 is a reminder that sledding has been a popular winter activity for generations of farm and village children. Children and adults skated on Bowmaker's Pond when it froze each winter. For a few years, the town enjoyed a downhill ski slope, but today, a favorite winter activity in Sharon is snowmobiling on designated trails. (Courtesy of Bruce Button.)

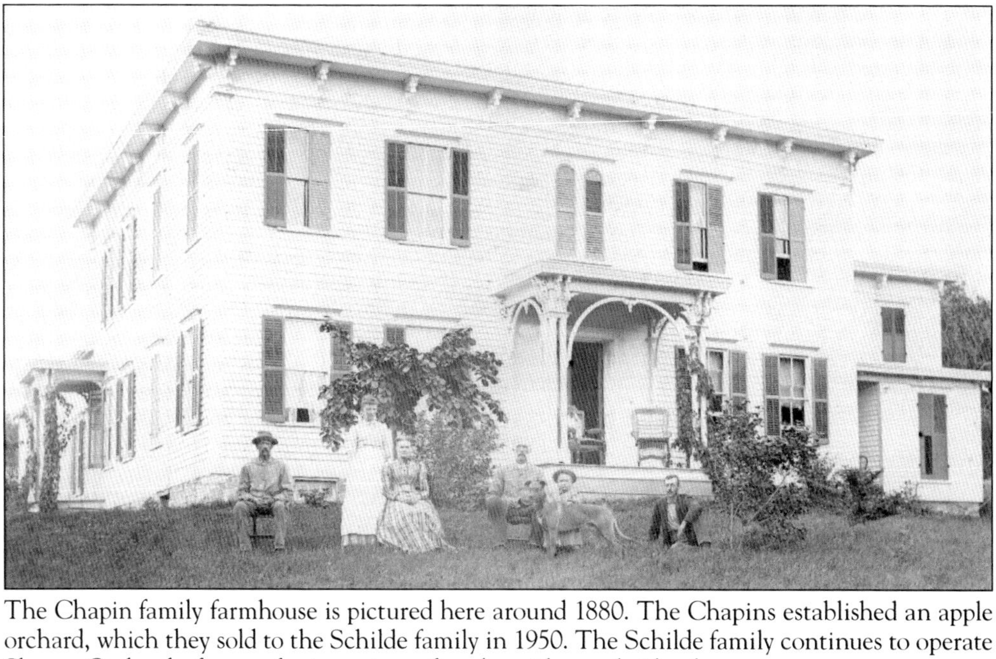

The Chapin family farmhouse is pictured here around 1880. The Chapins established an apple orchard, which they sold to the Schilde family in 1950. The Schilde family continues to operate Sharon Orchards, famous for its variety of apples, cider, and cider donuts.

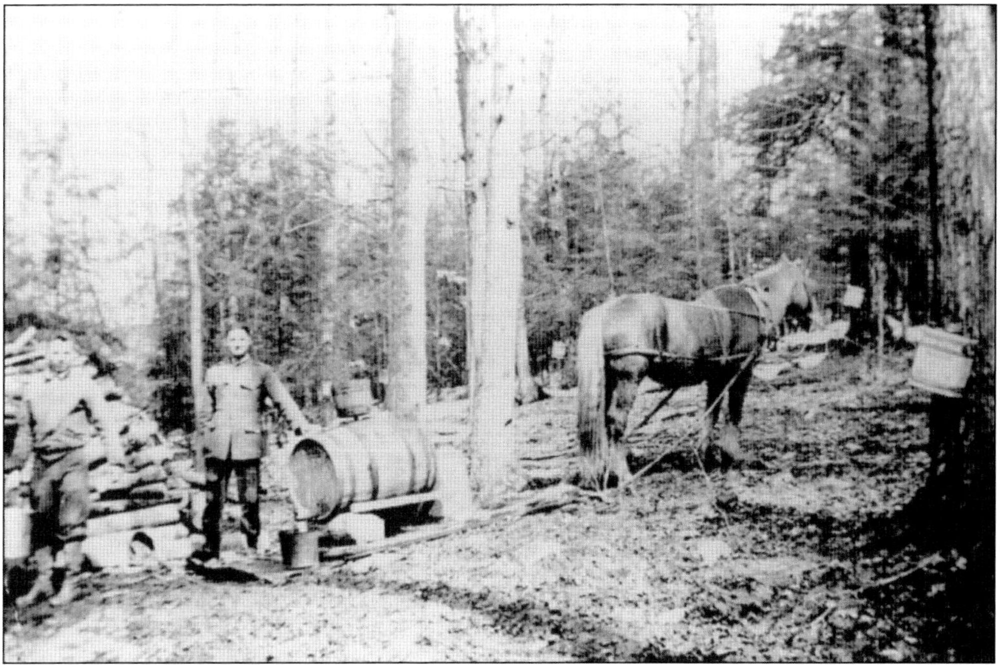

Maple sugaring on the Button farm is shown in the 1920s. Collecting sap and boiling it in large vats to create delicious maple syrup is still a thriving operation for Sharon's farmers in the 21st century. The Everetts' Stone House Farm has a special maple-sugaring barn, where pancake breakfasts are held each March. (Courtesy of Bruce Button.)

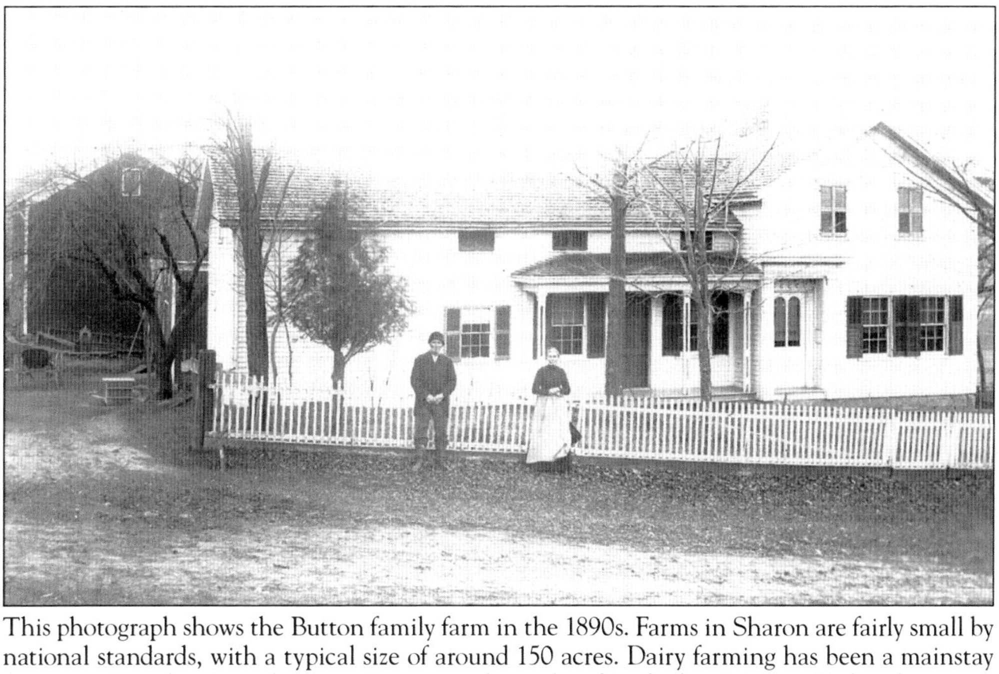

This photograph shows the Button family farm in the 1890s. Farms in Sharon are fairly small by national standards, with a typical size of around 150 acres. Dairy farming has been a mainstay for generations, but it can be precarious; many have closed in the last 50 years. Today, the yogurt and cheese industries of New York State provide a reliable market for local milk production. (Courtesy of Bruce Button.)

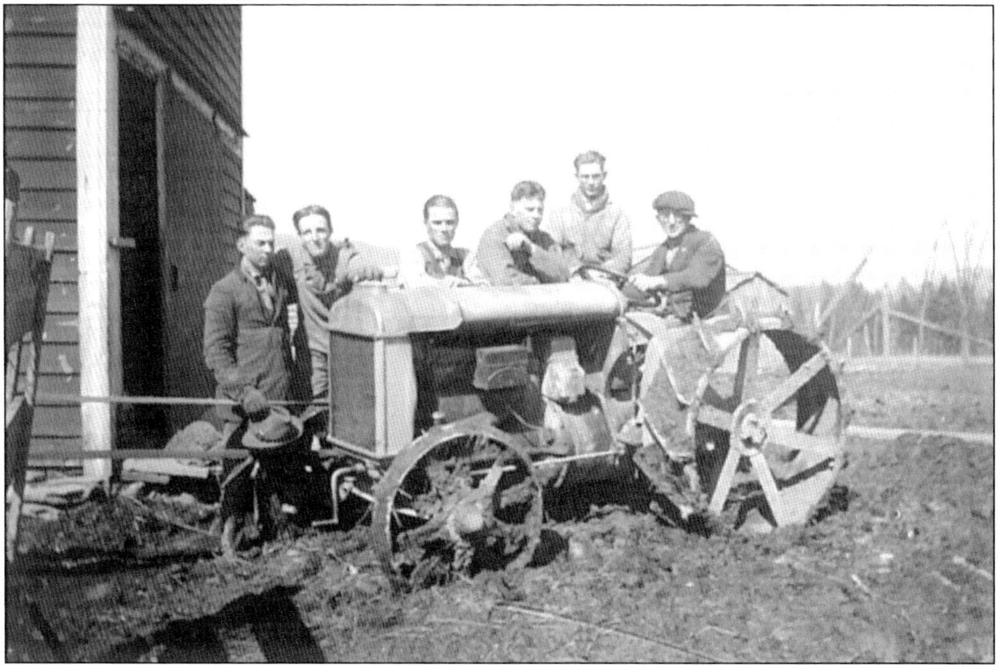

Brothers on the Button farm pose with their tractor in 1925. The advent of mechanized farming was often a mixed blessing: Machinery offered easier, more productive farming methods, but it also increased costs and brought the risk of injury or death from accidents. (Courtesy of Bruce Button.)

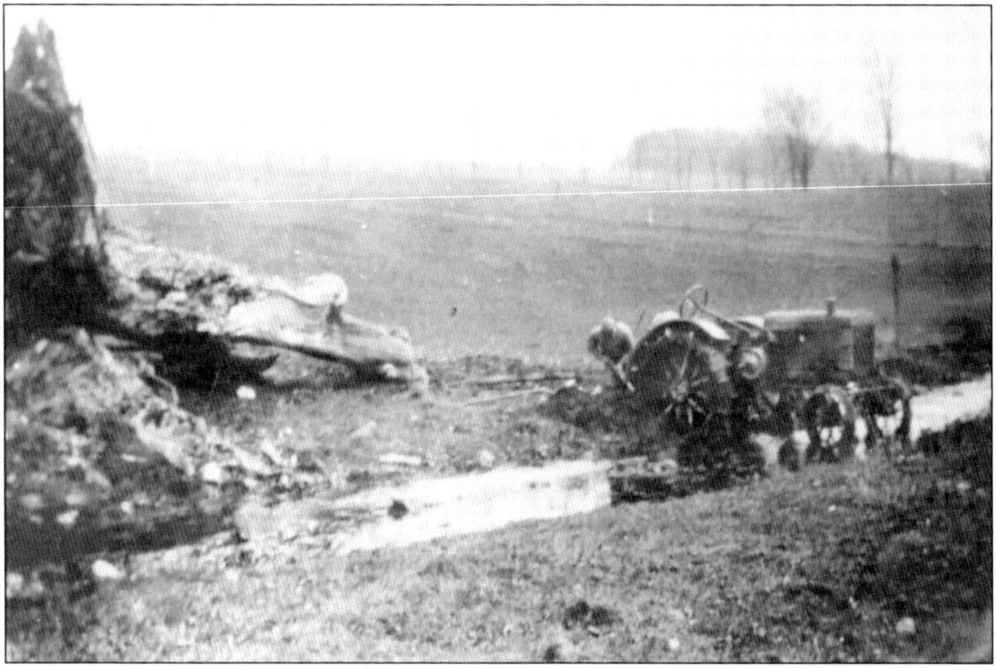

Mud is not the tractor's friend. Here is a typical field in early spring, with a farmer levering his tractor out of the mud, probably around 1935. Local people count five seasons: spring, summer, fall, winter, and mud! (Courtesy of Bruce Button.)

In December 1913, Scott Madison married Elsie Cross. They were blessed with four children, but, in December 1921, when the youngest was only two weeks of age, Scott was tragically killed when a tractor overturned on him as he was plowing the fields. (Author's collection.)

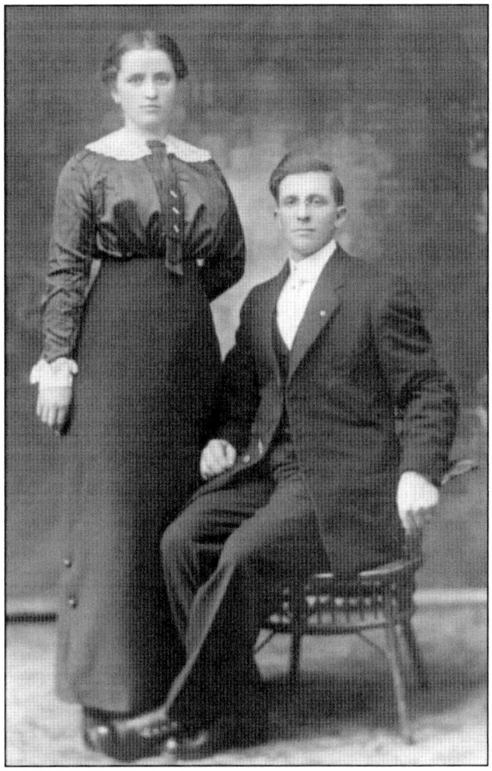

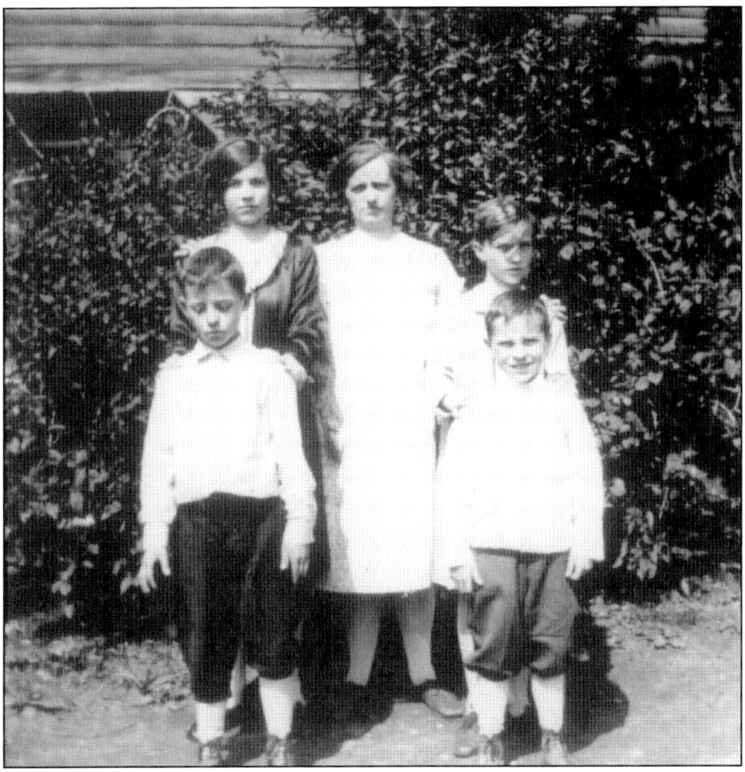

Pictured in 1927 are, from left to right, Raymond, Helen, Elsie, Grace, and Alton Madison. After Scott Madison's death, the family was able to stay on the farm, but the land and half of the house were rented out to a local farmer. Elsie worked in the school kitchen for many years and was affectionately called "Ma Madison" by the students. (Author's collection.)

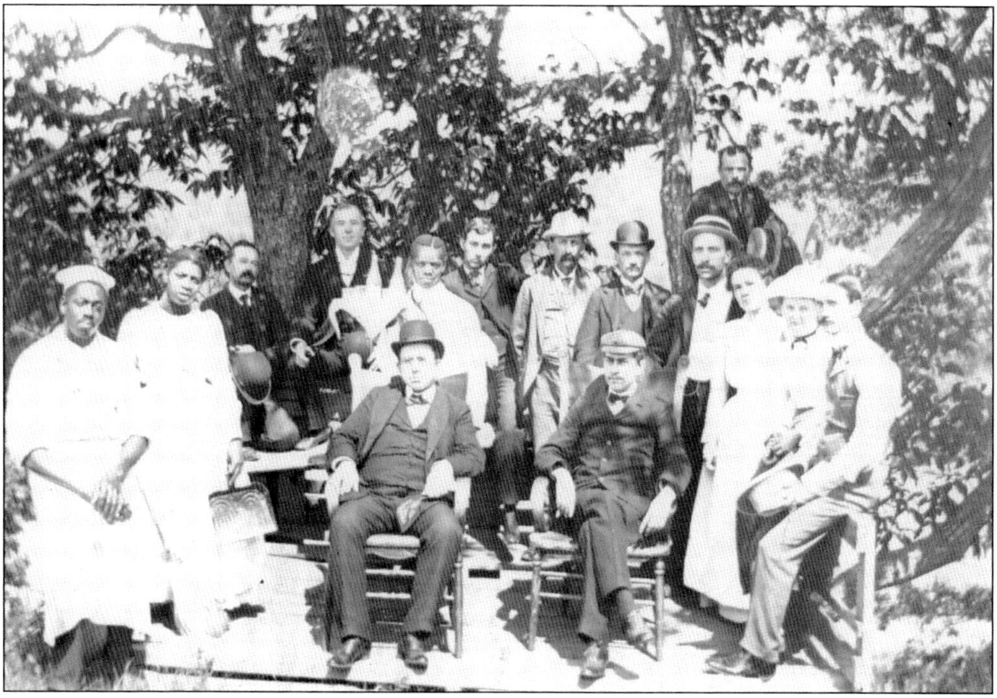

A photograph from the 1890s shows a hunting party and servants. The scene somewhat resembles that of an African safari, but it occurred in the town of Sharon. While hunting has continued to be a popular activity here, today's hunters are a lot more casual in their dress, and they do not employ servants.

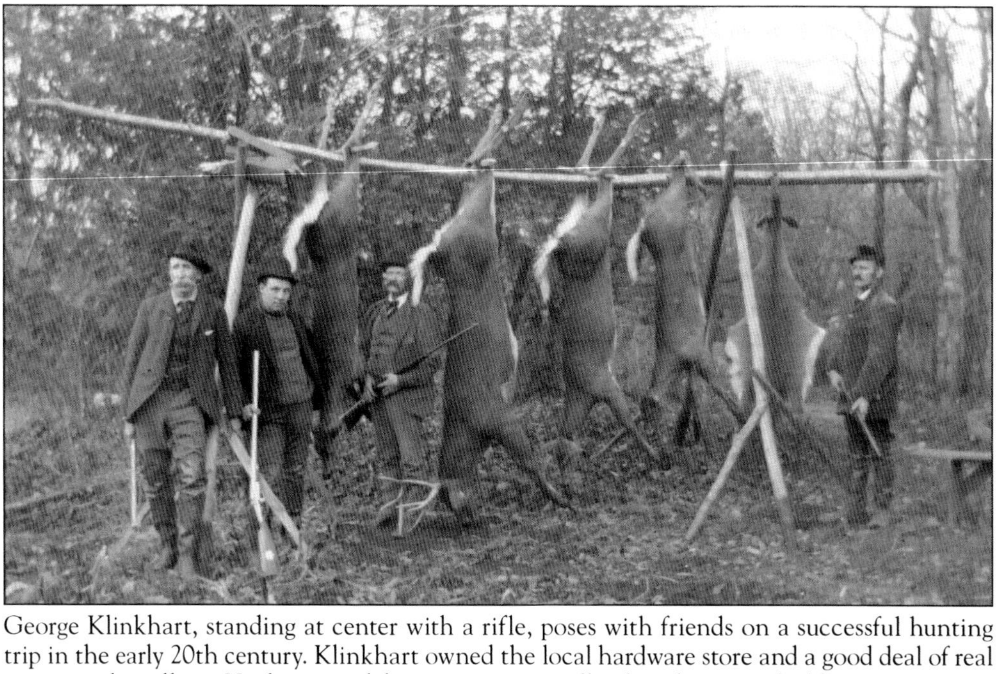

George Klinkhart, standing at center with a rifle, poses with friends on a successful hunting trip in the early 20th century. Klinkhart owned the local hardware store and a good deal of real estate in the village. His home and former store are still referred to as "Klinkhart's" a century after his death.

Lt. Alvin Lane fought in World War I and returned home to Sharon Springs to run the family dairy farm. He served on the school board for many years and was elected town justice.

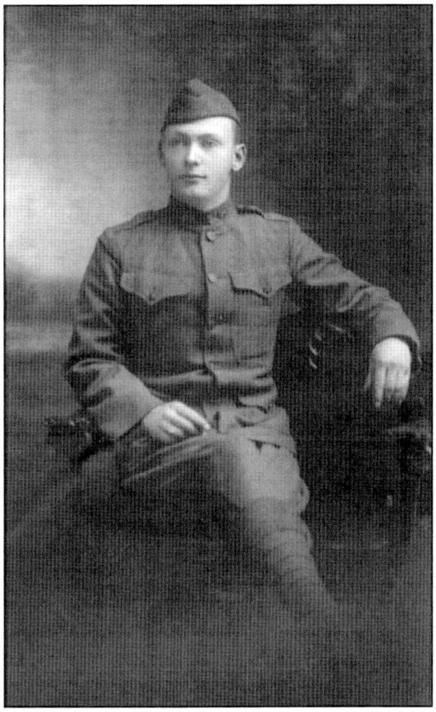

World War I draftees from the town of Sharon pose for a photograph around 1918. Although the population was small, many young men and, later, young women, answered the call to public service.

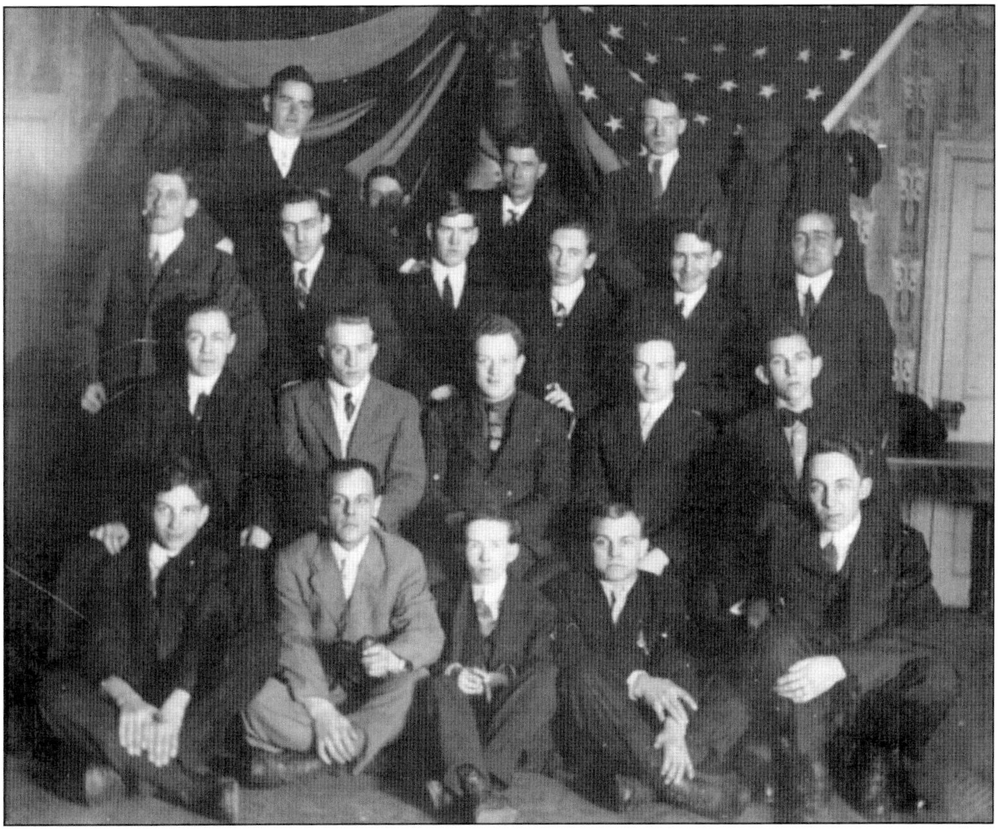

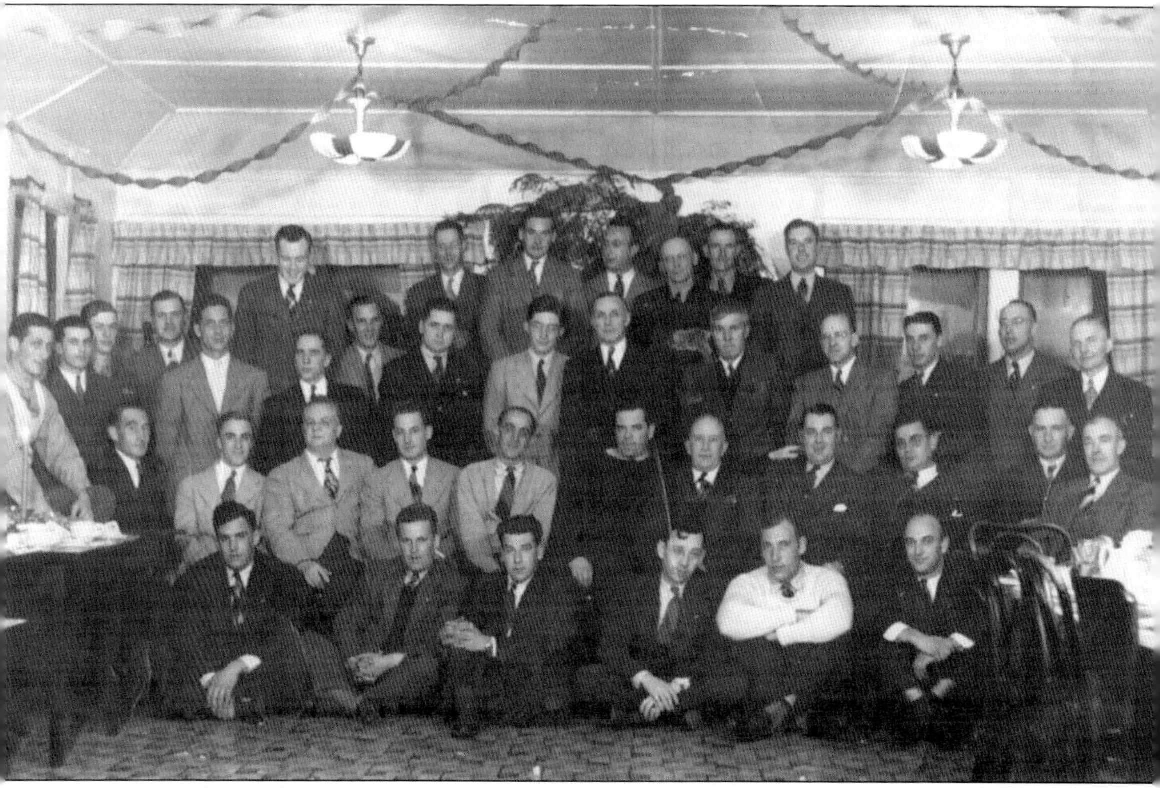

Following World War II, a celebration dinner was held to honor those local men who had served in the war. Many earned military honors, including George Bowmaker, who was awarded two Bronze Stars for bravery. Lawrence McFee spent several years as a German prisoner of war after his aircraft was shot down.

A group of town employees and board members poses for the camera in 1950 with road equipment. Although not seen here, an essential item in the town and village's fleet of equipment is the snowplow. Snowfalls of three feet and greater occur often in the winter.

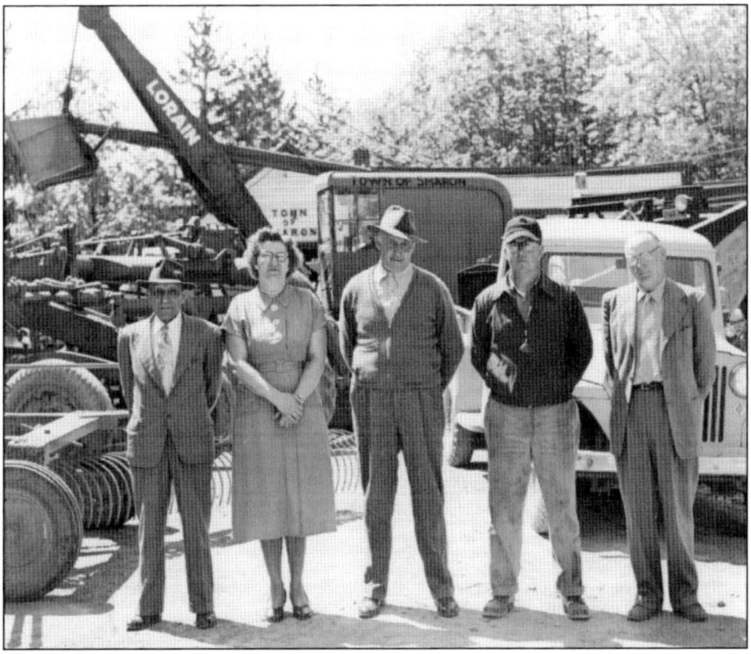

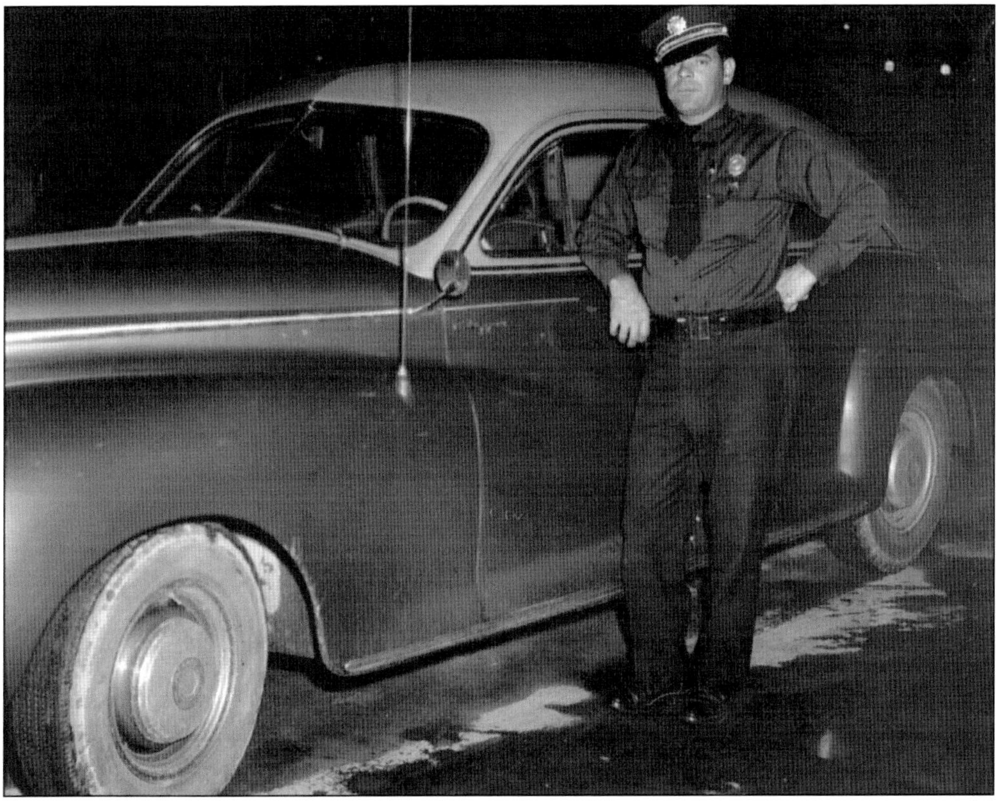

Well-liked "Babe" Farro, a long-serving village police officer, poses here in 1950. He was equally famous for writing speeding tickets and for his kind heart. He served in World War II, and the village has named a park in his honor. Farro's family emigrated from Italy in the early 20th century.

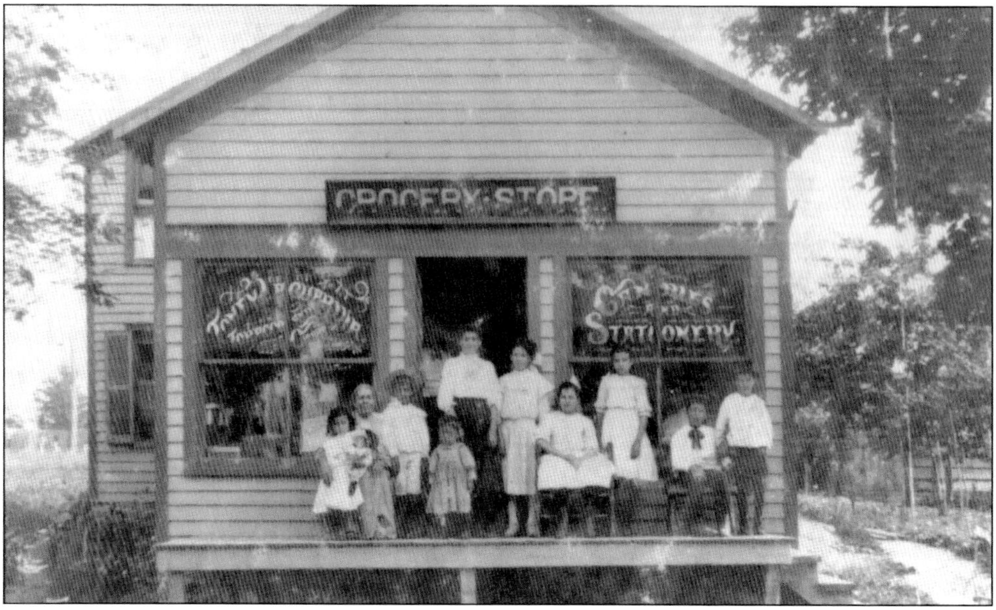

The LaGuardia family poses on the porch of their grocery store in the 1920s. They were one of the Italian immigrant families who moved to Sharon, where several generations continued to live. The area of Sharon where they settled attracted several Italian families, including the Carusos, Farros, Susis, and DiPaces.

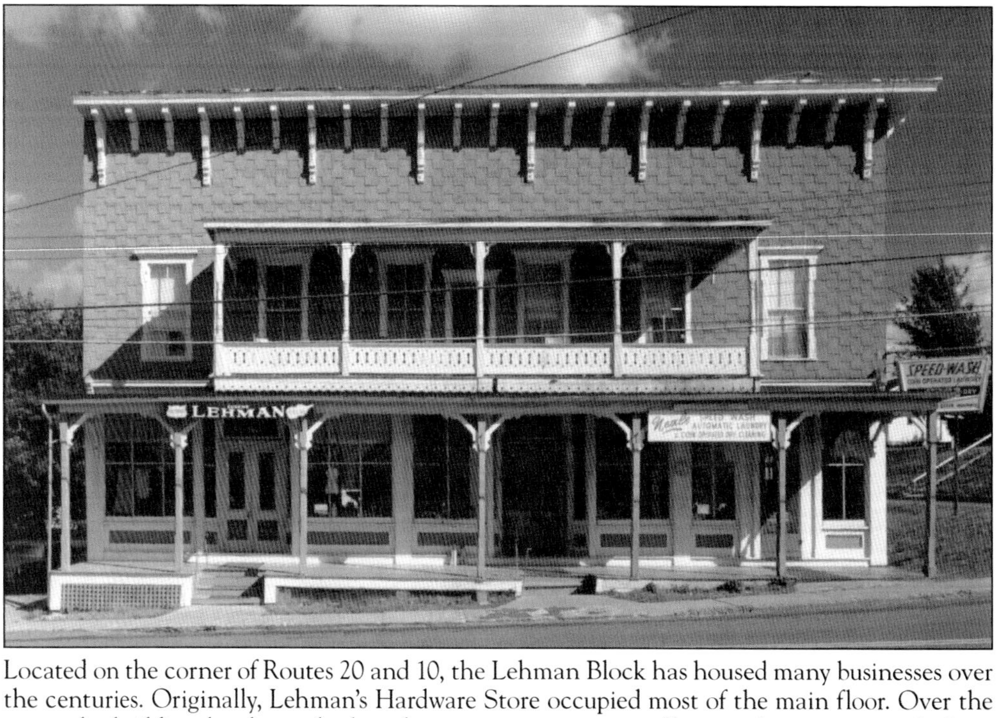

Located on the corner of Routes 20 and 10, the Lehman Block has housed many businesses over the centuries. Originally, Lehman's Hardware Store occupied most of the main floor. Over the years, the building has housed a laundry, grocery store, post office, appliance store, gift shop, liquor store, café, and apartments. The building continues to thrive today under owner Steve Larsen of Adelphi Paper.

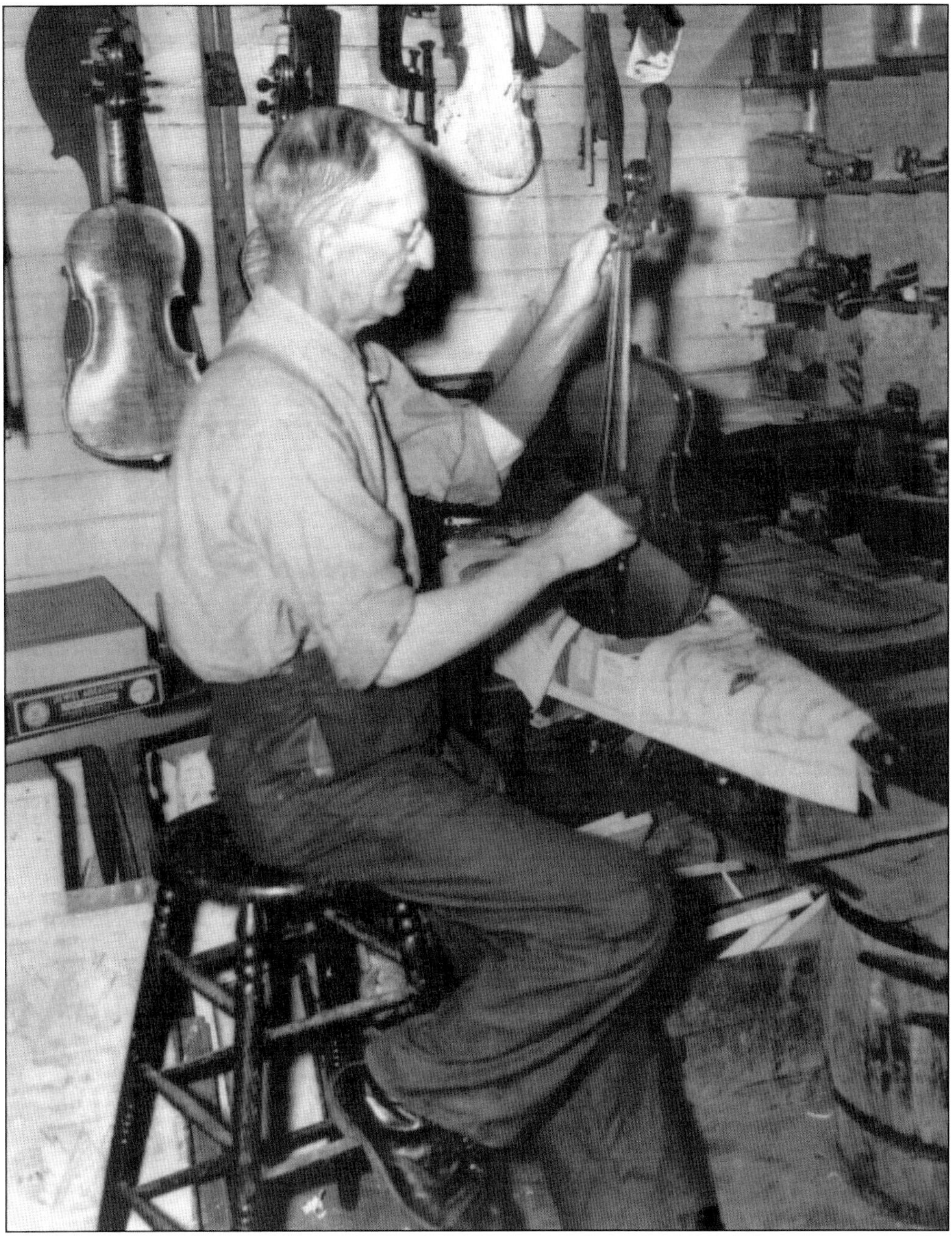

Eugene Lehman makes a violin in the 1950s. A true renaissance man, in addition to running the hardware store, Lehman made violins and had a small orchestra that played in venues around the area. He counted among his friends Rudolph Wurlitzer, who showed two of Lehman's violins at an exhibition in New York City. In 1942, of 130 million people in the United States, only 175 were violinmakers. Sharon Springs was proud to have one. Lehman was a community leader, a renowned musician, and an acclaimed family man.

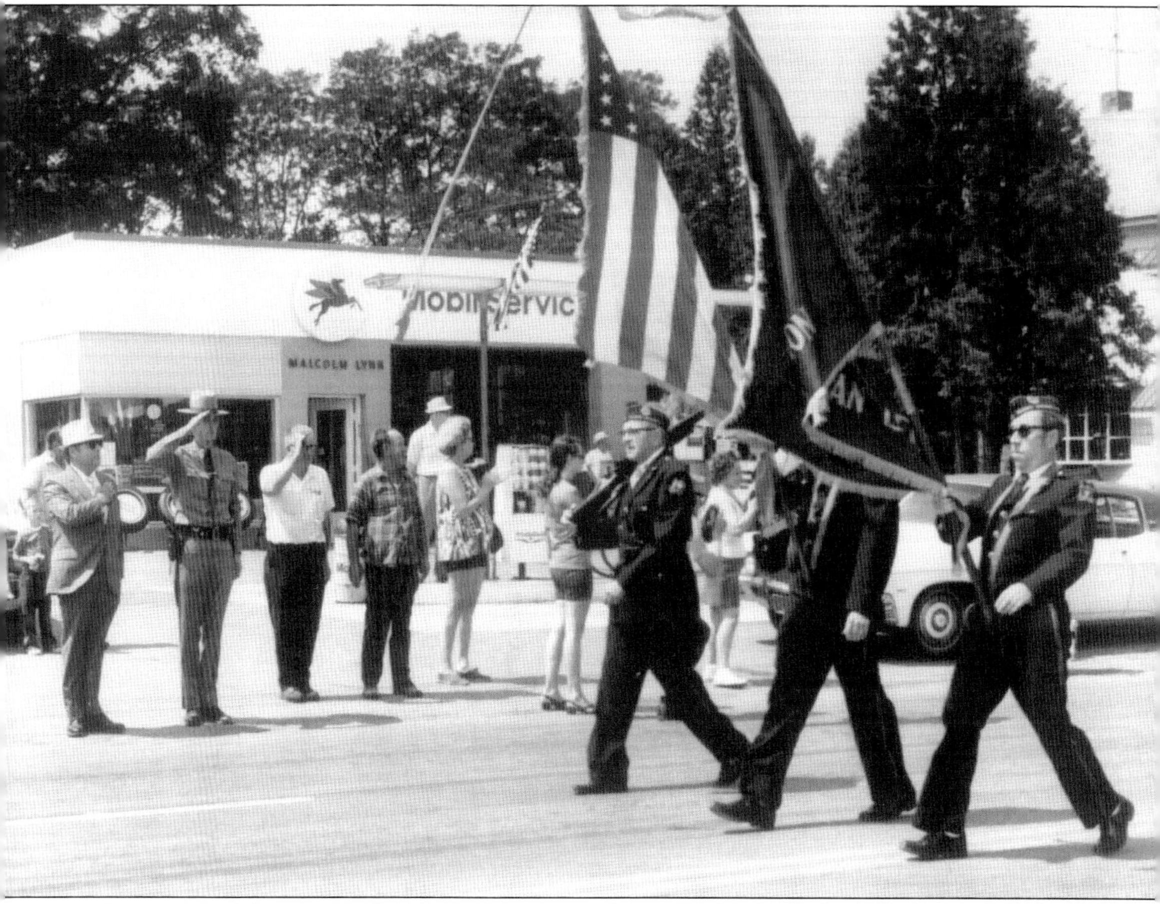

On Memorial Day 1970, the American Legion Honor Corps passes in front of Lynk's service station. For 40 years, Malcolm Lynk's Mobil station was a meeting place for the village men. The young people in town knew they could turn to "Mac" when they needed help with cars, family, or other problems. After Mac's retirement in 1980, the station was run by Herb Vrooman Jr. for seven years, then by Enders Oil Co. for several years, before it was sold to Stewart's Shops.

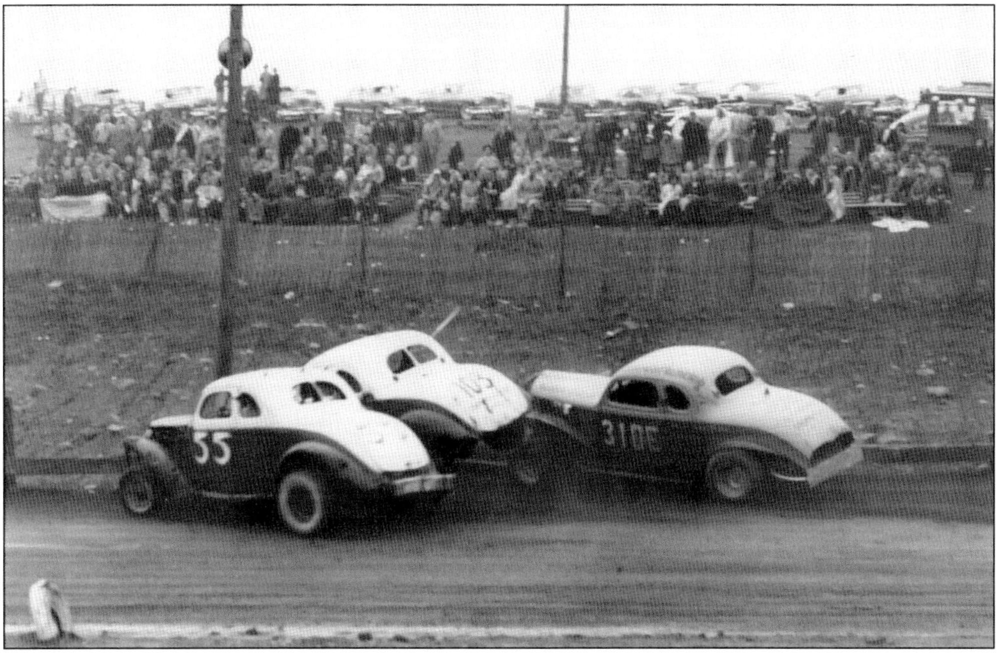

In the early 1950s, stock car races were held on Friday nights at the dirt track in the hamlet of Leesville. Local legend has it that, when the lights were brought up for racing, the local farmers often lost their electricity, which shut down their milking machines. Admission was $1.25 to this very popular venue during the summer months, but it only lasted for a few short years.

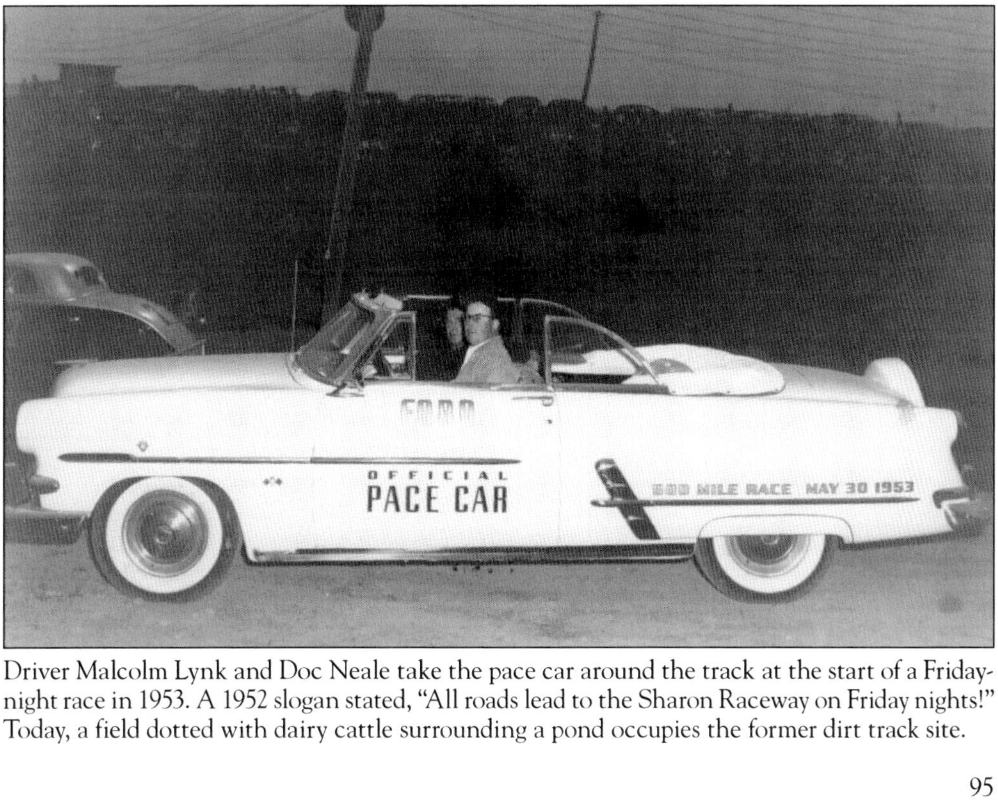

Driver Malcolm Lynk and Doc Neale take the pace car around the track at the start of a Friday-night race in 1953. A 1952 slogan stated, "All roads lead to the Sharon Raceway on Friday nights!" Today, a field dotted with dairy cattle surrounding a pond occupies the former dirt track site.

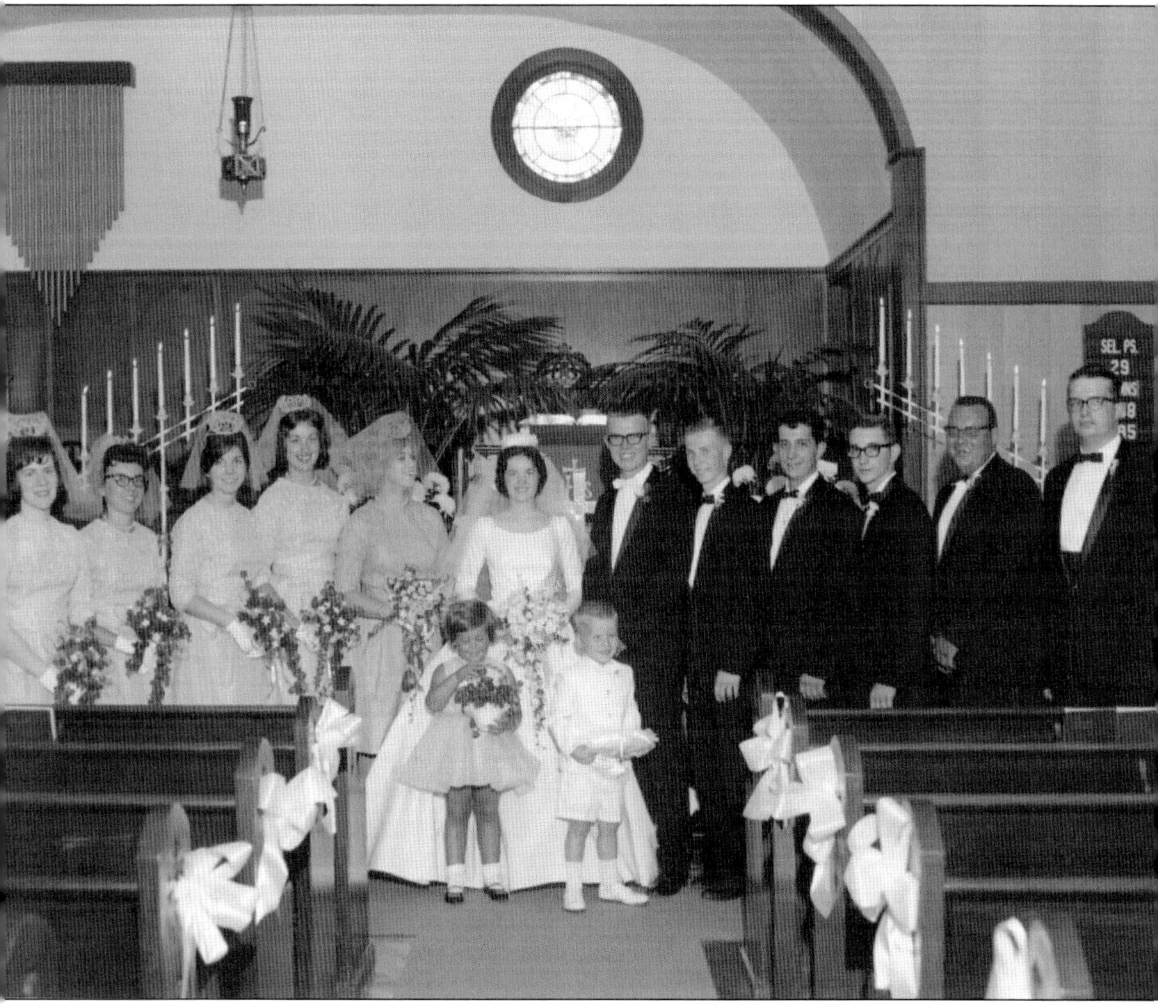

On July 27, 1963, Scott Lynk—whose ancestors on both sides date to the town's founding—married Gail Silvers, daughter of a Jewish Italian family who had moved to Sharon in the early 1950s. The flower girl is Marilyn Stein, and Howard Lynk is the ring bearer. The groomsmen are, from left to right, Ed Lynk, Anthony L. DiPace, Bruce Silvers, Paul Stafford, and Peter Melera. The maid of honor is Edie Lynk. The bridesmaids include Mary Lou Ullman (second from left) and Nancy DiPace (third from left). The wedding was held in Sharon Springs Methodist Church.

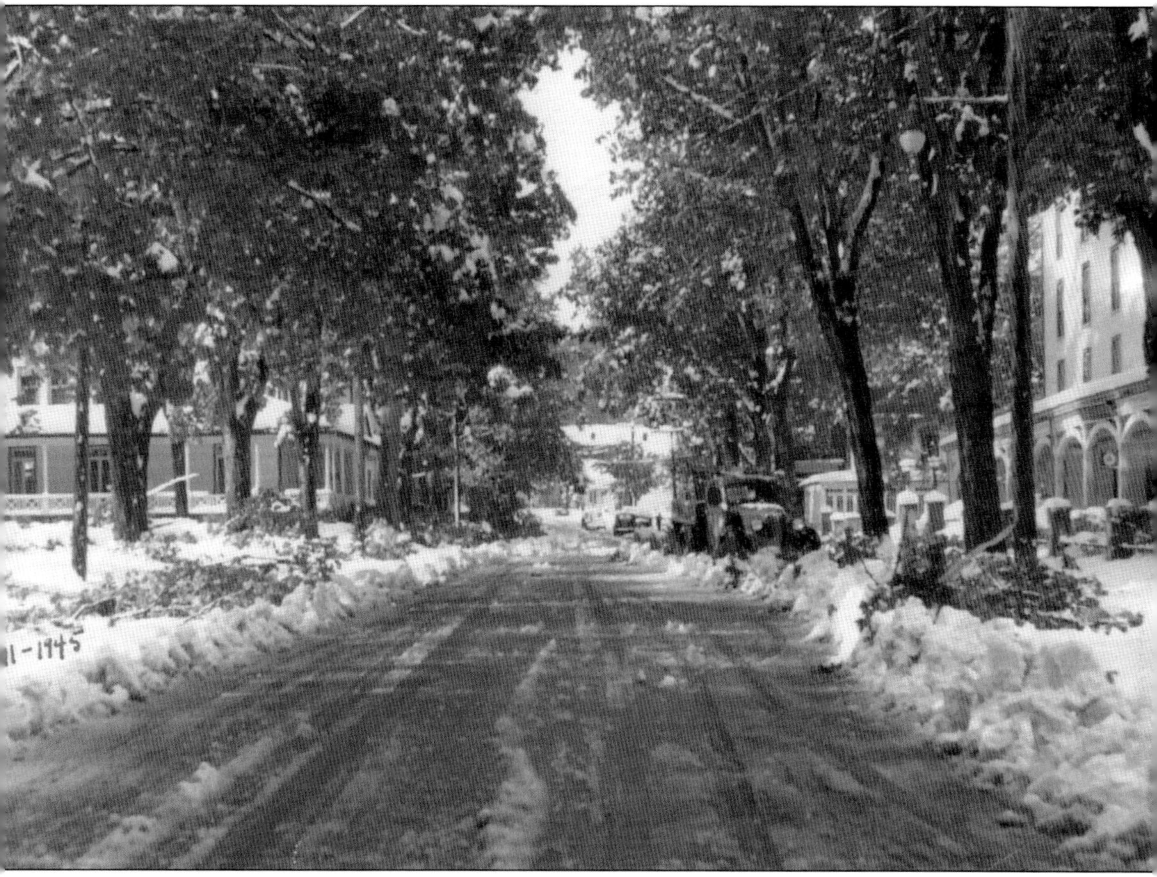

Sharon Springs is known for snowy winters. There have been occasions when Old Man Winter stayed around or bounced back unexpectedly. This photograph documents a snowstorm that took place on May 11, 1945. The Union Hotel is on the right. Local wisdom claims that planting should wait until after Memorial Day at the end of May.

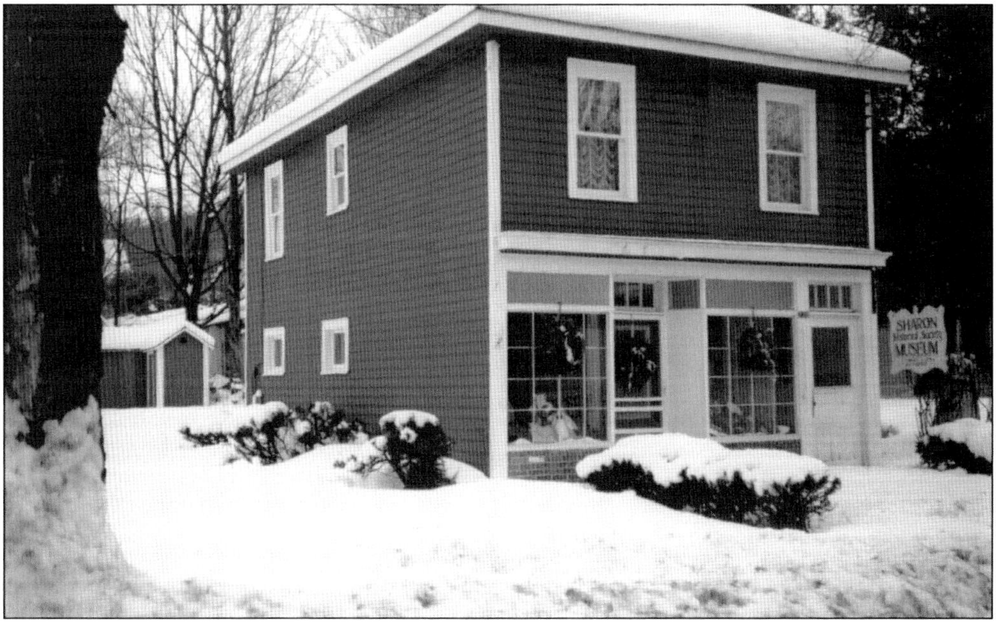

The Sharon Museum complex includes the museum building and storage barn donated in 1972 by Esther Sticht and a one-room schoolhouse and outhouse moved to the site in 1989. The museum is noted for its excellent collection of photographs and other memorabilia. The top floor has been furnished to resemble a Victorian home, with a parlor, bedroom, and kitchen displaying objects from that time.

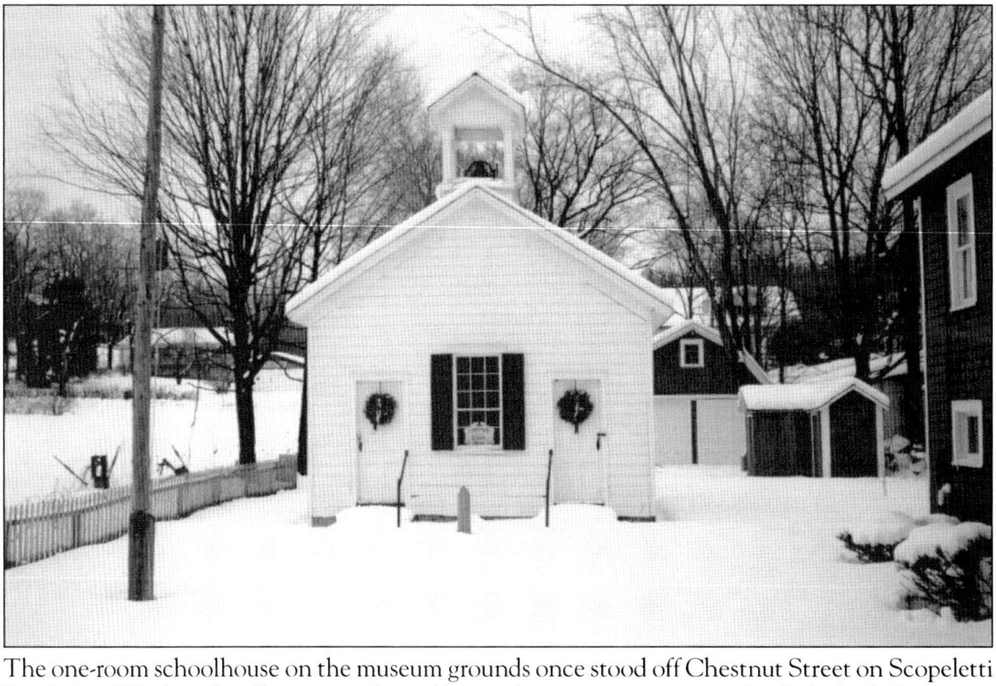

The one-room schoolhouse on the museum grounds once stood off Chestnut Street on Scopeletti Road. In 1989, the schoolhouse was ferried by truck to its present site and refurbished. Each year, second-grade students from the central school visit the museum and experience life in a school of bygone days.

Six

Challenging Times

Fortunes waxed and waned in the town and village over the centuries, leaving remnants of grandeur and swaths of decay. Many factors contributed to the decline of the spa and the once flourishing agricultural community.

Taking the waters for medicinal purposes had fallen out of fashion by the 1950s, bringing fewer guests seeking relief at the baths. Hotel owners neglected their properties and failed to modernize the once grand 19th-century buildings. Arson and other fires claimed many hotels, restaurants, and other commercial sites. The spa and hotel owners at one point deemed horse racing and gambling activities inconsistent with the image of a place for healing, further decreasing the number of visitors. There were many attempts to increase tourism in the 20th century, including a golf course, modernized swimming pool, ski slope (in hopes of a year-round clientele), concerts, street dances, and even a beauty contest.

Farming also faced a number of shocks, including competition from the industrialized farms of the Midwest and California, the blight on the hops, the short growing season, and mechanization. The cost to purchase and maintain tractors, reapers, and other power machines could bankrupt a small farmer, especially when crops failed or prices on grain fell sharply. While some fields remain fallow with abandoned farmhouses, other farmers found diverse ways to survive and prosper. The town government passed laws to become an agricultural district, which enabled farmers to obtain tax breaks and other government benefits.

The community sought ways to invigorate town life, with ventures like a racetrack in the 1950s, Founder's Day celebrations, a bicentennial parade and celebration in 1997, and other local festivals.

Since 2005, the baths and several hotels were closed after their purchase by Sharon Springs, Inc., a group of investors from South Korea. Shut down and neglected, in the absence of proper care, the buildings have crumbled. Nonetheless, the New York State Historic Preservation League declared 180 buildings in the lower village historic sites in 1994. Everyone interested in the village's history hopes to see these buildings renovated in the near future.

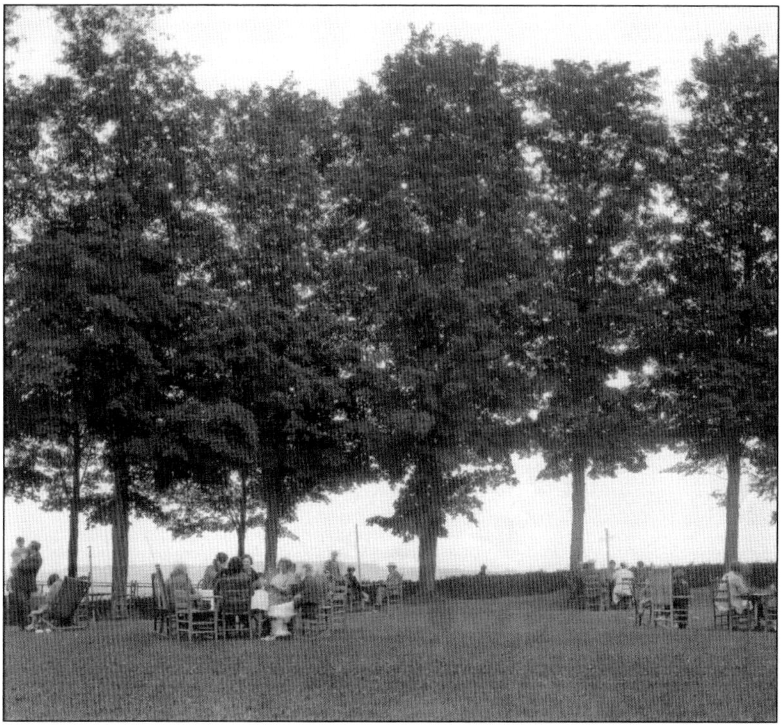

In the 1930s, the Pavilion Hotel offered kosher meals in an effort to attract more guests. This photograph of the lawn, where card games are in progress, is from the late 1930s, near the end of an era. By the late 1930s, the grand old hotel had become something of an anachronism, with most guests preferring the newer, small hotels or boardinghouses.

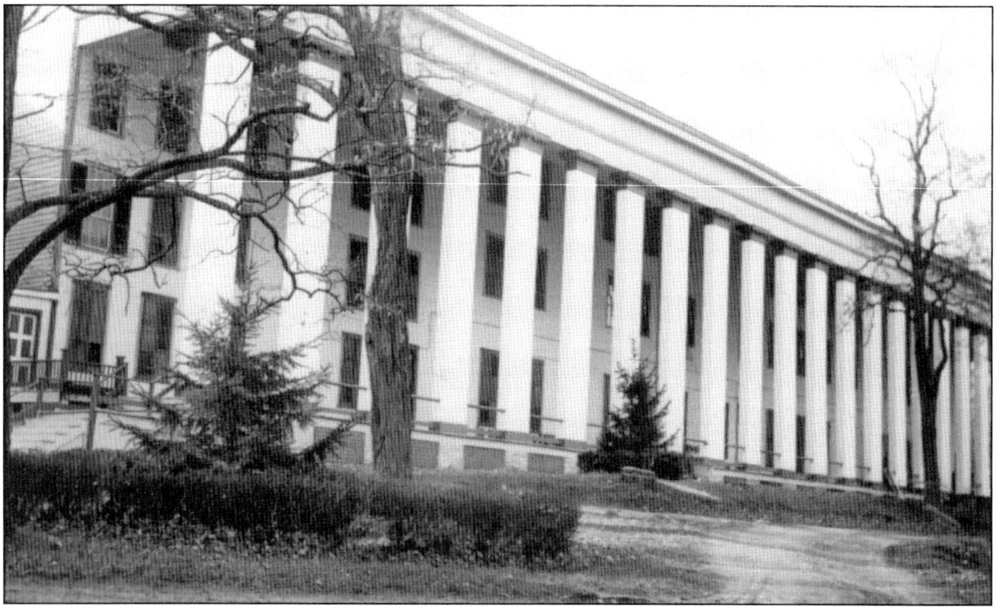

This 1940 photograph is one of the last of the famous Pavilion Hotel. The story goes that Mary Elizabeth Burchell Gardner, wife of Alfred W. Gardner, announced that year that, if Franklin Roosevelt won a third term as president, she would tear down her hotel. He did get elected, and she did tear down the hotel!

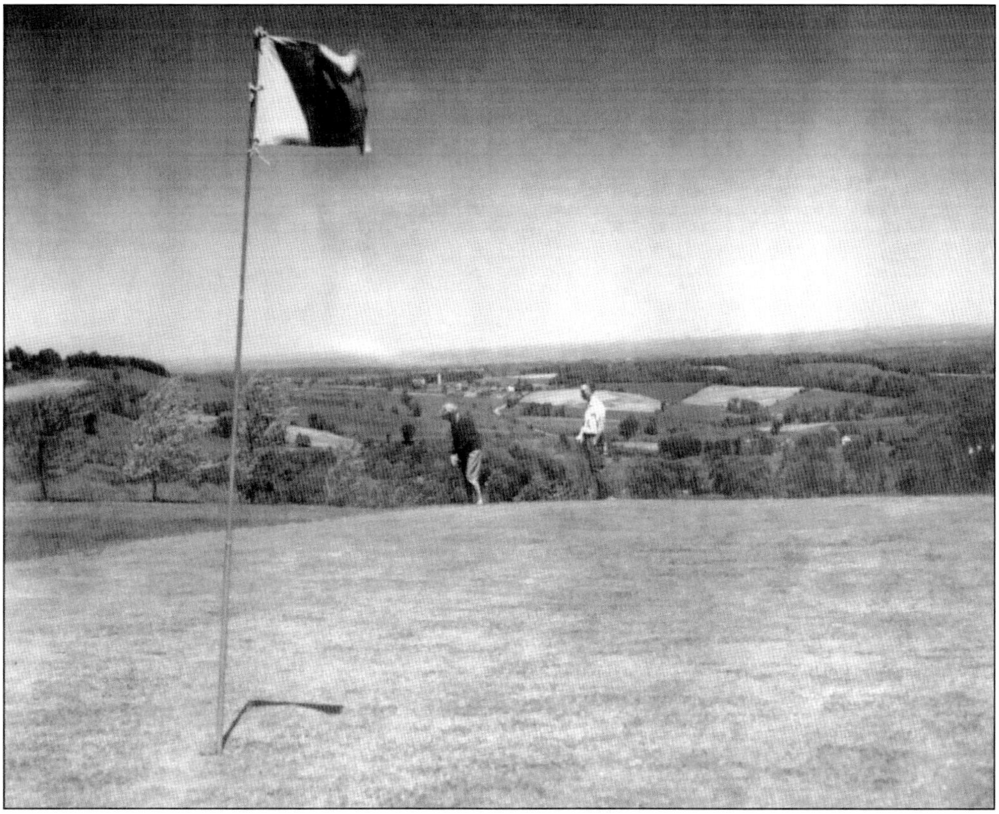

In 1925, a golf course was established on the grounds of the Pavilion Hotel in an effort to attract affluent guests to the spa. This 1950s photograph depicts the remarkably hilly terrain.

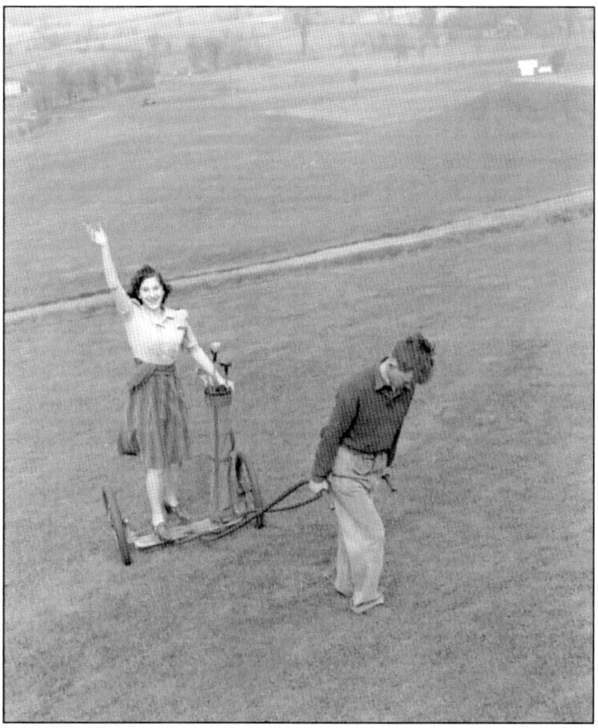

A publicity photograph from the 1940s shows Audrey Engle (daughter of the Park View owners) being pulled by Bill Long on a golf cart. Caddies were provided for golfers, and there were no mechanized golf carts. The course was abandoned by 1970.

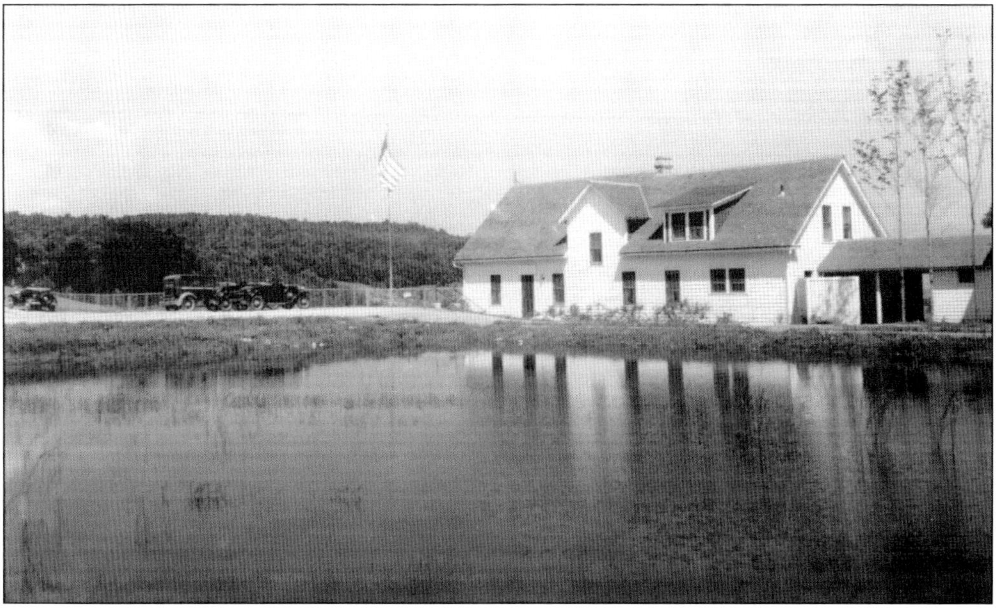

This pond next to the clubhouse was originally created to harvest ice during the winter months to supply the hotels in the summer. Eventually, this became what locals called "the mud hole," an informal swimming pool.

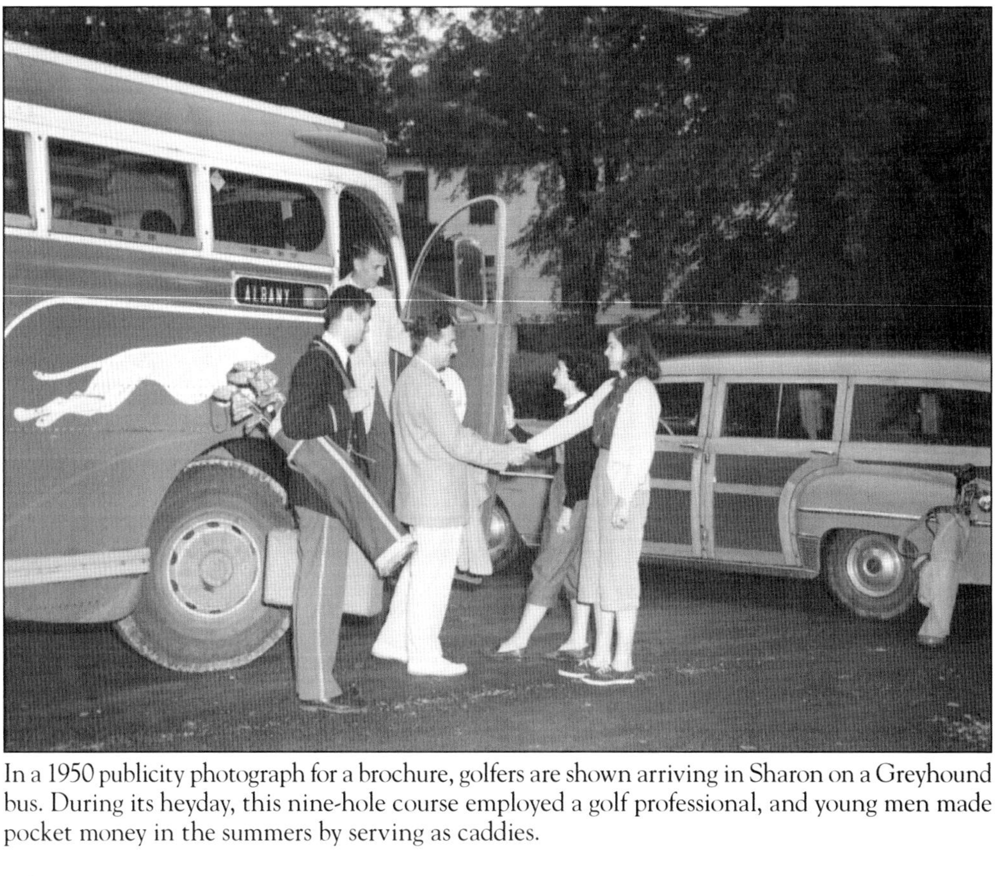

In a 1950 publicity photograph for a brochure, golfers are shown arriving in Sharon on a Greyhound bus. During its heyday, this nine-hole course employed a golf professional, and young men made pocket money in the summers by serving as caddies.

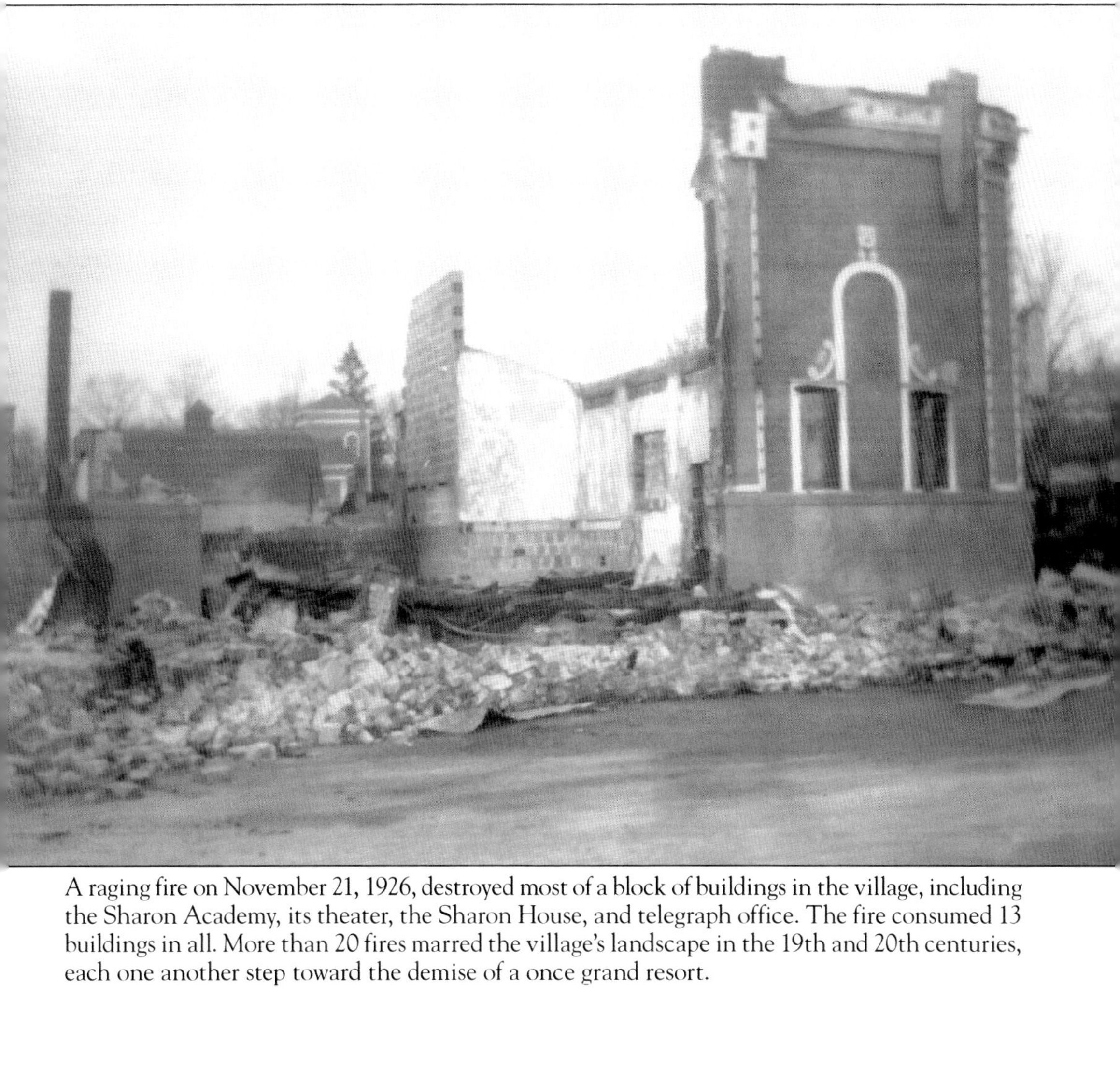

A raging fire on November 21, 1926, destroyed most of a block of buildings in the village, including the Sharon Academy, its theater, the Sharon House, and telegraph office. The fire consumed 13 buildings in all. More than 20 fires marred the village's landscape in the 19th and 20th centuries, each one another step toward the demise of a once grand resort.

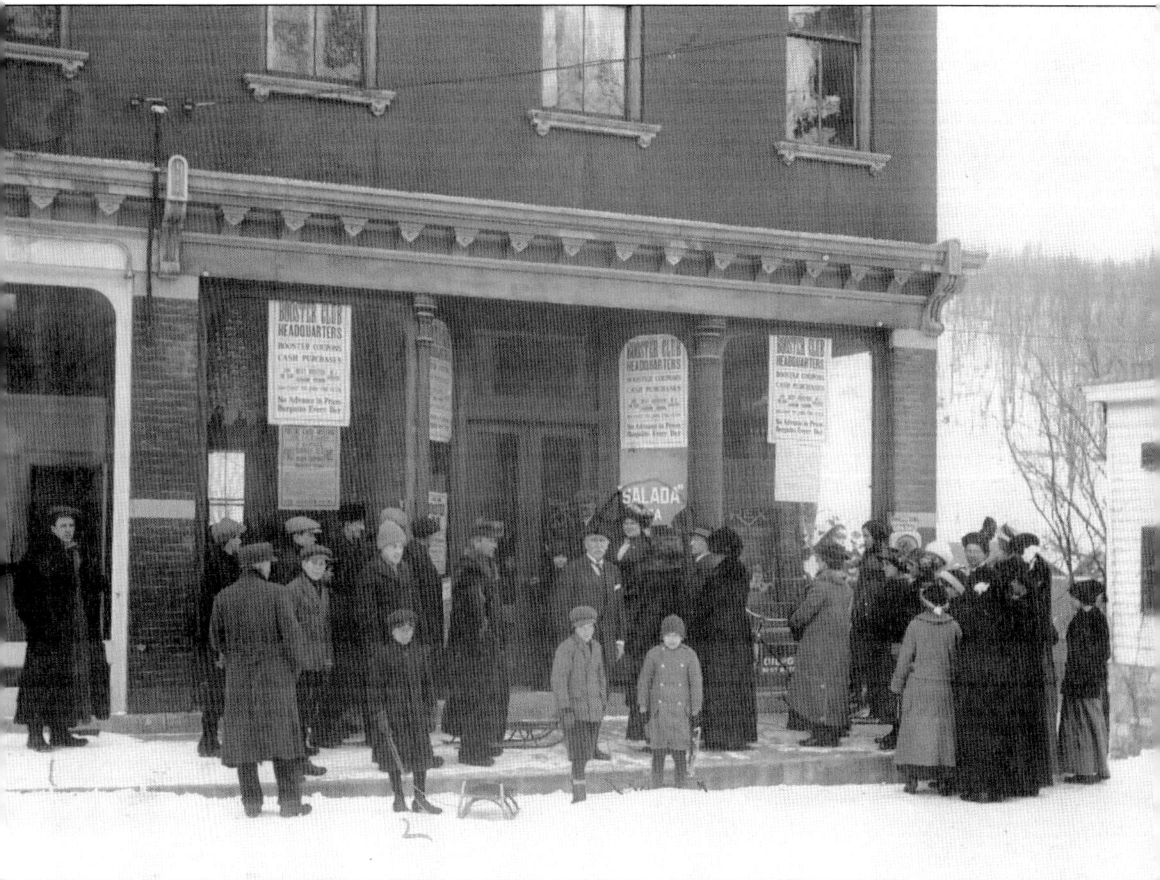

One of Sharon's more iconic buildings, Klinkhart Hall was built in 1886 on the site of George Klinkhart's first business. It was destroyed in the Empire Block fire of 1885. His new hardware store offered a multitude of items, including pianos, ammunition, and paint. An opera house on the second floor hosted parties, dances, and plays. In July 1911, Klinkhart was in the basement working with varnish when a candle ignited the liquid, severely burning his hands. He ran for help as his stock burst into flames. His wife, Louisa, ran back to save the receipts and was killed when the paint and gunpowder exploded. Klinkhart died in 1915. The Masonic lodge bought the building and used the second floor as its temple. The first floor became an auto showroom until 1925, then Smalley's Movie Theater until 1955. Today, it is poised for renovation.

The Recreation Center is shown (at right) in the 1950s, when it was one of the bathhouses. Originally part of the Pavilion Hotel complex, it was sold to the Spofford family with the rest of the Gardner estate in 1940. Eventually, the town was granted permission to use the building for community activities. During the daytime, it was used as a recreation center; dances were held there in the evening. Unfortunately, it burned down in 1996 (below) as a result of arson.

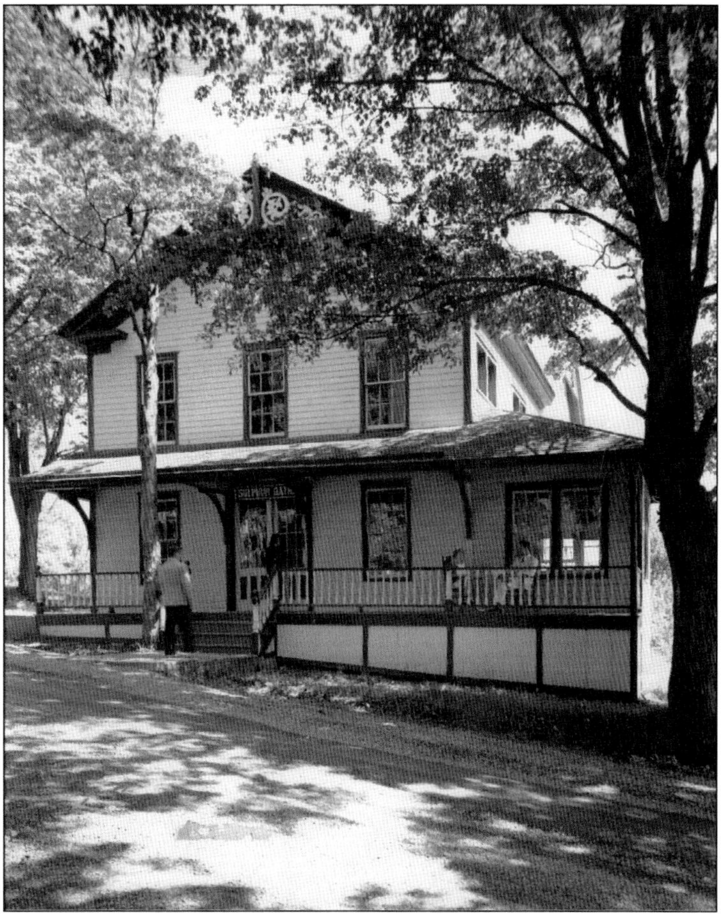

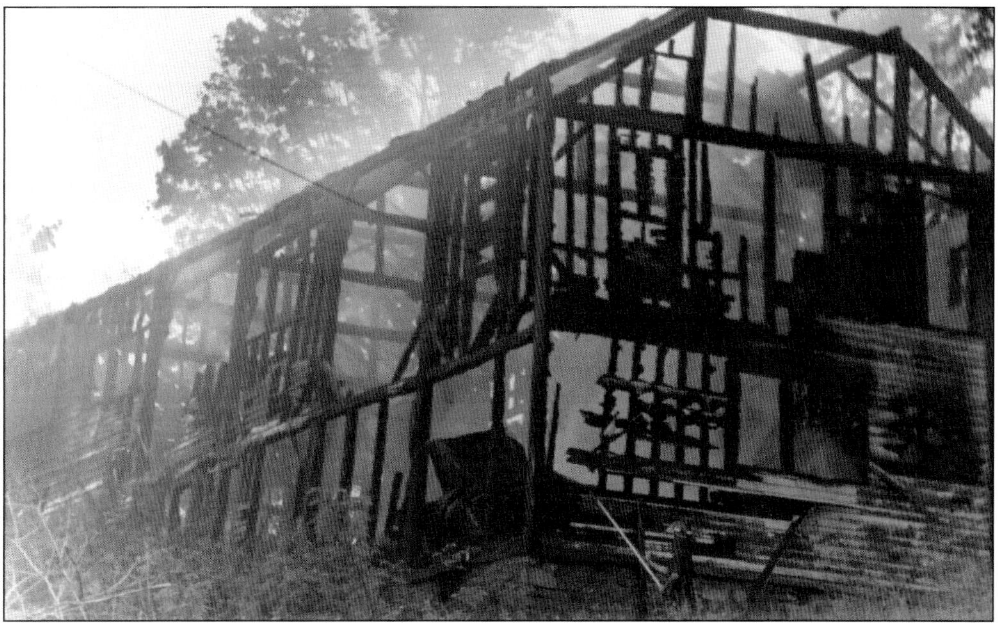

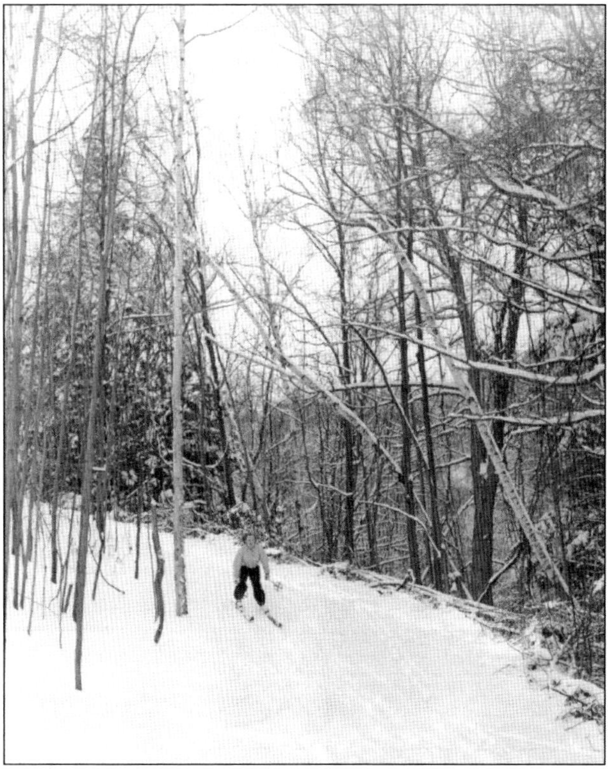

In the 1940s, the Spoffords, then owners of the White Sulphur Company, helped create a ski slope on their property, in hopes of expanding the resort's season into the winter months. The rope tow, the second in the United States (the first was built in Woodstock, Vermont), was built by Edgar Handy. This ski run was nicknamed "Suicide Hill."

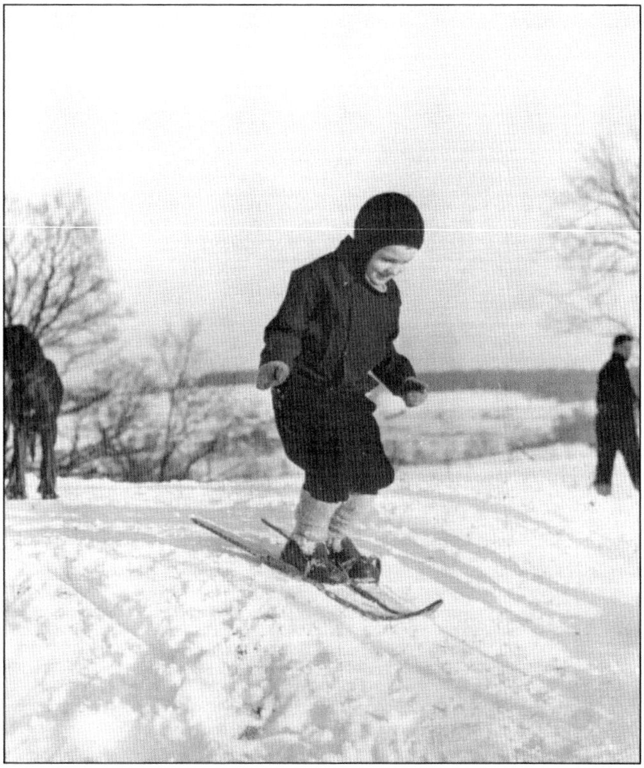

Sumner Miller III, shown here in 1941 at the age of three, was the son of the director of ski activities in Sharon. Young Sumner is shown inaugurating the 20-foot ski run for children, which adjoined the adult ski slopes and trails.

This photograph was taken for a 1950s advertising brochure to illustrate recreational activities available in the village, including horseback riding. The stables were located on Pavilion Avenue and still stand today, although they are now vacant. The horse, once prevalent for farm labor, has returned as a recreational outlet; many former dairy farms are today horse-breeding farms.

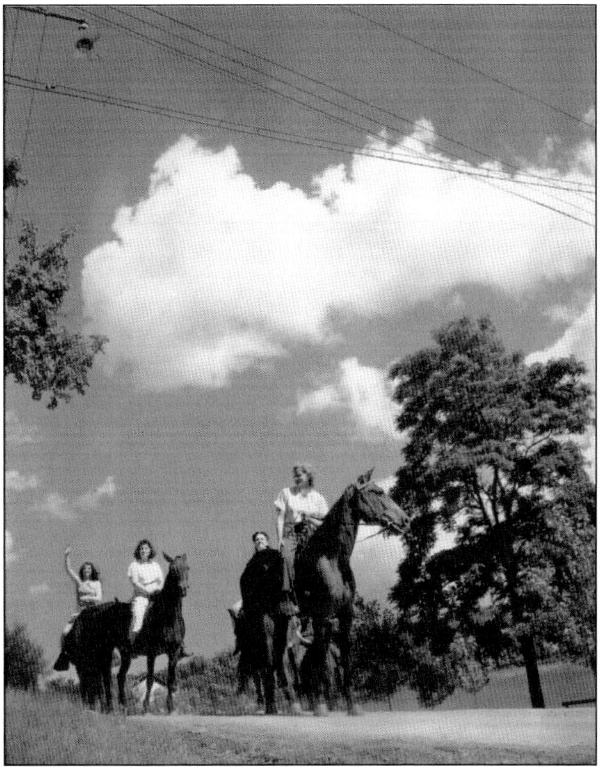

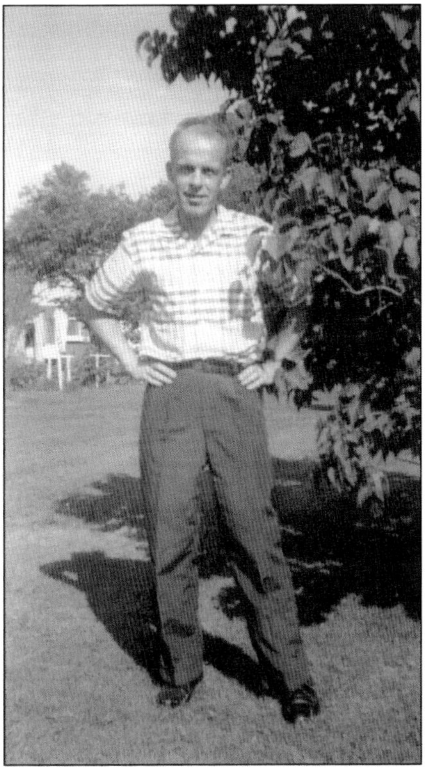

James Bowmaker, a well-known local chef and restaurant owner, served as the village mayor in the 1970s. He agonized over hotel owners who refused to pay taxes and allowed their properties to disintegrate in order to lower assessments. Bowmaker had a great sense of humor and often told the story of visiting the kosher hotels, announcing he had just put several hams in to roast. He then waited for the hotel staff to sneak into his restaurant to eat ham, in violation of their dietary rules.

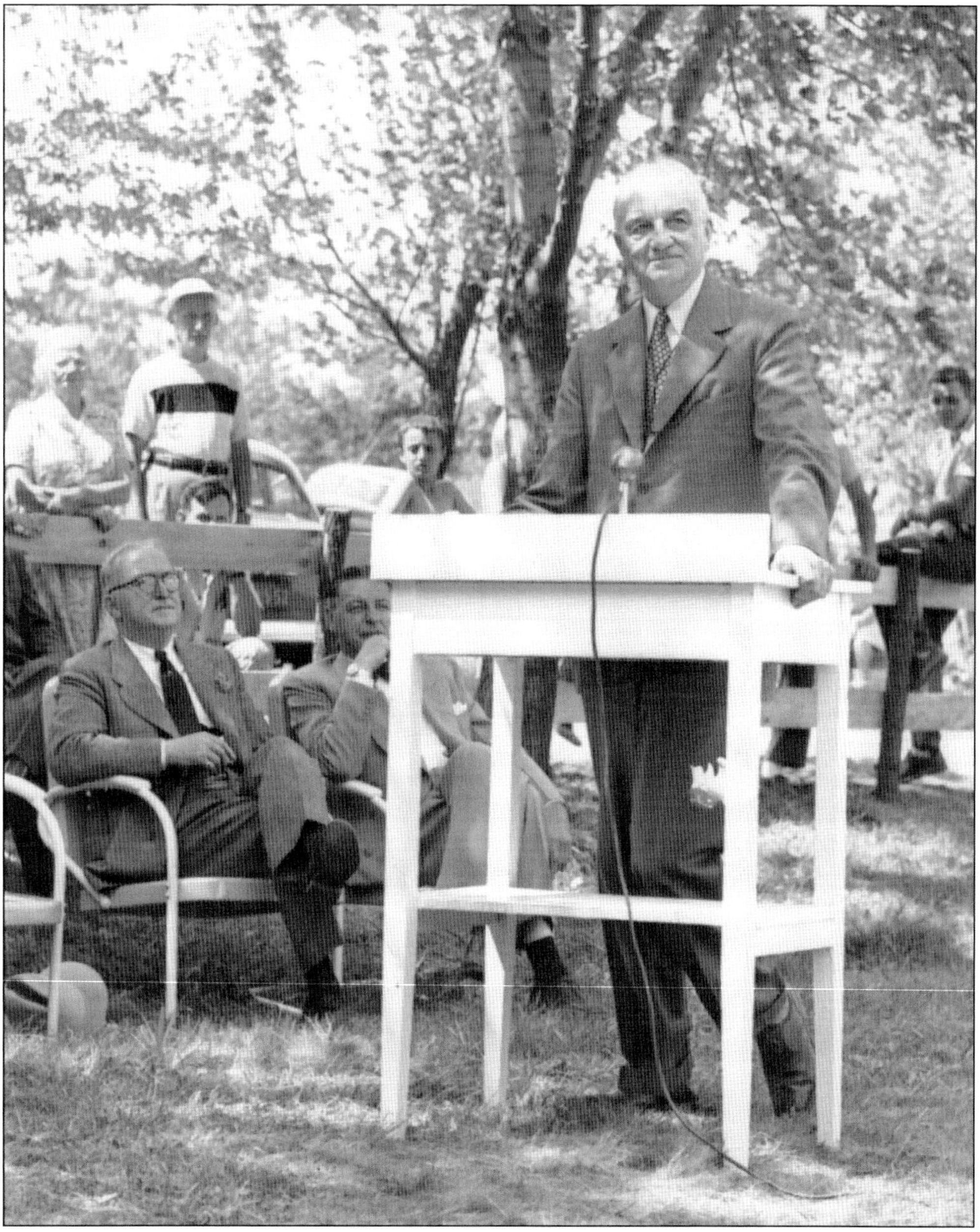

At the dedication of the public pool in 1950, Sharon Mauhs is seated at left. His father, Fritz, had been tragically killed in 1911, after which Sharon and his family struggled to survive. Sharon moved to Cobleskill after the tragedy and went on to become a noted prosecutor who brought down several mob figures in New York. Homer Spofford is credited with convincing Sharon Mauhs to become involved again in the village of his birth. The speaker is General Electric head Owen D. Young. Well-known local barber Keith Mallery stands in the background.

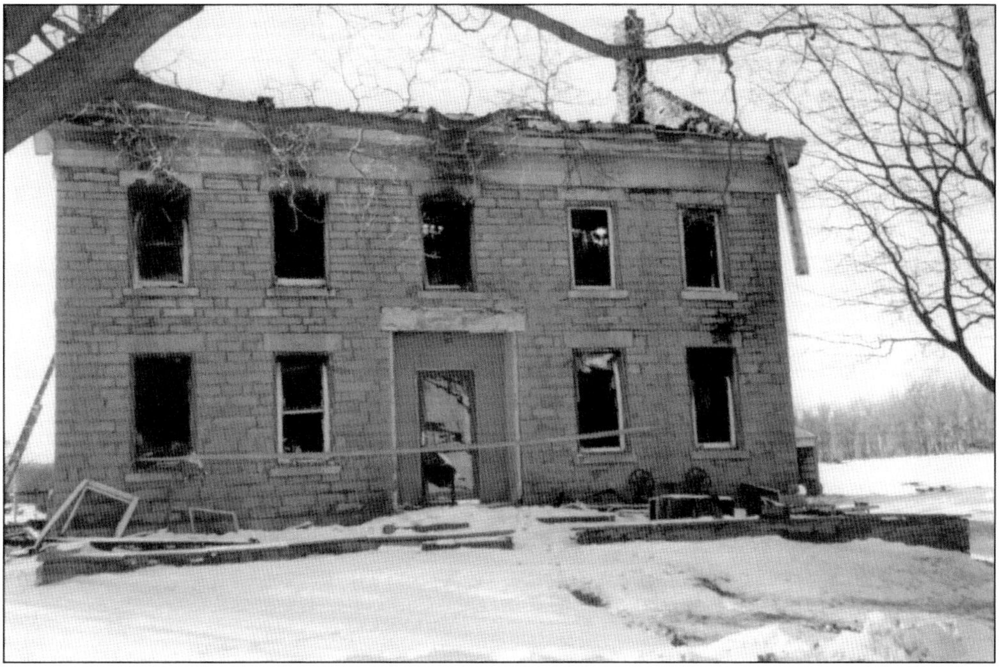

In 2005, the magnificent Stone House Farm was destroyed by fire. The Walrath family built the original home around 1850 with stone quarried on the farm, hauled by horses, and hoisted in place with pulleys over two large beams used in the attic until the fire of 2005. Current owners Tim and Patti Everett made the decision to rebuild; today, the house stands as a reminder that rebirth is possible. The Everetts were awarded the Otsego 2000 Preservation Award in 2010 for their reconstruction. They continue to operate a successful dairy farm and popular maple-sugaring enterprise today.

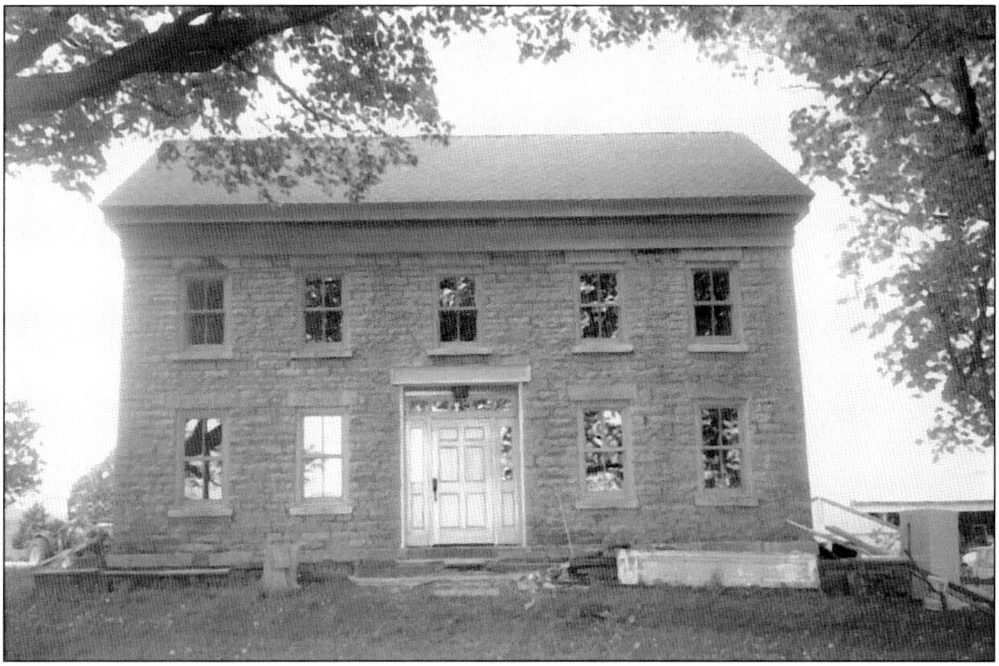

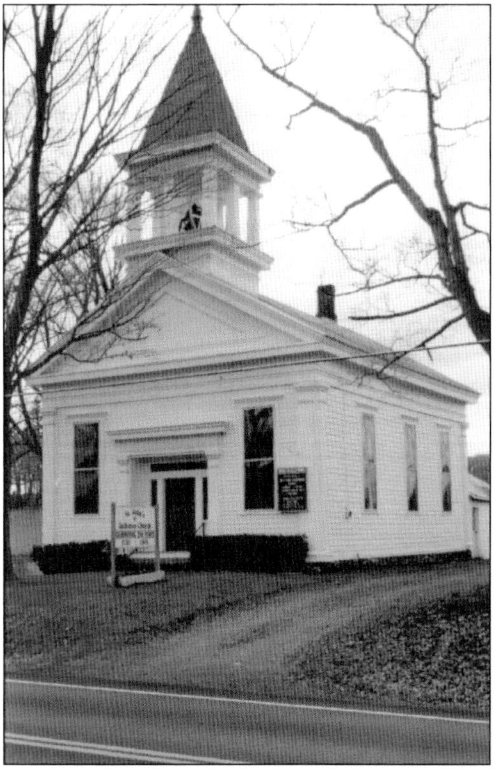

The Lutheran congregation of St. John's, one of the oldest in the town, was organized in 1745 by Rev. Peter Nicholas Sommer. The edifice shown here was dedicated in 1861. Noted for its frescoes, the church offered its last service in 2011 before being sold to Michael Buchanan. There were too few congregants to pay for maintaining the building. The congregation merged with Zion Lutheran Church in Seward.

The decaying Sulphur Temple is seen here in 2014. It has been abandoned to the elements since 2005, when the property was sold to Sharon Springs, Inc. The investors have allowed the facade to crumble and the pipes, which fed the famous mineral waters into the fountain for more than a century, to become so clogged with dirt and debris that they no longer function. The temple is a far cry from its heyday magnificence (see page 50). (Author's collection.)

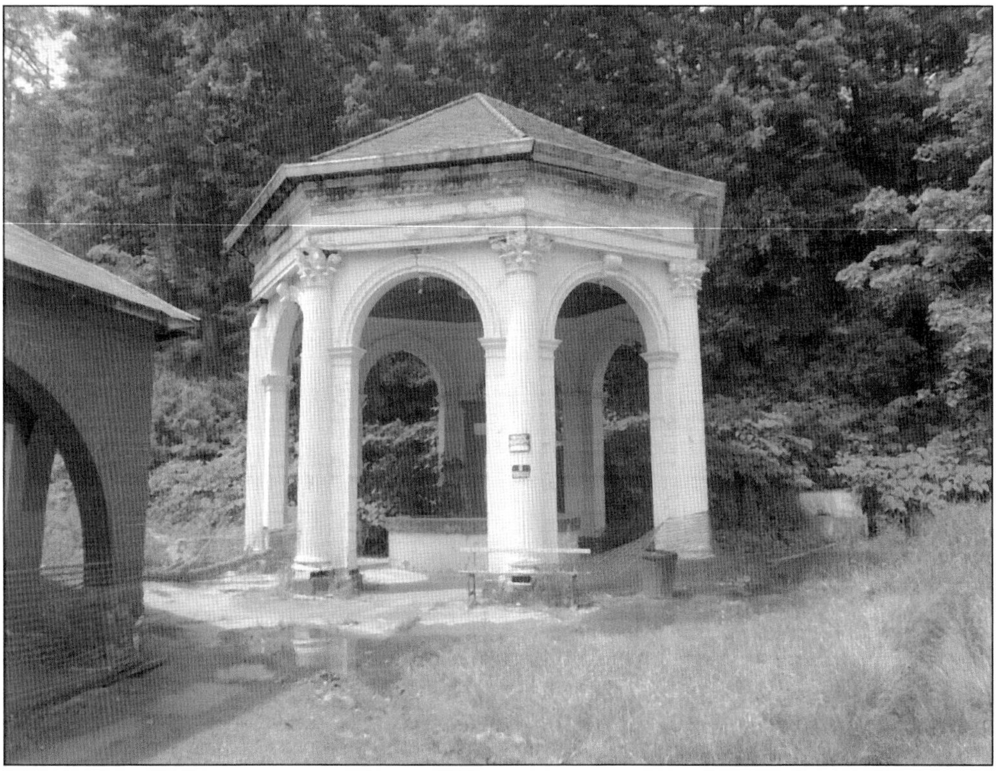

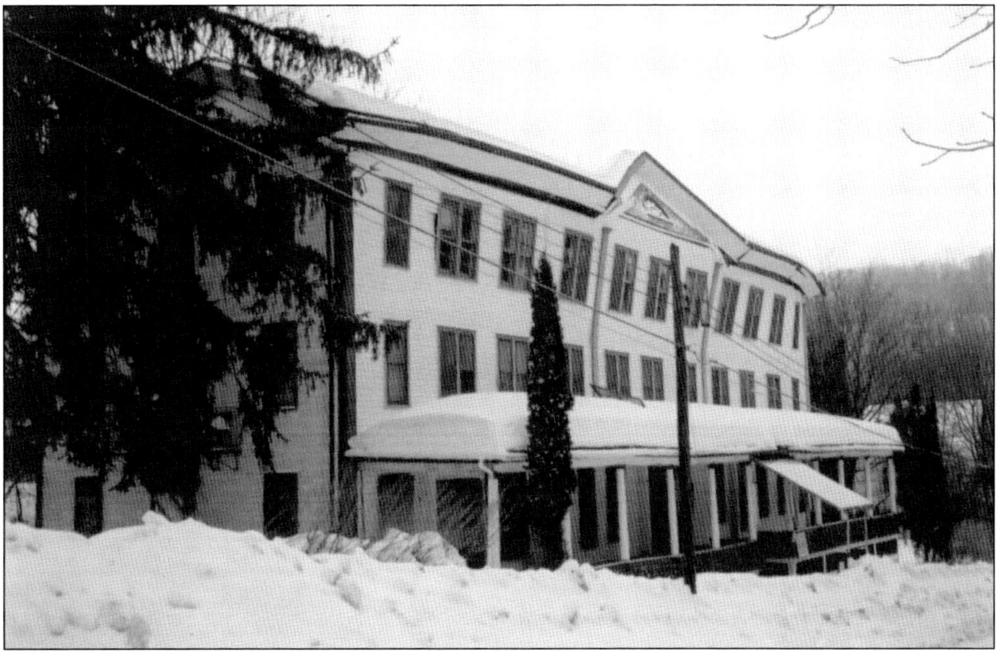

By 2003, when this photograph of the Hotel Washington was taken, many hotels and boardinghouses had been abandoned and left to the elements for several years. Wooden structures are especially vulnerable to snow and ice; if not attended to, the building eventually collapses, as seen here. The Washington was torn down in 2013.

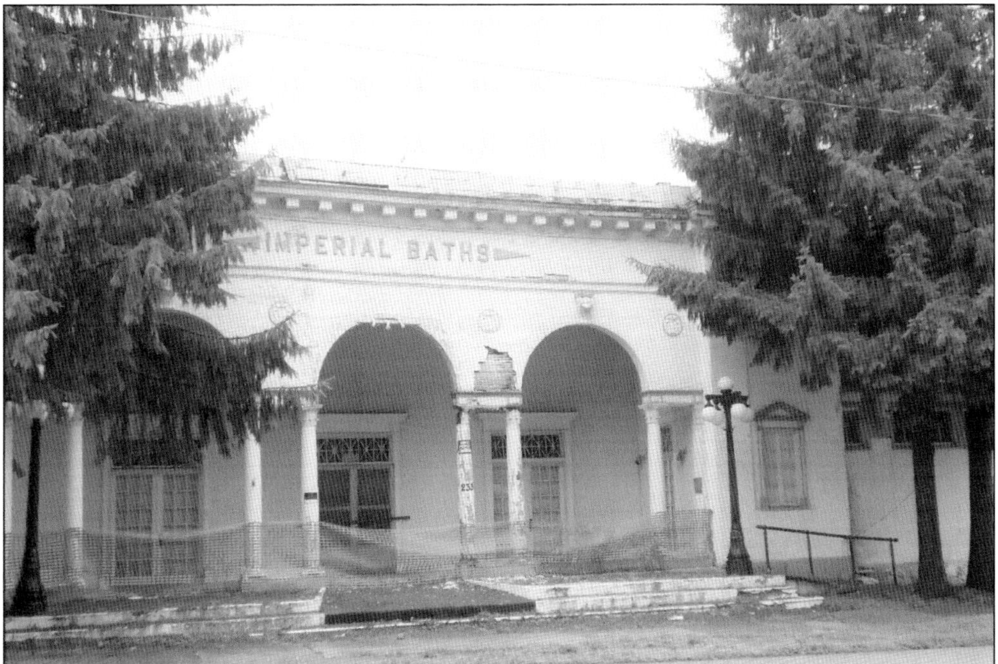

The Imperial Bathhouse is shown in its dilapidated state in 2014. Sharon Springs, Inc. closed the facility nine years earlier and has neglected its maintenance and upkeep. Time, weather, and vandalism have taken their toll on this once magnificent structure. (Author's collection.)

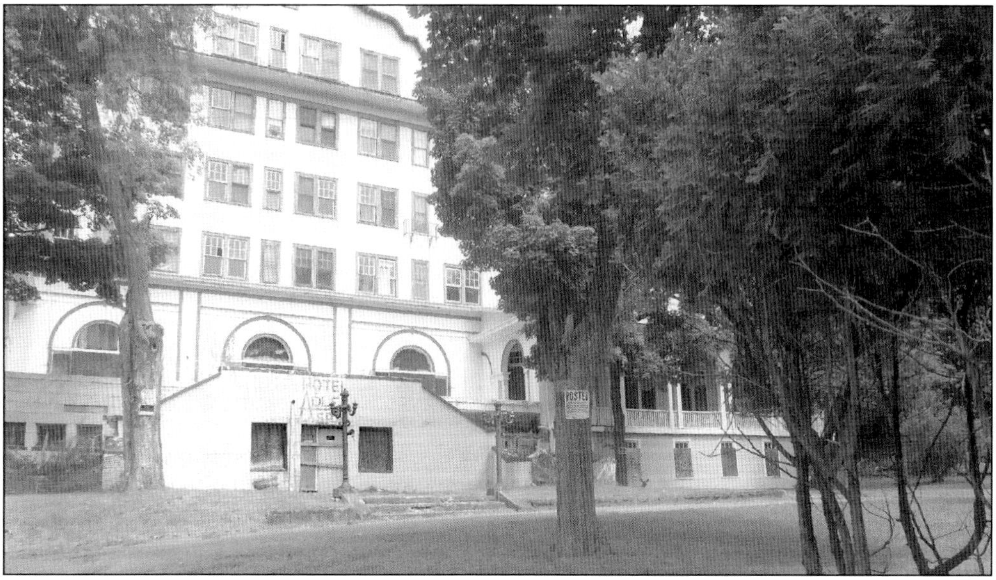

The once grand Adler Hotel, seen here in 2014, shows the result of several years of neglect. Thieves have broken in and removed the copper wiring as well as the chandeliers and other items of value. No longer will Jewish ladies promenade along the walkways or sunbathe in the solariums. The ballroom remains eerily quiet, with no orchestra, dance band, or well-dressed guests. The kitchens are closed up and silent. Like several of the other properties now owned by Sharon Springs, Inc., the building has deteriorated. The basement has become a home for foxes, and below, a deer reclines peacefully in the shadows. The Adler Hotel in its heyday is seen on page 48. (Both, author's collection.)

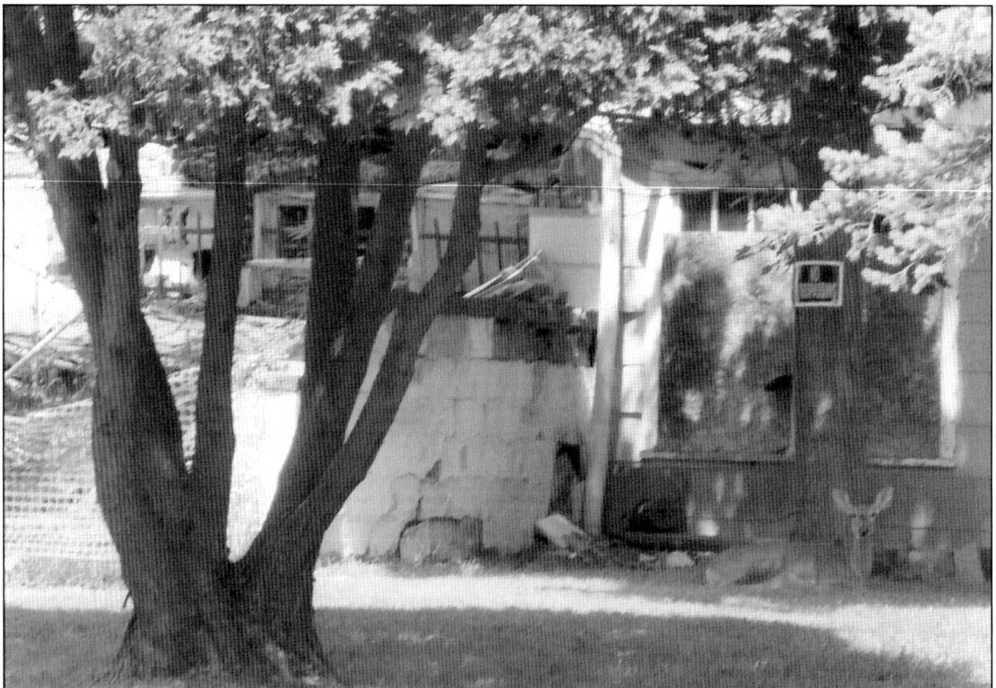

Seven

Hope and Renewal

Although the springs and most of the hotels continue to decay, elsewhere, the town and village are experiencing a renaissance, with cafés, restaurants, a boutique hotel, bed-and-breakfasts, shops, a day spa, organic farms, a reality television show, an influx of artists and artisans, festivals, media coverage, and community involvement. Anchoring this renewal are several businesses that have persevered over the years. The Log House, along Route 20, and the Sharon Tavern, east of the village in Sharon Hill, are two businesses that have thrived for more than 50 years. Although not pictured here, they are true survivors.

Doug Plummer and his husband, Garth Roberts, have been instrumental in sparking this current revival. In 1993, they opened the Rockville Bakery, a successful café in the upper village. By 2001, they had restored and opened the American Hotel, a linchpin in the transformation of the village, which is now home to many other successful gay couples and others attracted by reasonably priced real estate and a lively community.

The popular television show *The Fabulous Beekman Boys* chronicles the challenges faced by Josh Kilmer-Purcell and Dr. Brent Ridge as they attempt to turn the former Beekman estate into a profitable farm and retail business. The show has brought new visitors to the town and village. Often, they say, "I came because of the show, but I come back because of the people!"

None of this new growth would be possible without the ongoing commitment of the community. Teachers, shopkeepers, volunteers, and farmers are the true linchpins in the town's survival. Sharon and Sharon Springs are places where people are welcoming and stop on the street to chat. Thousands of visitors attend the many festivals in the village each year.

From before written history, when native tribes congregated at the springs, through the early Dutch and German settlements, the American colonists of English descent, the 19th-century "elite" families, the mingling of Italian, Eastern European, and Jewish cultures in the 20th century, to today's gathering of artists, artisans, and entrepreneurs, Sharon Springs has enjoyed a unique history, offering residents and visitors a wider window onto the world.

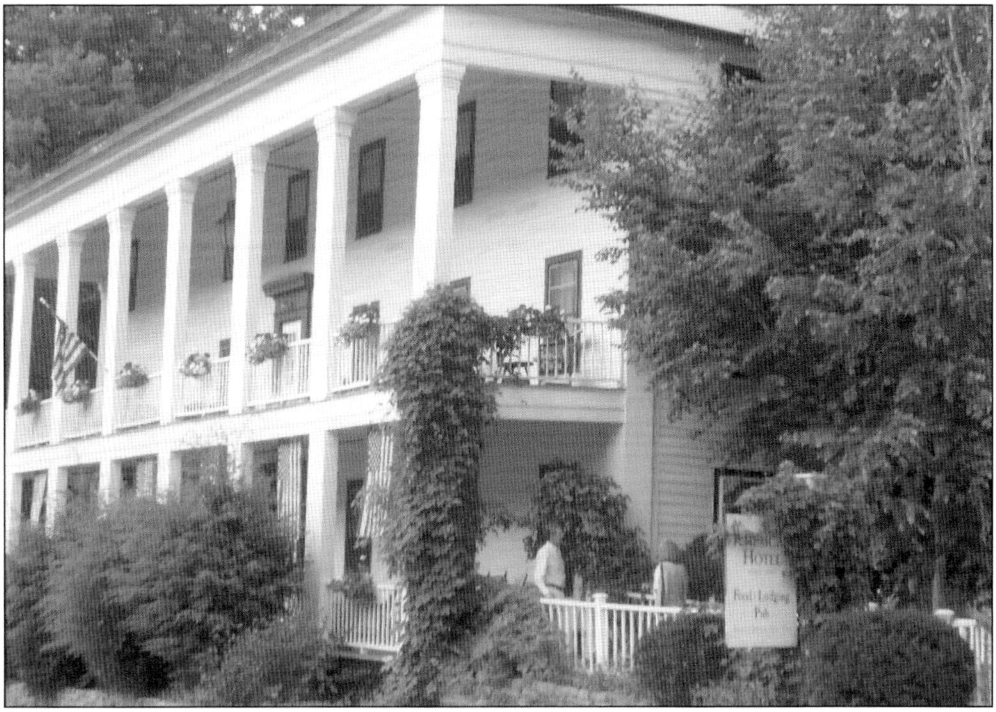

The lodestar of the renaissance in Sharon Springs, the renovated American Hotel, opened its doors in 2001. Owners Doug Plummer and Garth Roberts have created a thriving restaurant and hotel business, spurring other entrepreneurs to join the renewal. This jewel of the renewal of the village has been featured in many magazines and in the *New York Times*. (Author's collection.)

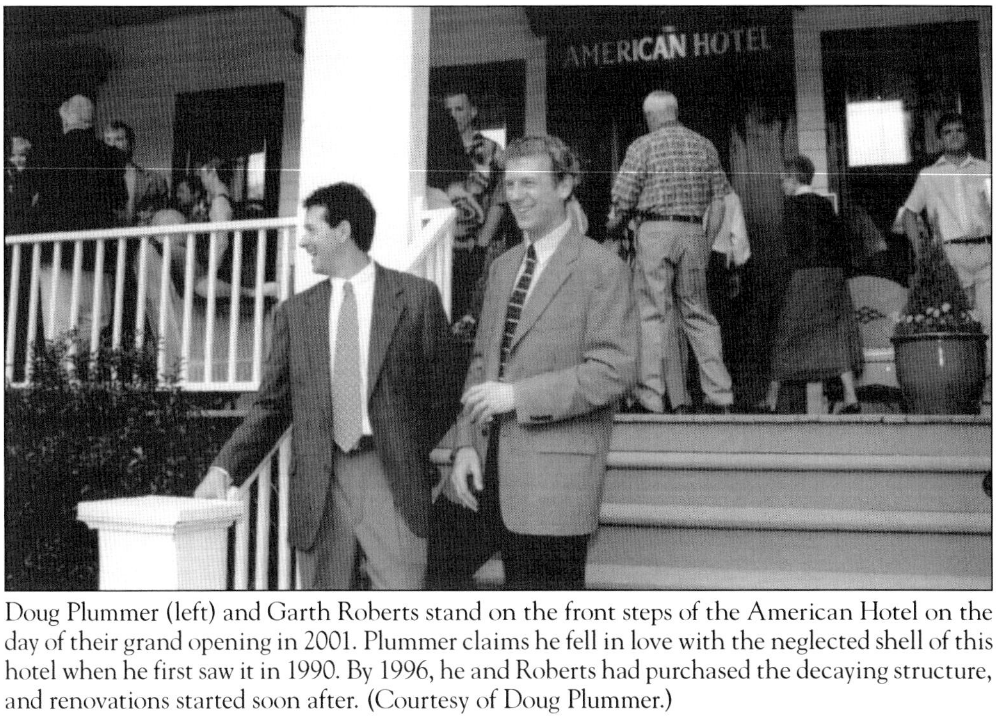

Doug Plummer (left) and Garth Roberts stand on the front steps of the American Hotel on the day of their grand opening in 2001. Plummer claims he fell in love with the neglected shell of this hotel when he first saw it in 1990. By 1996, he and Roberts had purchased the decaying structure, and renovations started soon after. (Courtesy of Doug Plummer.)

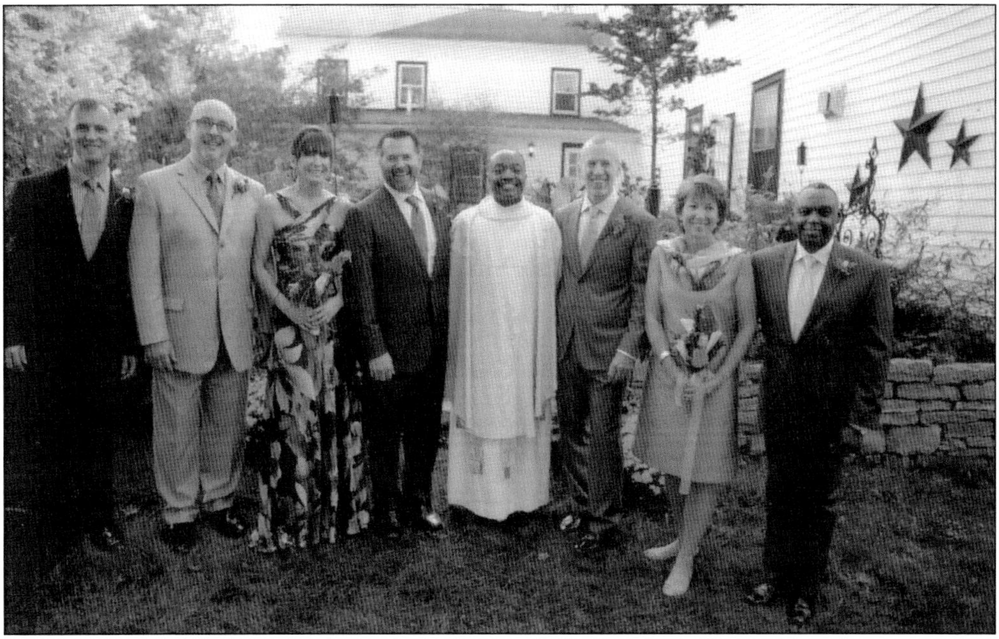

Doug Plummer (fourth from left) and Garth Roberts (third from right) pose with members of their wedding party on their big day, September 10, 2011. They were wed just a few months after the New York State Legislature approved same-sex marriage. Plummer was elected village mayor in 2013. (Courtesy of Doug Plummer.)

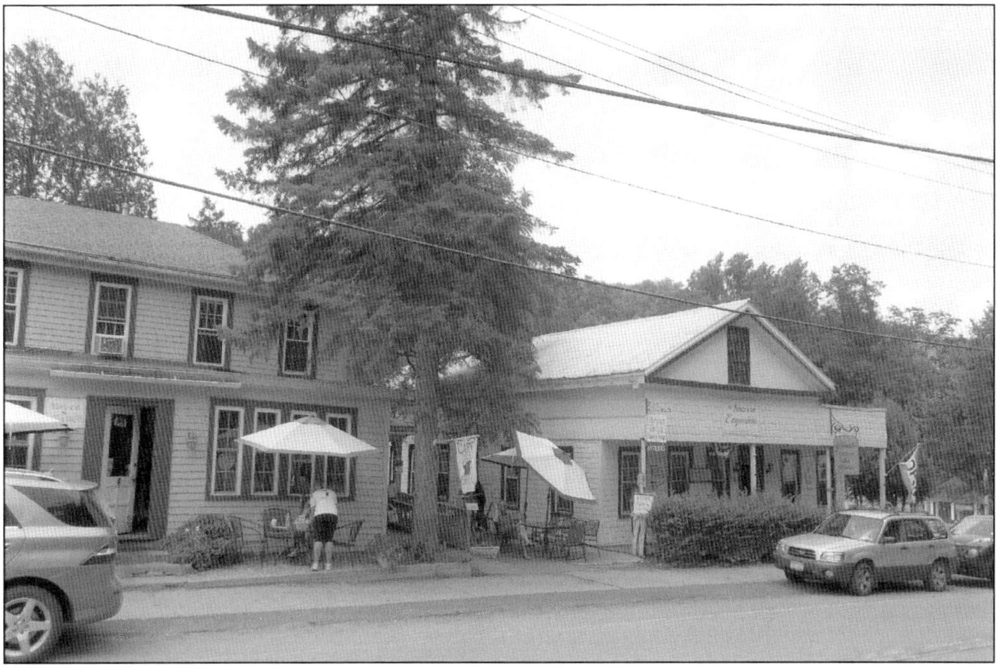

Directly across the street from the renowned American Hotel, visitors will find the Black Cat Café, Finishing Touch, McGillicuddy's Naturals, Flo's Fabrics, and other small shops. These shops lend a festive air to the rebirth of the village. Tony Daou's Black Cat Café provides the picnics for the Glimmerglass Festival in nearby Cooperstown during the summer. (Author's collection.)

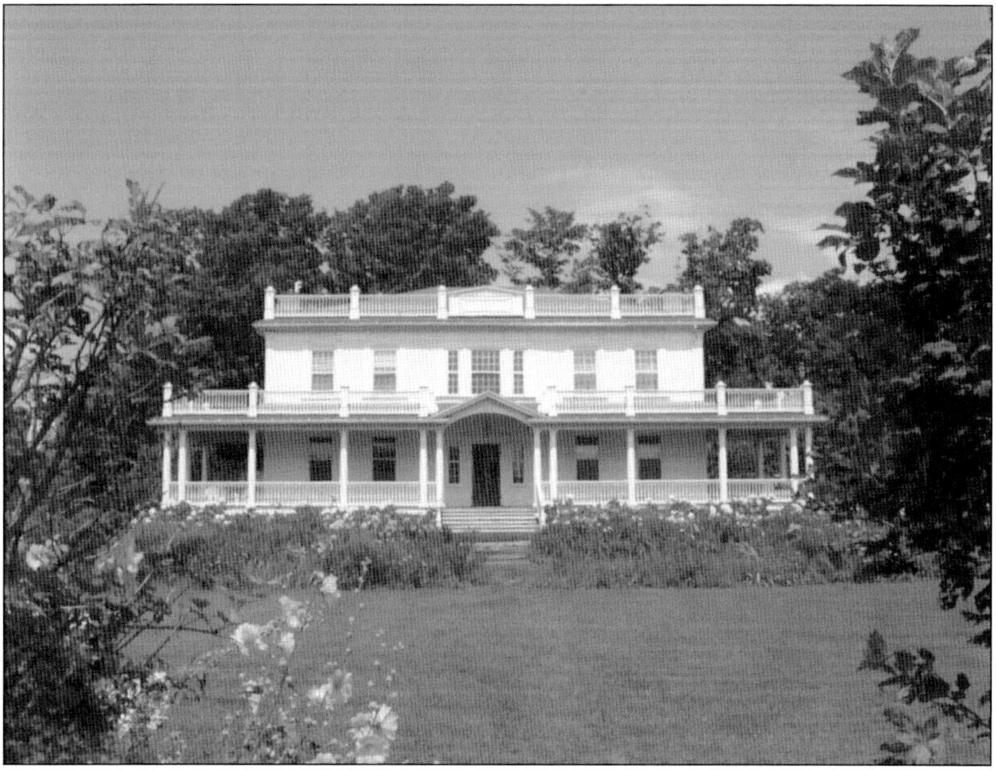

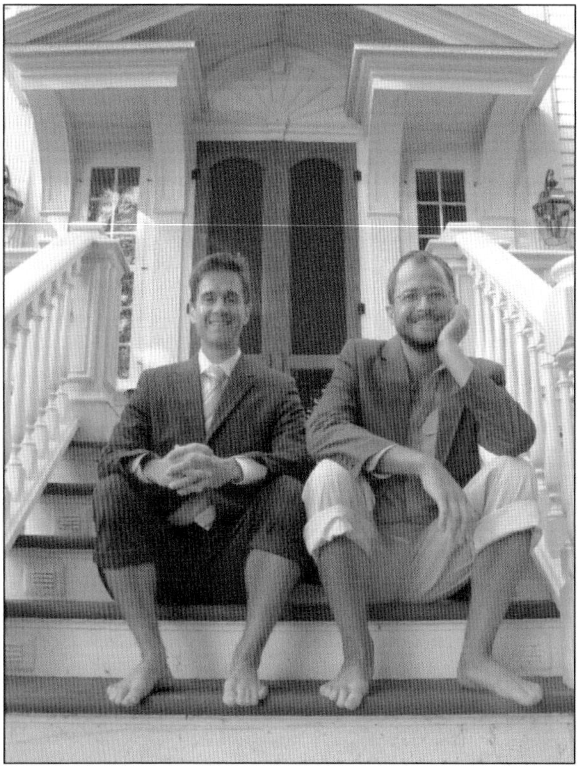

This 1802 masterpiece was lovingly restored in the 1990s by Frederick Selch and purchased in 2006 by Josh Kilmer-Purcell and Dr. Brent Ridge, "The Fabulous Beekman Boys." One of Sharon's most loved homes, it had suffered several years of neglect before being rescued by Frederick Selch and his wife, Patricia. Today, it has acquired new fame and has been featured in many magazines, including the December–January 2011 issue of *Country Living.* (Courtesy of Josh Kilmer-Purcell.)

Seated on the front steps at their Beekman mansion in 2012, Josh Kilmer-Purcell (right) and Brent Ridge, known as the "Fabulous Beekman Boys," contemplate their next big move with the Mercantile Store. Kilmer-Purcell has written a lively book chronicling their first year as owners of the Beekman estate, *The Bucolic Plague.* (Courtesy of Josh Kilmer-Purcell.)

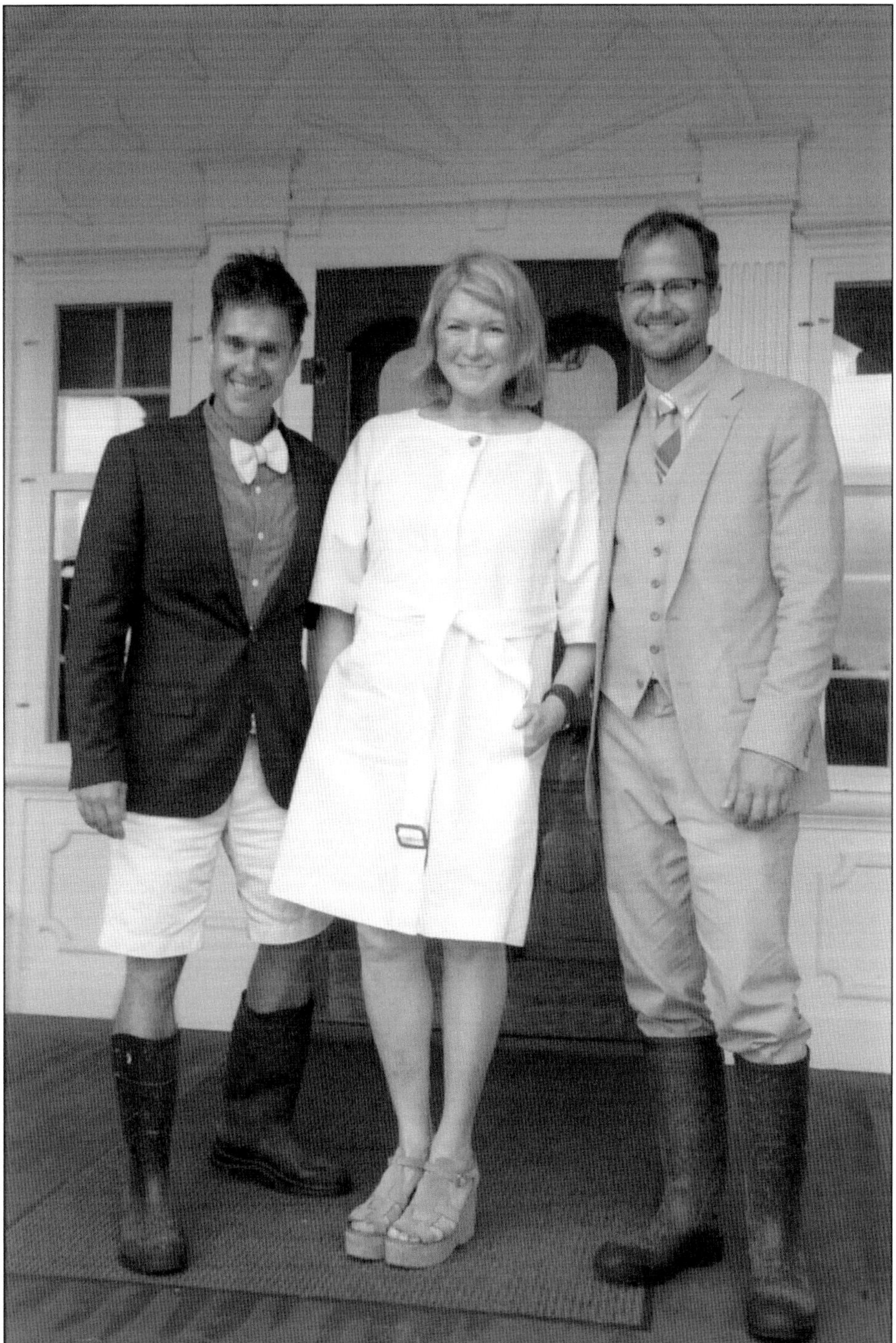

A special guest came to the July 2013 wedding of Josh Kilmer-Purcell (left) and Brent Ridge. Martha Stewart has become a big fan of Sharon Springs and especially the Beekman 1802 Mercantile. It was her advice that tempted the men to buy the mansion in 2006 while Ridge was working for Stewart's company. (Courtesy of Josh Kilmer-Purcell.)

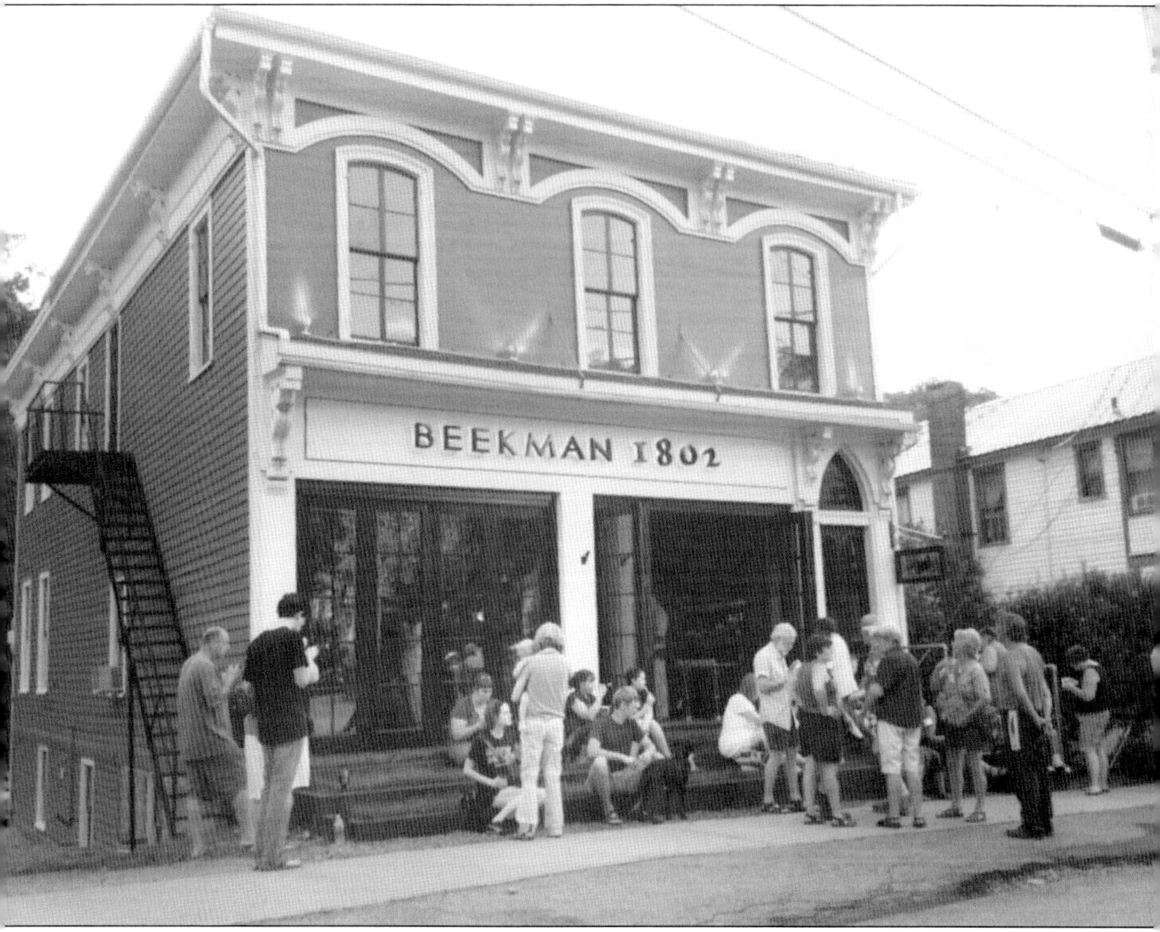

The flagship store for Beekman 1802 Mercantile is pictured here during a festive Saturday night in the lower village in August 2013. The occasion was an ice-cream social. The building itself has seen many manifestations. Originally located several blocks away, it started out as a mercantile shop in 1850. In 1894, the village purchased the building and moved it to its present location, where it served as a jail, library, firehouse, town hall, and general meeting room. In 2008, Leila and Philip Durkin purchased and transformed it into the Village Hall Gallery. The Durkins sold the gallery in 2012 to Kilmer-Purcell and Ridge, who had just won the CBS television contest *The Amazing Race*. The Beekman 1802 Mercantile opened in May 2013 and inaugurated a furniture line with Bloomingdale's in 2014. (Courtesy of Josh Kilmer-Purcell.)

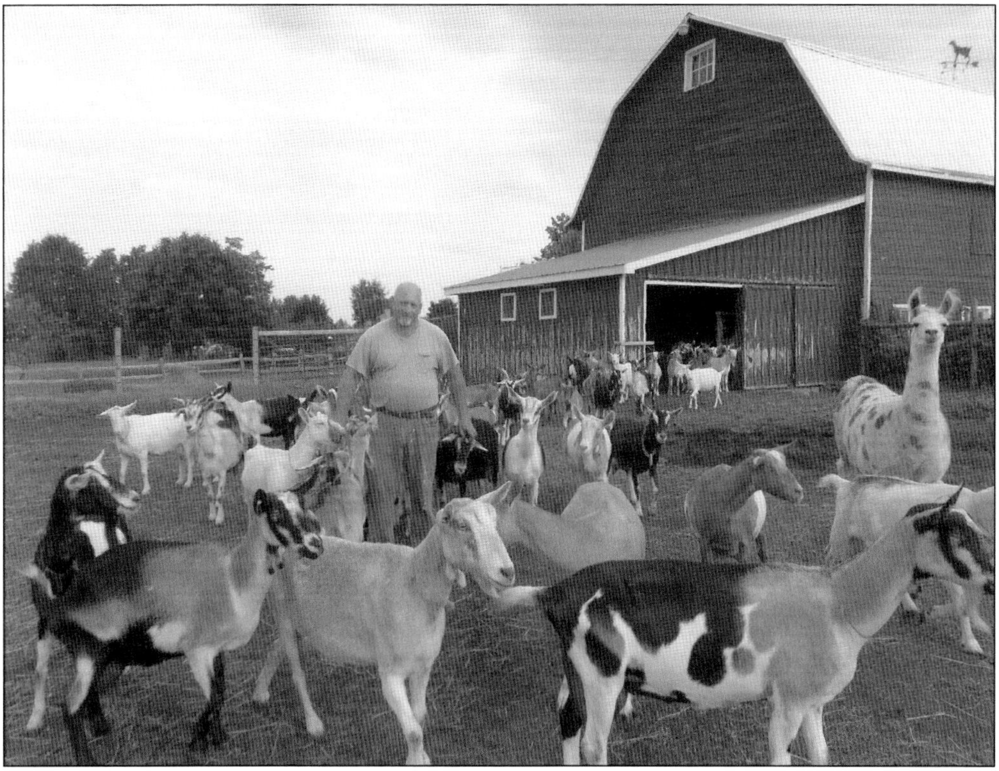

Today, John Hall, perhaps Sharon's best-known farmer, is seen here with his herd of goats and persnickety llama, Polka Spot, outside the Beekman barn. Hall graduated from the State University of New York at Cobleskill, which named him Distinguished Alumnus of the Year in 2014. Hall and his goats supply the lifeblood of farming techniques, work, and milk to Beekman 1802. (Author's collection.)

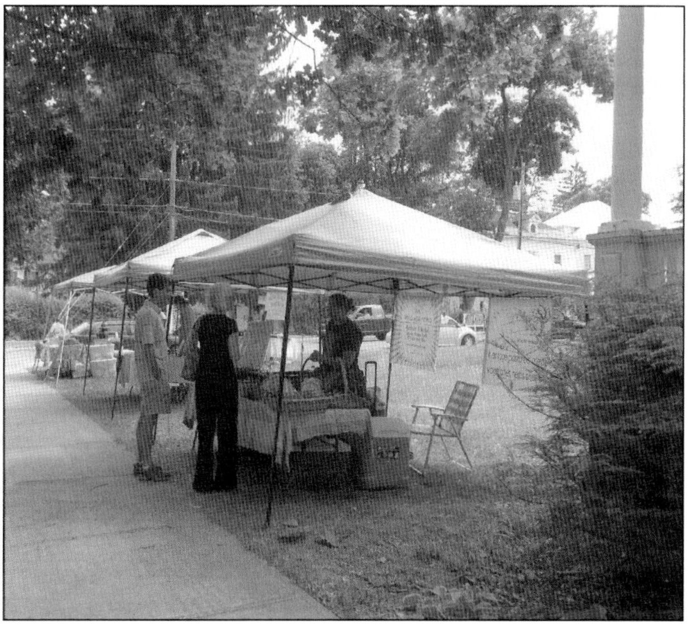

Several local organic farmers have organized a weekly Saturday market. Weathertop Farm, the Everett Stone House Farm, Parson's Farm, Melody Spring Farm, and others are actively engaged in the "farm-to-table" movement, bringing local produce to several markets as well as supplying area restaurants with fresh ingredients. In yet another move forward, hops production is reappearing on several local farms, to be sold to local breweries. (Author's collection.)

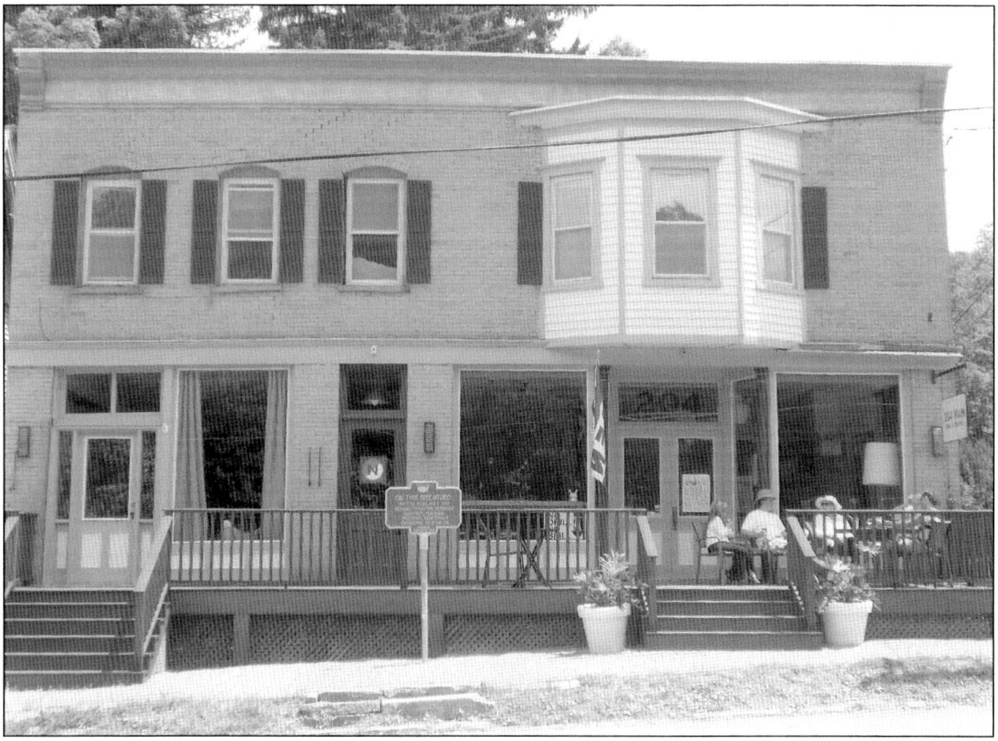

A new addition to the ambience in the lower village, 204 Main Bistro serves locally sourced meats and vegetables. Chef Norm Phenix, and his partner, Jim Grinchis, have created a state-of-the-art restaurant with a boutique hotel. The bistro is located in the former post office, grocery store, and bank building. (Author's collection.)

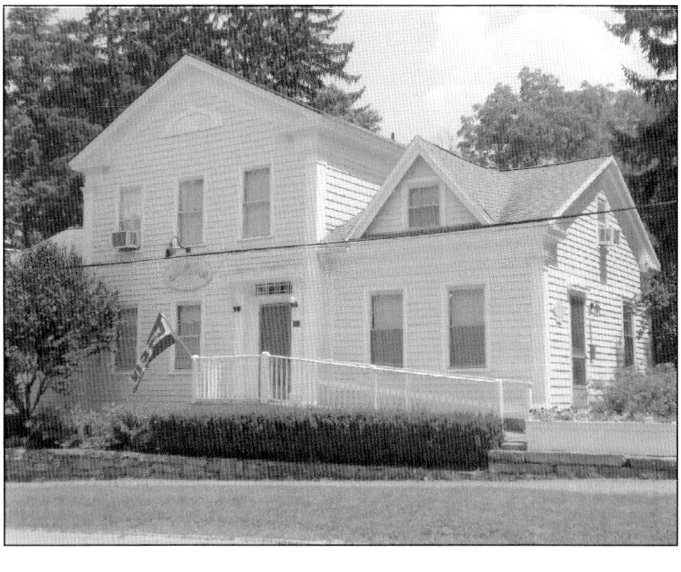

Craig and Cheryl Rosen opened the Spring House Spa in July 2011, giving Sharon Springs a return to its heritage for the first time since the baths closed in 2005. Formerly known as the Monticello Cottage and built in 1840, the building has seen many transformations over the centuries, from a doctor's residence to a kosher boardinghouse, a gift shop, and now a world-class spa with guest apartment on the second floor. (Author's collection.)

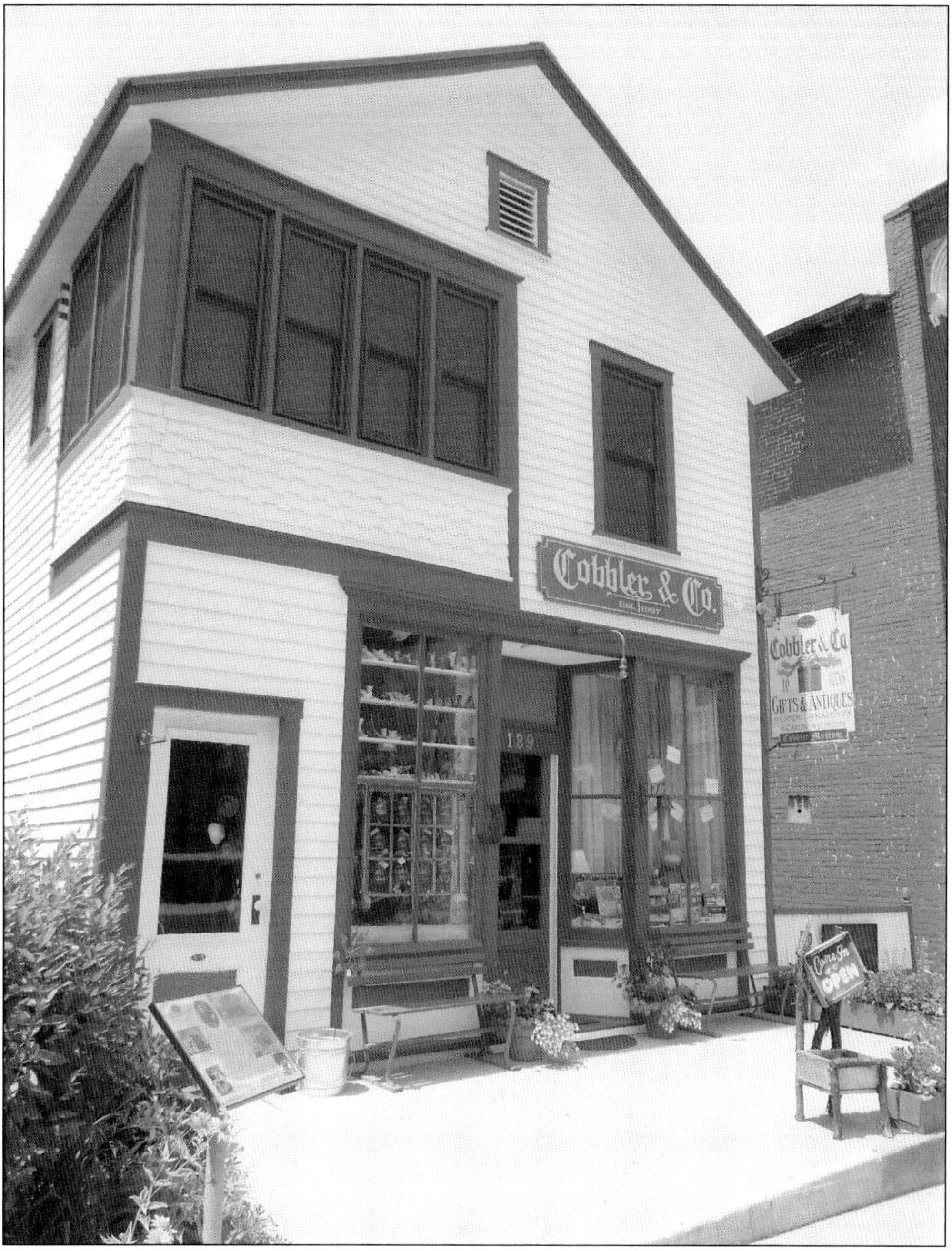

A mainstay among the shops in the village is Maureen Lodes's Cobbler & Co., an eclectic gift shop operating since 1997. Lodes's leadership in the Sharon Springs Chamber of Commerce, school board, and many other community organizations has helped invigorate the commercial center of the town and village. This delightful shop started life as Florence Fonda's millinery shop in 1898; she sold the premises to an Italian shoemaker, Frank D'Amico, in 1930. He operated his cobbler shop and a boardinghouse in the rest of the building (called Florence's Cottage) until the 1970s. The building stood vacant until it was purchased by Lodes, who opened Cobbler & Co. in 1997. Today, the cobbler's equipment remains as a tribute to the past. (Author's collection.)

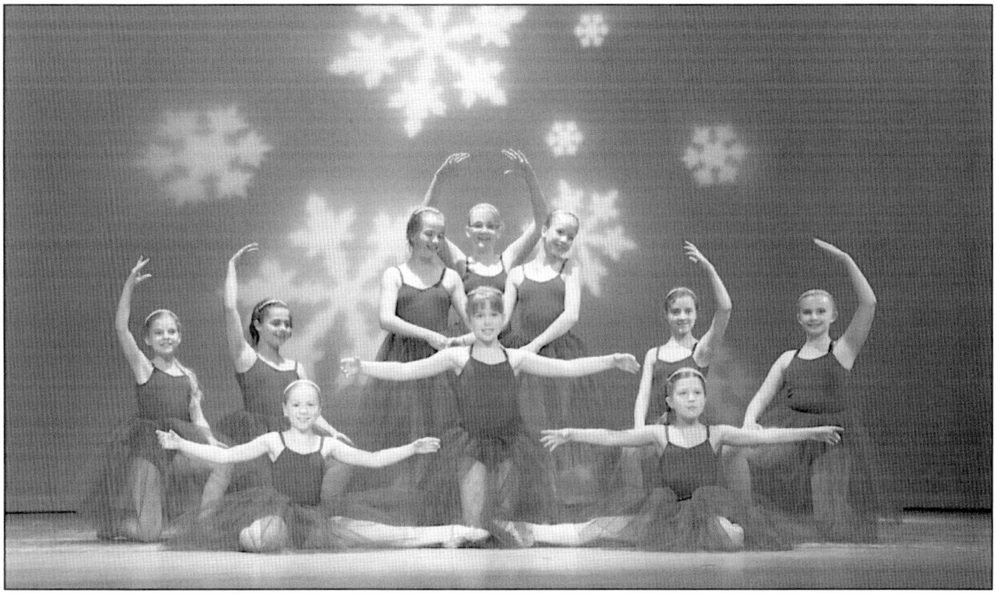

Betty Gavin Singer has been teaching dance at Studio North in the village for 20 years. This highly successful dance studio attracts students from miles around, offering acrobatics, ballet, hip-hop, jazz, tap, modern dance and more. Here, 10 young ballerinas pose for the camera before their recital. (Courtesy of Betty Gavin Singer.)

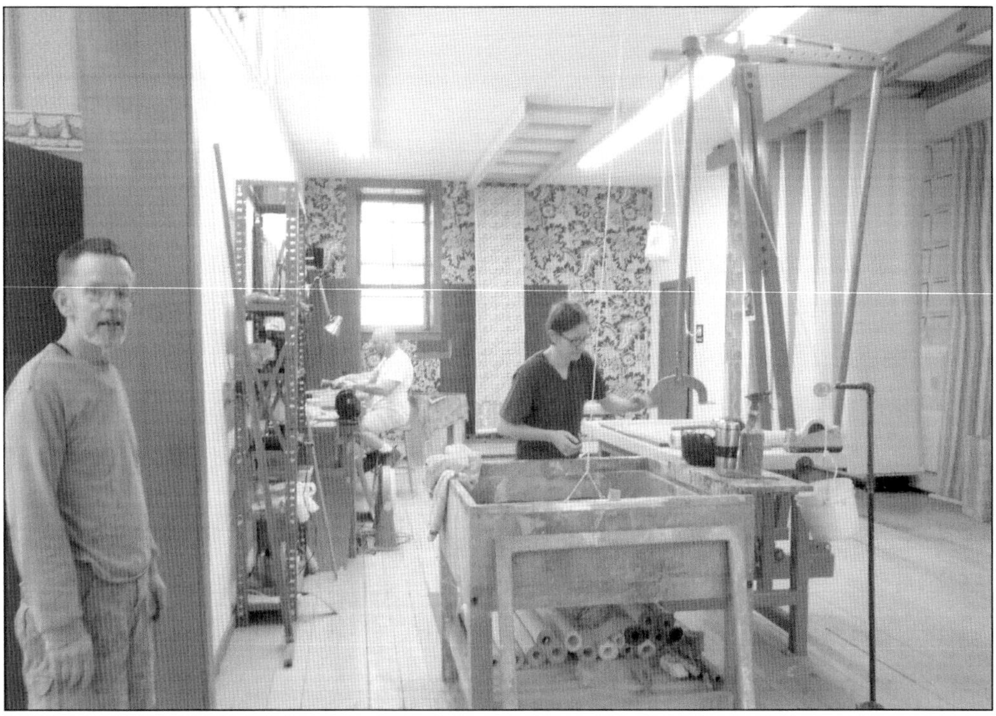

Adelphi Paper Hangings is located in the former Lehman Block at the top of Main Street. Steve Larsen (left) and crew design and create custom wallpaper for clients as diverse as Thomas Jefferson's Monticello, 204 Main Bistro, George Washington's Mount Vernon, Beekman 1802 Mercantile, and houses in Britain. (Author's collection.)

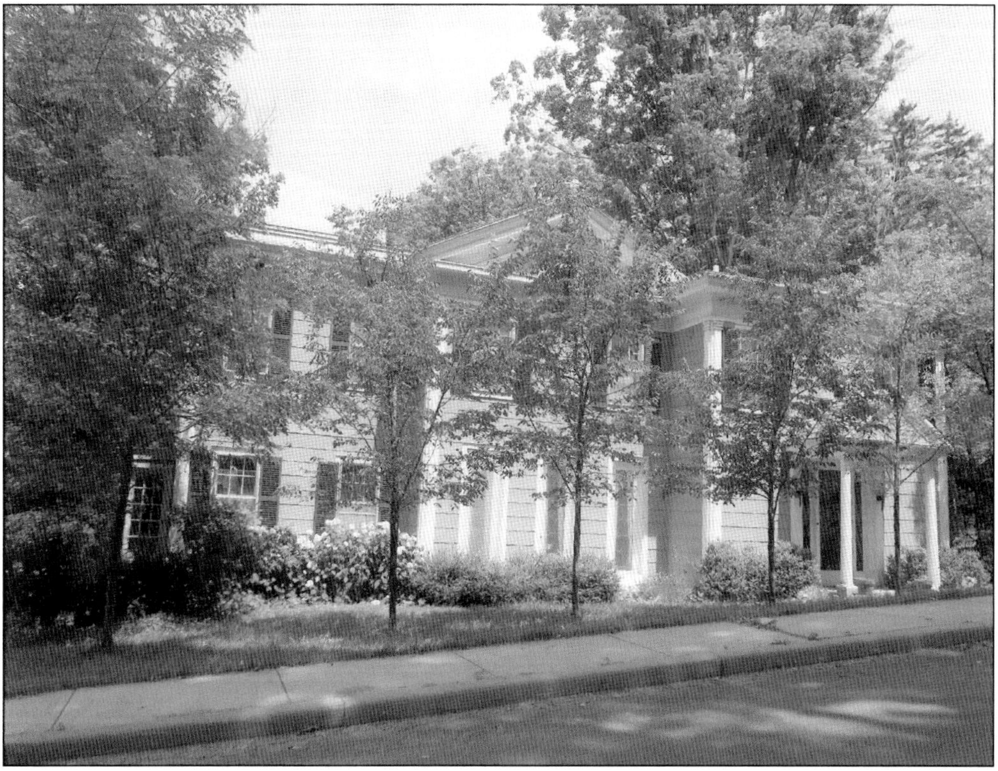

Featured in the November 1998 issue of *Colonial Homes,* Dan and Dave Wood's Edgefield bed-and-breakfast is a favorite retreat for many opera buffs. The village is located a mere 20 miles from the Glimmerglass Opera House in nearby Cooperstown, which hosts a festival of opera every July and August and has helped spur resurgence in hotels and bed-and-breakfasts in Sharon Springs. (Author's collection.)

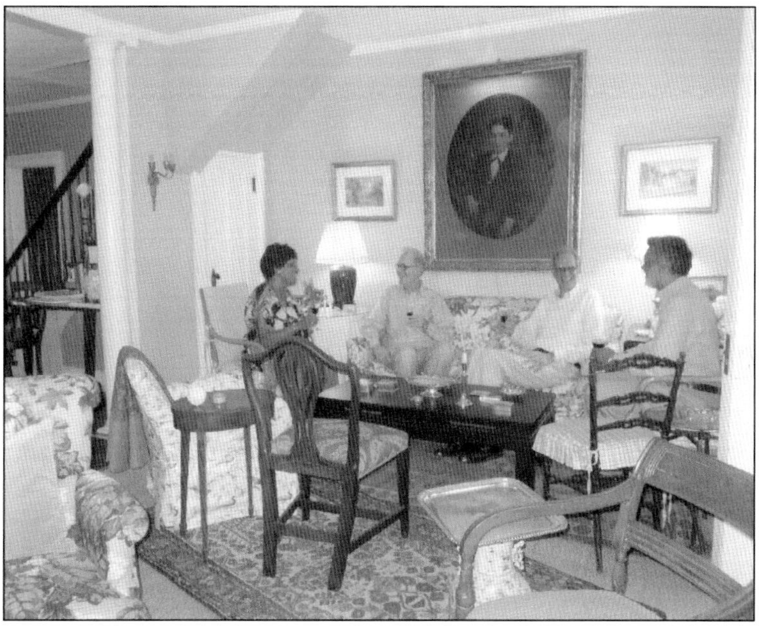

Dave Wood is a noted architect, and Dan Wood favors interior design. Together, they have created an elegant space in the old Curry House on Washington Street in the lower village. In addition to breakfast, Edgefield hosts afternoon tea and sherry parties. Shown are, from left to right, Dr. Hueldine Webb, Dan, Dave, and Lester Blair. (Author's collection.)

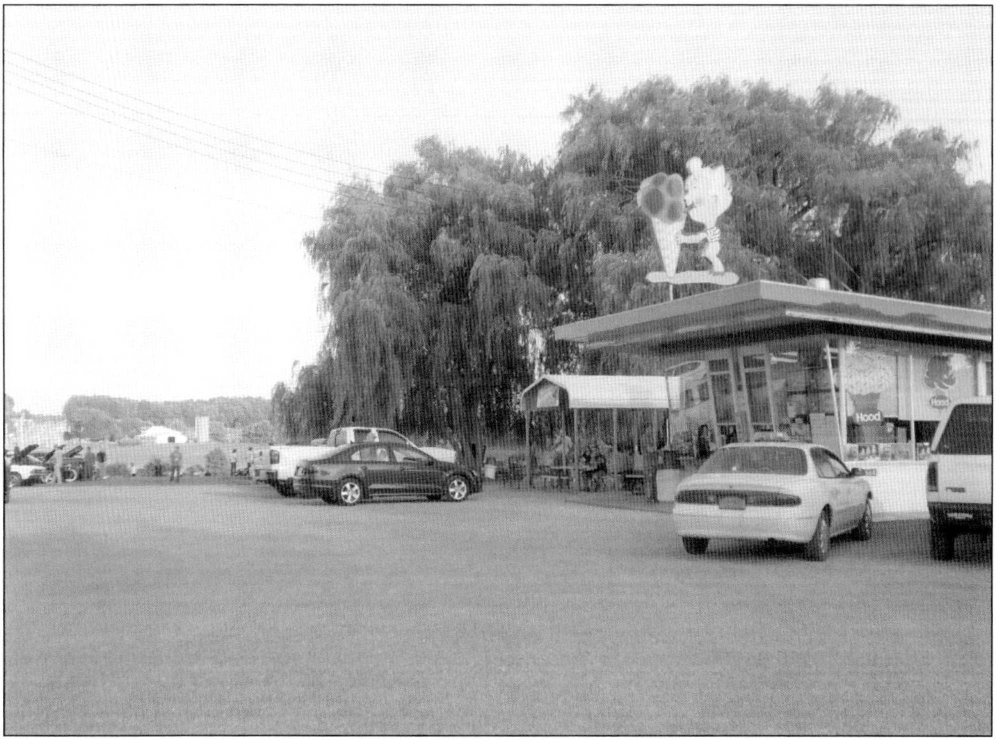

Since opening its doors in 1963, Dairyland has been a popular spot in the summer months. One of the first roadside snack bars in the area, it serves burgers, fries, and ice cream to townsfolk and visitors alike. Friday nights feature Big Al's Cruise-In with "Oldies' Music" and a chance to vote for a favorite restored vehicle. The current owner of Dairyland is Cyle Conley. (Author's collection.)

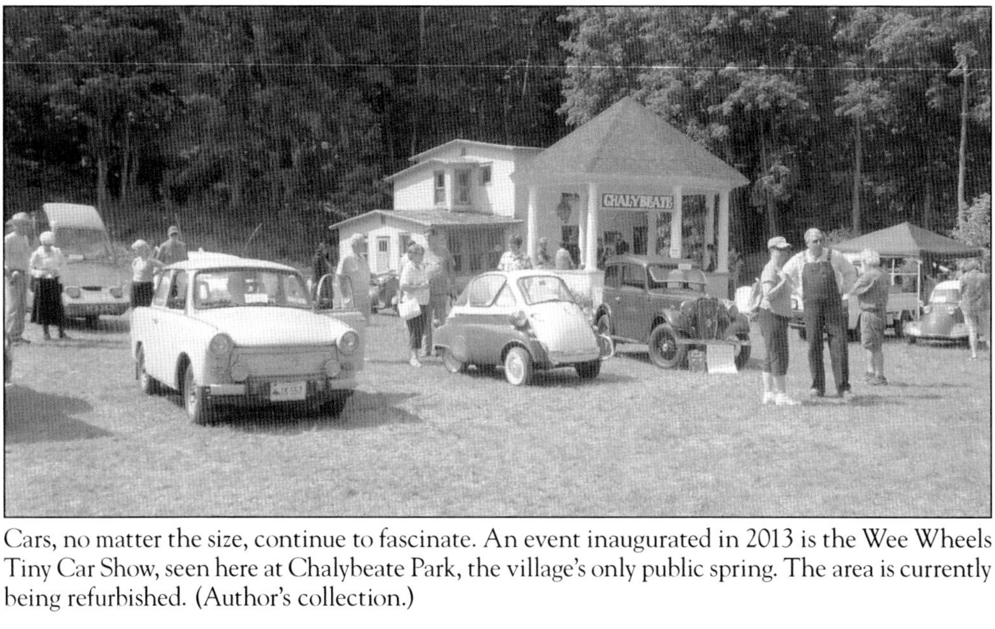

Cars, no matter the size, continue to fascinate. An event inaugurated in 2013 is the Wee Wheels Tiny Car Show, seen here at Chalybeate Park, the village's only public spring. The area is currently being refurbished. (Author's collection.)

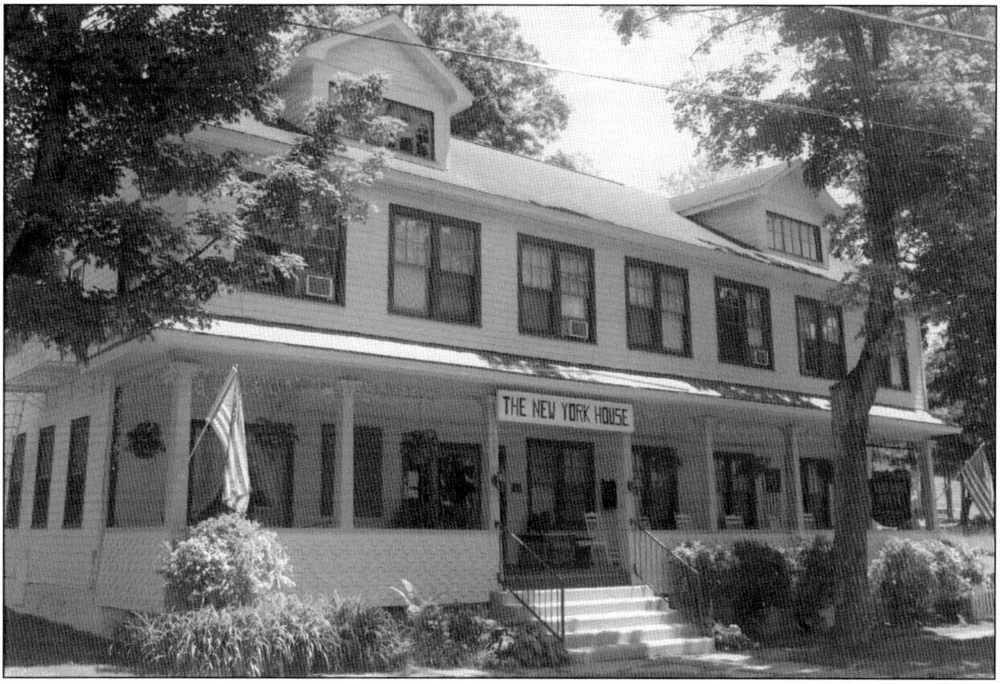

Another excellent restoration, the New York House, reopened in 2009 under the capable hands of Bruce and Kelly Button. The Buttons have modernized a former boardinghouse, built around 1885. Originally, this was operated as a German boardinghouse with German kitchen. Today, the Buttons offer a full-service bed-and-breakfast. (Courtesy of Bruce Button.)

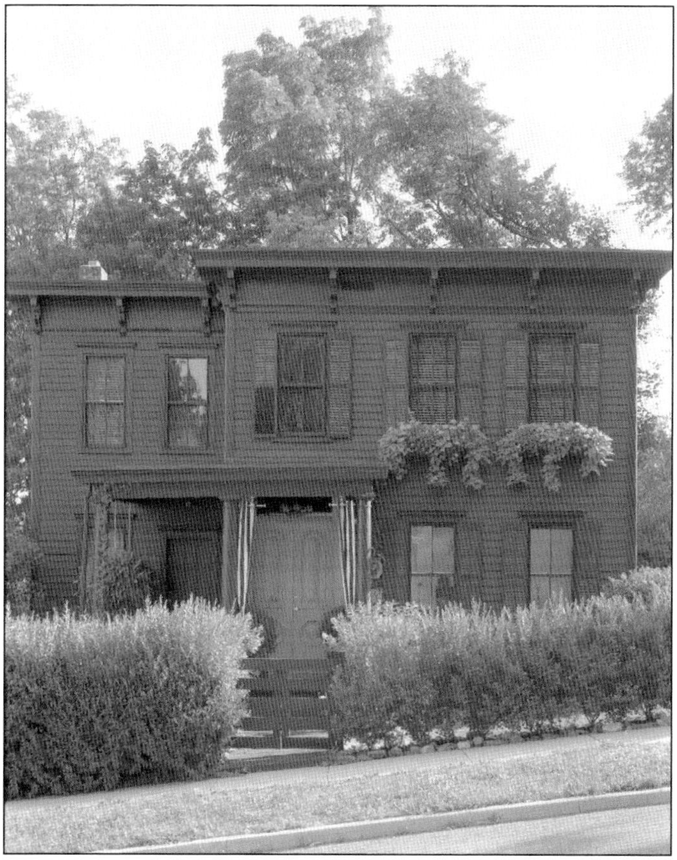

Among the village's newest residents are Chris and Roger Stout-Hazard, known for their television shows *Sell This House* and *Sell This House Extreme*. Since moving to Sharon, they have renovated one of the older 19th-century homes in the lower village. (Courtesy of Chris Stout-Hazard.)

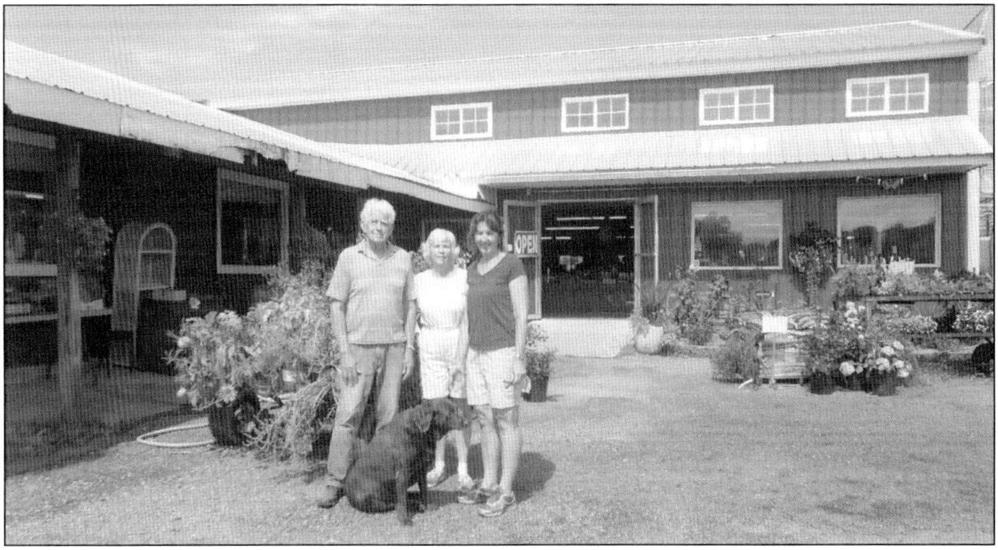

The Schilde family expanded its apple business with Sunnycrest Orchards and Greenhouses in 1978, after purchasing the former Kling farm and orchard. Today, the baton has been passed to a third generation. Milt and Carol Schilde are seen here with their daughter, Laurie Schmidt, who plans to add an apple-cider barn. (Author's collection.)

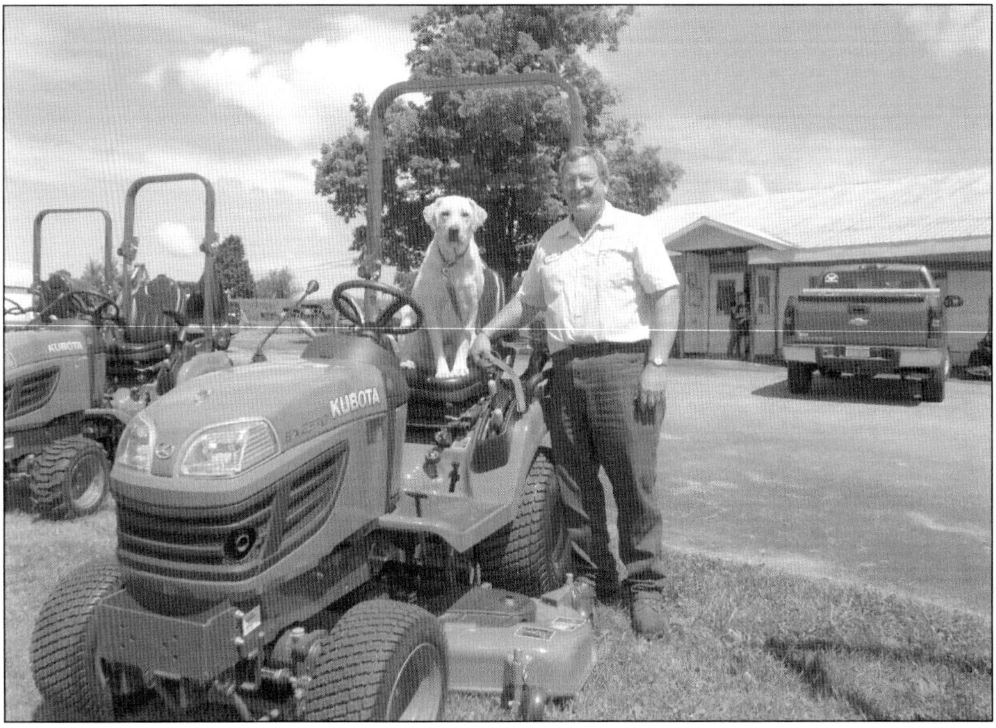

Originally located in the lower village near the Adler Hotel, the Sharon Springs Garage is now located on Route 20, east of the village, and has been operated by the Handy family for several generations. It is now under the leadership of Dave Handy, seen here with his dog, Kubota. In recent years, the garage has opened satellite stores in Oneonta and Troy. Handy shares ownership with his brother-in-law Robert Spohn. (Author's collection.)

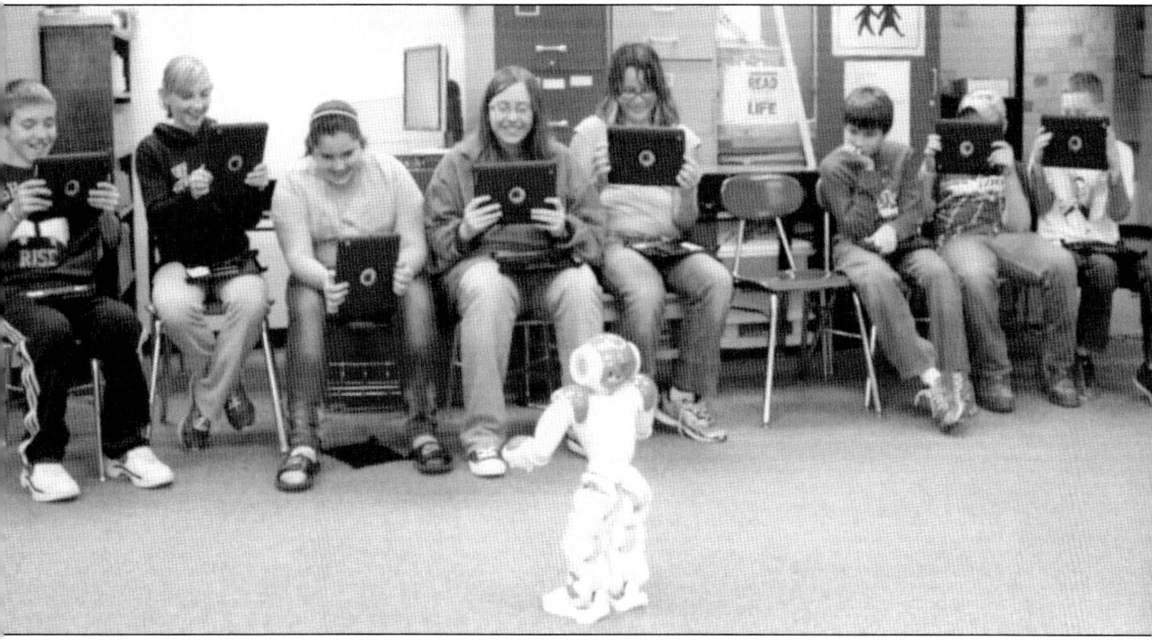

When Sharon Springs Central School District implemented the one-student-to-one-iPad program in November 2013, it was awarded the Apple Distinguished Program because of its successes in enhancing and extending teaching and learning with thoughtful and innovative implementations of technology. The iPads are used throughout the day in a range of subjects, from math to social studies to language arts, allowing students to participate in such features as online discussion boards and virtual field trips. All 160 students in grades 6 through 12 have iPads for their personal use during the school year. The students shown here attempting to program a robot with their iPads are, from left to right, Isaac VanArsdale, Abby Reynolds, Darienne Roberts, Ashley Coons, Amber Miller, Owen Rohac, Anthony Stabler, and Jayden Kendle. (Courtesy of Tom Reynolds, Sharon Springs Central School.)